Recommended by
The World Wildlife Fund

By the same author

Mammals, Reptiles and Amphibians, 1955
Hallwag

Short History of Earth, 1955
Hallwag

Simba: The Life of the Lion, 1962

The Wilderness is Free, 1963

S.O.S. Rhino, 1966

Giraffes

Man and Wildlife

C. A. W. Guggisberg

Foreword by Dr. F. Vollmar,
Secretary-General
of The World Wildlife Fund

Arco Publishing Company Inc.
New York

Published 1970 by Arco Publishing Company Inc.
219 Park Avenue South,
New York, New York 10003

Maps by Dennis Ranston

Library of Congress Catalog Number 76–110614
Standard Book Number 668–02282–5

Printed in Great Britain

Contents

Colour Plates

Acknowledgements

I should like to thank Dr. F. Vollmar, Secretary-General of the World Wildlife Fund, for providing me with valuable information; Christine Hankinson of Evans Brothers Limited for the trouble she has taken over the illustrations for this book, and my wife, Rosanne, for the invaluable help she has given me on all my safaris through Africa's National Parks and game reserves, and for undertaking the tedious job of typing my manuscript.

For permission to reproduce black and white illustrations in Chapters 1-5, the author and publishers are indebted to: The American Committee for International Wildlife Protection (page 96); Ashmolean Museum, Oxford (page 79); British Museum/Freemans (Photographers) (pages 21, 65), British Museum (pages 48, 49), British Museum (Natural History) (pages 34, 38, 47), British Museum (Natural History) for reproductions from their publications *Man the Toolmaker* (page 40), *Fossil Birds* (pages 85, 87), British Museum (Natural History)/Freemans (Photographers) (pages 20, 51 [upper and lower], 101); His Grace the Duke of Bedford (page 132); Bruce Coleman Ltd. (page 99)/Des Bartlett (pages 104, 125)/Sven Gillsater (page 137)/Russ Kinne (page 92)/Tom McHugh (page 131)/Graham Pizzey (page 103)/W. L. Puchalski (page 63)/Alan Root, Armand Denis Productions (page 77)/World Wildlife Fund (page 133)/Zoological Society of London (page 83); Crusade Against Cruelty to All Animals/Mondadori Press, Milan (page 66), Crusade Against Cruelty to All Animals/Tierbilden Okapia, Frankfurt (top picture, page 67), Crusade Against Cruelty to All Animals (lower picture, page 67, pages 74, 75); Editions Payot, Paris, from their publication *La Chasse Prehistorique* by Lindner (pages 41, 43); Stuart Hertz/Freemans (Photographers) (page 64); India Tourist Office (page 120); Kennedy Galleries, New York (page 106); Lee Conservancy Catchment Board (page 81); Macmillan and Co. Ltd., from *Ancient Hunters* by Sollas (pages 42, 45); National Film Board of Canada (pages 109, 112); Netherlands National Tourist Office (page 124); New York Public Library (page 29); New Zealand High Commission (page 100); Novosti Press Agency, London (pages 121, 135); Radio Times Picture Library (pages 69, 95); Rijksmuseum van Natuurlijke Historie (page 89); Smithsonian Institute (page 27, left-hand picture page 69); South African Information Service (page 113); South African Tourist Corporation (page 115); Swiss National Tourist Office (page 110); United States Information Service (pages 32, 61, 71, 78, 80, 107, 108).

For permission to reproduce colour transparencies: Africana Museum (Johannesburg) for Plate iv; British Museum (Natural History)/Freemans (photographers) for Plate x; Bruce Coleman Ltd/H. M. Barnfather for Plates xvi and xviii;/Bob Campbell for Plate xv;/Peter Jackson for Plate xiv;/Russ Kinne for Plate xiv;/Chas J. Ott for Plate xvi;/Alan Root for Plate xi;/Simon Trevor for Plate xx. International Society for the Protection of Animals for Plates viii and ix; Japanese Tourist Office for Plate xix; Lee Conservancy Catchment Board for Plate vi; Paul Popper Ltd for Plate iii; Smithsonian Institute for Plate i.

Foreword

Man and Wildlife presents a telling history of man's relationship with his natural environment which began with his own fight for survival. He survived and conquered, domesticating animals for his own use, laying claim to a dominance of the natural world as his birthright. The chapter devoted to the massacres in the Bering Sea, on the Mascarene Islands and on the North American prairies show this relationship at its worst.

But such results of man's mastery are by no means inevitable: man has already begun to take steps to halt the destruction of animal life. This new direction to save animals from extinction springs from a new awareness of man's deep commitment to wildlife. The instincts which led man from hunter to sports-

man, can now be redirected into the more constructive role of preserver. The maintenance of the ecological balance is not only a more responsible use of man's power, but also a fundamental expression of the realisation that man is part of his natural environment; a loss in the world's stock of wildlife is a loss in man.

Man and Wildlife is presented in the lucid and scholarly manner that typifies Dr. Guggisberg's work. Its aim is to propagate the cause of conservationists and conservation organisations throughout the world, not least, the objects of The World Wildlife Fund which exists to save the world's wildlife and wild places for the benefit of man.

Dr. F. Vollmar
Secretary General of the
WORLD WILDLIFE FUND

Morges, Switzerland 1970

Animals have been Man's longest and most fundamental preoccupation. For the greatest part of his existence on Earth his survival has depended on his skill as a hunter. Animals were closely connected with his first excursions into the spiritual world, and they formed the subjects of his most ancient artistic endeavours. Primitive hunters felt closely akin to the beasts they had to slay in order to live. It was only after Man had begun to produce food crops from the soil, thus taking the first tentative steps on the road to undisputed mastery of the Earth, that he began to feel superior to animals. Man the Hunter became Man the Master, Man the Unique. He enslaved a certain number of animal species, he killed others wholesale for meat, for furs, feathers and ivory, for their glandular secretions, for the raw materials he was able to extract from their carcases, even for superstitious reasons. He deprived innumerable animals of their habitats, he slaughtered them because they fed upon his crops or competed with his domestic stock. Where formerly he had hunted out of necessity, he now did so for sport, for enjoyment. To safeguard their enjoyment, hunters often protected game animals and thus became instrumental in saving certain species from extermination.

This ruthless exploitation of nature led, in the course of the last century, to a new phase in Man's attitute to the animal world. In order to stem the devastating advance in civilization he became Man the Preserver. The creation of Yellowstone National Park in 1872 started a movement that has, with steadily growing momentum, embraced the world, all national barriers. Despite the tremendous popular support conservation has gained in recent years, the battle for the preservation of wildlife is, however, by no means won. Indeed, it has hardly begun, for very many species of animals are today very close to extinction.

C. A. W. Guggisberg
Nairobi 1970

An exploring party had meanwhile discovered that the naturalist had once again been right and that the expedition had come to grief, not on the coast of Kamchatka and within easy reach of Petropavlovsk, but on an island not yet marked on any map. It was, in fact, the island now known as Bering Island which, with the neighbouring and smaller Copper Island, forms the Commander or Komandorskie Group. The castaways had to resign themselves to spend the winter as best they could and to set out for Petropavlovsk the following year in a boat built from what remained of the *St. Peter*.

Vitus Bering died on December 8th and to all practical purposes leadership of the expedition went to the energetic and resourceful Steller. Without him few, if any, of the sailors would have lived through the winter, but he supervised the building of adequate huts, tended the sick, encouraged the downhearted, explored the natural resources of the island, organized hunting parties and was, without any doubt, the only one among all those men who thoroughly enjoyed himself. To be marooned for ten months on this unknown bit of land in a stormy northern sea was, to Steller, a 'fortuitous accident', and I think that any keen naturalist who reads the account he has given of Bering Island as it then was, will be inclined to agree with him wholeheartedly. In all their misfortunes, Bering's men had at least had one phenom-

enal stroke of luck, for their island, inhospitable though it had looked from the sea, was teeming with animal life. There were flocks of ptarmigan, big colonies of sea birds and, all along the coast, sea otters, northern sea lions and fur seals could be found in enormous numbers. Steller's enthusiasm reached its climax when he discovered a marine mammal entirely new to science. He recognized it as some kind of manatee, or sea cow, but much larger than the West Indian animal which had been described by Hernandez and by Dampier, the famous buccaneer-naturalist. The manatee of the tropical seas was reported to be about 2·5 to 4·5 m. long and to weigh 140 to 300 kg., the sea cows of Bering Island measured a good 7·5 m. from nose to tail flipper, had a body circumference of 6·2 m. and attained a weight of 4,000 kg. Steller was fascinated by these huge, inoffensive creatures and made a thorough and most meticulous study of them without, however, neglecting any of the other animals and birds that surrounded him in such profusion. No wonder that he secretly blessed the navigational blunders which had led to the wreck of the *St. Peter*.

The situation was, of course, not without its drawbacks. Steller made great efforts to impress upon his companions the wisdom of hunting with care and moderation, so that the animals, which at the beginning showed absolutely no fear of man, would not

Map showing Bering Island, where the 'St. Peter' ran aground

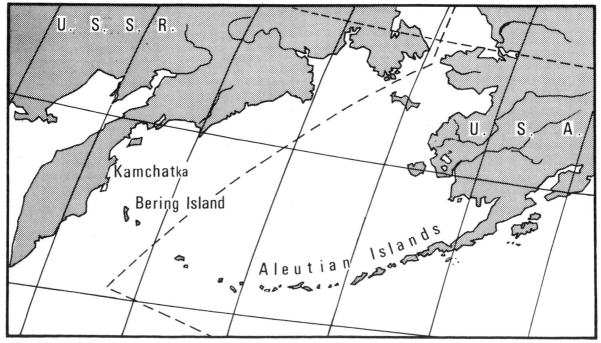

Steller's drawing of the sea-cow (far right) and two fur seals

be unduly disturbed, but, as usual, he found himself preaching to deaf ears. The sailors slaughtered the sea otters for their precious furs, leaving the bodies to rot, they killed seals for the sheer fun of it, and the consequences of their insane behaviour was soon only too obvious. The animals, rapidly losing their misplaced trust in humanity, deserted the beaches within easy reach of the camp, and hunting trips became increasingly longer and more arduous.

Winter went by, and work was started on the construction of a small, but seaworthy vessel from the timbers of the *St. Peter*. The expedition eventually put to sea on August 14th sailing into Avatcha Bay on the 27th of the same month.

Steller spent two more years in Kamchatka, in the course of which he paid another visit to Bering Island. In 1751 his copious and detailed notes on the animals observed during Bering's expedition were published in a book entitled *De Bestiis Marinis* and it was through this work that the sea cow was introduced to the scientific world.

'The animal never comes out upon the shore,' Steller wrote, 'but always lives in the water. Its skin is black and thick, like the bark of an old oak, and so hard that one can scarcely cut it with an axe. Its head, in proportion to the body, is small, and falls off from the neck to the snout, which is so much bent that the mouth seems to lie below, towards the end of the snout; it has no teeth, but only two flat white bones one above, the other below . . . The animals go in droves in calm weather near the mouths of the rivers, and though the dams oblige their young always to swim before them, the rest of the herd covers them upon all sides, so that they are constantly in the middle of the drove. In the time of flood they come so near the shore that one may strike them with a club or spear, nay, even stroke their backs with the hand.

'These gluttonous animals eat incessantly and because of their enormous voracity keep their head under water with but slight concern for their life and security, so that one may pass in the very midst of them in a boat even unarmed and safely single out from the herd the one he wishes to hook. All they do while feeding is to lift the nostrils every four or five minutes out of the water, blowing out air and a little water with a noise like a horse snorting. Half the body, that is their back and sides, is always above water, upon which flocks of crows settle and pick the lice [crab-like crustaceans of the genus *Cyamus*] out of their skins. They do not feed upon every herb, but just upon sea cabbage, which has a leaf resembling soroys; secondly, upon cabbage resembling a club; thirdly, upon cabbage resembling thongs; and fourthly, upon a waved kind of cabbage [these are various species of kelp]; and wherever they have been, though but for one day, heaps of roots and stalks are thrown out upon the shore. When they have eaten their fill, they lie asleep upon their backs. As soon as the ebb begins, they retire to the sea, fearing to be left upon the shore. In the winter time they are frequently crushed by the ice against the rocks, and thrown upon the beach. This happens during a storm, when the wind is upon the shore. At this season they are so lean that one may count all their ribs and vertebrae.

'When one of them is struck, and struggles to clear himself of the hook, those of the herd that are nearest to him come to his assistance. Some overturn the boat by getting under it, others lay themselves

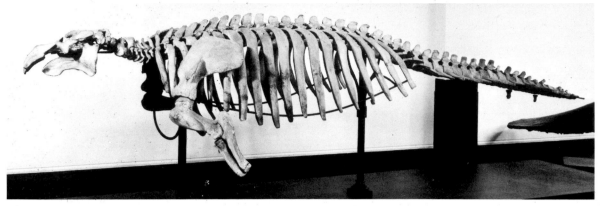

Skeleton of Steller's sea-cow in British Museum (Natural History)

upon the rope as if they could break it, and others endeavour to strike out the hook with their tails, which sometimes succeeds.

'Their flesh, though it takes a long time to boil, tastes well, and is something like beef. The fat of the young resembles pork, and the lean is like veal. The flesh is easily boiled, and swells so much that it takes up double the space when boiled than it did raw. It is impossible to boil the fat about the head and tail; but the ribs and back are very delicate. Some pretend that the flesh of this animal will not keep in salt, but we found the contrary, it appearing to us little inferior to salted beef.'

It is difficult to assess the actual number of sea cows present in Steller's time, but there may have been not more than 1,500 to 2,000 animals, frequenting about 15 suitable feeding grounds around Bering and Copper Islands. But whatever the total population may have amounted to in 1741 and 1742, by the time the lines quoted above went into print, Steller's sea cow, *Hydrodamalis gigas*, as it came to be known, had almost disappeared from Copper Island and was rapidly approaching extinction on Bering Island. Twenty-seven years later, in 1768, the very last representative of the species became the victim of a party of Russian sealers.

After the survivors of Bering's expedition had reached Petropavlovsk, tales of the fantastic riches in furs and seal skins that could be gathered on the Komandorskie Islands spread rapidly through the Russian Empire. From 1743 to 1763 no less than 19 hunting parties, each numbering 20 to 50 men, wintered on Bering Island, and many more on Copper Island. Ships bound for the Aleutians and other sealing and otter-hunting grounds called at the Komandorskies in order to replenish their provisions. There was a ceaseless massacre of sea otters,

fur seals and sea lions, while the sea cows were being killed off not only for their meat, but also for their thick, tough skins, out of which the sealers made primitive, but very serviceable boats. And so these harmless, kelp-eating mammals became totally extinct a mere 27 years after they had been discovered! They have never been found anywhere else; a 'sea cow' reported near Bering Island in 1854 turned out to have been a female narwhale.

Except for Steller, no other naturalist has had an opportunity to study the sea cow, and if he had not been a member of Bering's expedition, almost nothing would be known of its appearance and habits. A few museums have pieces of sea cow skin, which they count among their greatest treasures. Anyone interested in the anatomy of this animal has at his disposal about a dozen complete skeletons, as well as a number of skulls and a considerable number of odd bones.

In July 1962, Russian whalers reported having seen half a dozen strange marine mammals off Cape Navarin on the Siberian coast, and from the description given by the men, it seemed possible that they might have been sea cows. At the time of writing nothing further has, however, been heard of this 'discovery', and it is to be feared that the resuscitated sea cows were no more substantial than the yeti, the sea serpent and the surviving mammoths, which have been rumoured from time to time!

The sea otter, *Enhydra lutris*, Steller's sea lion, *Eumetopias jubatus*, and the northern fur seal, *Callorhinus ursinus*, are still with us because they were all distributed over a vast area of the northern Pacific. But in addition to the sea cow, Bering Island lost one of its sea birds, the spectacled cormorant, *Phalacrocorax perspicillatus*, which succumbed to hunters and egg collectors around 1852.

Plunder of the Mascarenes

While Steller's sea cow was being ruthlessly exterminated amidst the storms and fogs of the Bering Sea, a similar, though somewhat more protracted, tragedy was drawing towards its end in the blue, sunlit reaches of the Indian Ocean. It ran its course on three volcanic islands situated due east of Madagascar. The largest was named Ilha do Cisne, the Isle of Swans, by its discoverer, Pedro de Mascarenhas, and is now known as Mauritius. Réunion, once called Bourbon, is the wildest and most rugged island of the Mascarene group, Rodriguez the smallest and most easterly.

When the Dutch fleet under Admiral van Neck landed on Mauritius in 1598, the island was a superb tropical paradise uninhabited by man. Dugongs, Indian Ocean cousins of Dampier's manatee and Steller's sea cow, bobbed up outside the reefs, giant tortoises ambled over the beaches, and the chronicler of the expedition was especially impressed with the great number of birds. There was 'an abundance of feathered folk', he wrote, 'such as turtle doves, parrots and others.' He went on to say: 'In addition, there are large birds, as big as our swans, but with bigger heads.' A woodcut shows the sailors running riot, riding on tortoises, firing off their guns in all directions, knocking down the unsuspecting doves and parrots with sticks, while between the trees one of the swan-sized flightless birds can be seen waddling along. They were very numerous, and van Neck's men called them *walghvogels*—nauseous birds—because they were not at all fond of eating them, asserting that the meat became steadily tougher, the more it was being boiled. Breast and stomach alone made a tolerable meal, they said, but perhaps they simply preferred the turtle doves, which they killed by the hundreds. About the time the report on van Neck's expedition was being published, in 1601, another Dutch fleet, commanded by Wolphart Hermanszoon, had dropped anchor off Mauritius. On board one of the ships was an artist whose sketches of birds have fortunately been preserved in the Utrecht library. Several of them represent the *walghvogel*,

The woodcut from van Neck's journal published in 1601

21

which Dutch authors now began to call *dronte*. English sailors came to know it as dodo, using a Portuguese word meaning 'simpleton'.

Flightless birds of a similar type were reported from Réunion and Rodriguez, and we now know that each island had its own dodo-like species. The dodo, *Raphus cucullatus* (formerly *Didus ineptus)* of Mauritius was very clumsily built, had a grey plumage, a large head, a heavy, hooked bill, short, sturdy legs and a very small tail consisting of just a few curly feathers. The solitaire, *Pezophaps solitaria*, of Rodriguez, had a rather goose-like appearance, somewhat less clumsy than the dodo, with longer legs, a longer neck, a smaller head and a more slender bill. The brownish-grey males stood about 2 ft. 9 in. high, the lighter coloured females attained 2 ft. 3 in. The third species, which is usually, and rather confusingly, called the solitaire of Réunion, *Raphus solitarius*, seems to have been mainly white, with yellow legs and a yellow beak. All three are generally regarded as pigeons which, in an insular environment without

Solitaire of Rodriguez, Pezophaps solitaria

predators, gradually lost their power of flight. It must, however, be mentioned that a German zoologist, J. Lüttschwager, has recently produced evidence that they might have been more closely related to the rails than to the pigeons.

Unfortunately the aversion towards eating dodos displayed by van Neck's sailors did not persist very long. The negro slaves imported into Mauritius ate them with relish, and Europeans, too, began to consider them palatable. Passing ships made full use of the island for replenishing their provisions. As one Willem Ysbrandtz wrote in his journal:

'We found there also a quantity of geese, pigeons, grey parrots and other sorts of birds, numbers of tortoises, of which there were sometimes twenty-five under the shade of a tree. We took of all these animals as many as we wanted, for they did not run away. There were also some dodos, who had small wings but could not fly. They are so fat they could hardly move, because as they went they dragged their bottoms along the ground. But that which was most pleasant was that when we had a parrot or other bird and teased it to make it cry out, all the others which heard it assembled around to defend it and let themselves be taken. We returned on board with a quantity of these birds.'

Like the tortoises, the dodos were apparently taken on board alive and eaten gradually as the voyage progressed. They seem to have been easy to keep, and some did reach Europe, the first of them probably on one of van Neck's ships. There is no doubt about an occasional live specimen having been seen in London. One day in 1638, Sir Hamon Lestrange, attracted by the picture of a weird-looking creature hung out on a canvas cloth, entered a room and was shown a bird 'somewhat bigger than the largest turkey cock, and so legged and footed, but shorter and thicker', which, the keeper told him, was called a dodo. It may have been this very bird which afterwards figured in the catalogue of the 'Collection of Rarities preserved at South Lambeth' by Tradescant, the botanist-gardener, as a 'Dodar from Mauritius; it is not able to fly, being so big.' Tradescant's stuffed dodo passed into the possession of Willoughby, the naturalist. After changing hands several times more, it was finally incorporated into the Ashmolean collection. By 1755 it had, however, become so moth-eaten that the curator of the Ashmolean Museum ordered it to be destroyed—but fortunately the head and right foot were cut off, and these precious relics can still be seen in Oxford.

Dodos displayed in Holland were painted from life

The dodo of Mauritius as painted by Roelandt Savery

by famous artists, such as Brueghel and his pupil, Roelandt Savery from Courtray. The latter seems to have been especially fascinated by these exotic birds for there are over half a dozen canvasses in existence, either definitely bearing his signature or at least ascribed to him with considerable certainty. One of them is in the possession of the Zoological Society of London, while another belonged to Sir Hans Sloane and is now in the British Museum of Natural History.

This great artistic interest in the birds turned out to be most fortunate, for in their homeland they served not only as food for colonists and sailors, but great numbers were also destroyed by pigs and dogs which had escaped from the Dutch settlements. By 1681, not quite 100 years after it has first been described, the species became extinct, leaving us with the expression 'as dead as a dodo' to denote complete oblivion! No stuffed specimen has been preserved, and our knowledge of its outward appearance is based almost entirely on the paintings of Savery, Hoefnagel and some of their colleagues.

They were never studied by a naturalist of Steller's calibre, but a fair amount of information can be gathered from the works of various navigators and voyagers. By far the best account available deals with the solitaire of Rodriguez and was written by François

Leguat, a Frenchman of considerable education who settled on Rodriguez in May 1691. Leguat took a great interest in the natural history of his new home, filling the pages of his journal with descriptions of birds completely unknown to scientists in Europe. He paid special attention to the local representative of the dodo family, to which he gave the name 'solitaire', for, he tells us, 'it is very seldome seen in company though there are an abundance of them.' Leguat went on to write:

'The bones of the wings are thickened towards the end and have underneath the feathers a spherical mass of bone, somewhat like a musket ball, which in addition to the beak, they use to defend themselves. It is difficult to catch them in the forests, but in the open, where a man can run faster than they, this can be done quite easily. From March to September they are very fat and of excellent flavour, especially the young ones. Among the males, some may weigh up to 45 pounds'.

Leguat discovered that the nest consisted of a heap of palm leaves, a foot or more in height. The single, large egg was incubated for seven weeks, the parents taking turns in sitting on it.

No modern naturalist will ever be able to watch the whirling-dervish dance of the courting solitaire, so graphically described by Leguat, for, alas, the bird has gone.

Of the three species of dodo-like birds, the solitaire of Réunion is the least known. While various museums are in possession of a considerable amount of skeletal remains of both the dodo and the solitaire of Rodriguez, not a bone of the Réunion solitaire has ever been found. C. Keller, a Swiss naturalist, who visited Réunion, during the 1880s, thought that the very mountainous nature of the island might account for this strange fact. He could find no marshy flats, like the famous Mare aux Songes of Mauritius, where bones of extinct birds had been dug up in such large quantities, and he assumed that the deposits containing remains of the Réunion solitaire had long ago been washed out to sea by heavy tropical rains.

There can, however, be no doubt about the actual presence of a dodo-like bird on Réunion. It was first

Top: *the skin and skull remains of the head of the dodo.* Bottom: *its reconstructed form*

mentioned by John Tatton, who visited the island in 1613 and saw big, fat, short-tailed birds 'of the signe of a turkie', as he put it. Four years later Bontekoe, the Dutch navigator, called them 'dodos', thus perhaps indicating that they resembled the species found on Mauritius more closely than the solitaire of Rodriguez. A certain Du Bois, who spent several years on Réunion, gave a fairly detailed description of the plumage, and a 17th century painting, done from a live specimen by Peter Withoos, depicts a bird with a big head and a strong, hooked beak not unlike a dodo. Even though it was referred to as 'solitaire' by the colonists, and also acquired the specific designation of 'solitarius', taxonomists have, on the basis of the very scanty evidence available, placed it in the same genus as the dodo. It seems to have become extinct about 1746.

It is now almost impossible to visualize the Mascarenes as they looked at the time of their discovery. Early visitors talk of dense, bushy forests, the destruction of which must have begun just as soon as settlements were established. It did not take long for the natural vegetation to be replaced by introduced and cultivated plants, with pitiful remnants of the former forest splendour persisting precariously on mountain tops and in inaccessible ravines. The birds, already suffering from ceaseless hunting pressure and from the depredations of pigs, dogs, cats and rats, found themselves deprived of their habitat, and the islands lost not only the dodo and the two solitaires, but between 17 and 20 other species as well.

To give the reader an idea of the depletion the Mascarene fauna has undergone, it may be mentioned that of the 11 to 12 indigenous land-birds of Rodriguez only two can still be found today. One of them, the Rodriguez Fody, *Foudia flavicans,* apparently just maintains its population level; the other, the Rodriguez bush warbler, *Brebrornis rodericanus,* is very rare and probably on the verge of extinction.

The dugong and the tortoises, so numerous at the time of Admiral van Neck's expedition, have, of course, also gone from the islands, but they can still be found elsewhere.

The history of the Mascarenes is a very sad tale; one of ruthless destruction and devastation. Mauritius, Réunion and Rodriguez, today, can only be considered as pitiful ruins and this dismal picture is in no way brightened by the fact that man has replaced a large part of the highly interesting endemic fauna with a considerable number of animals foreign to the islands, some introduced by the settlers, while others established themselves accidentally. The human invaders not only brought their domestic animals, but also released deer, hares, squirrels, guinea fowl and francolins for sporting purposes. Indian mynahs were imported in an effort to control the locusts, which were increasing dangerously in numbers, probably owing to man having completely upset the islands' ecology. House sparrows arrived as stowaways, and so did rats, European snails and various other pests.

Today Rodriguez has seven species of introduced land birds—grey francolin, barred ground dove, Indian mynah, yellow-fronted canary, red-eared waxbill, house sparrow and Madagascar fody—all of which are present in flourishing populations. The island is thus not without bird life—but can sparrows and mynahs be regarded as an adequate replacement for the solitaire, for the flightless night heron, the blue rail and all the other birds which Leguat found and which became lost to the world so soon afterwards? I am sure that a majority of cultured people will agree that they cannot, and that something valuable and irreplaceable has gone from Rodriguez, leaving it a desert, despite the noisy mynahs, the chirping sparrows and the twittering canaries.

Frank B. Gill, an ornithologist who recently made a study of the birds of Rodriguez Island, discovered that two introduced species—the guinea fowl and the Madagascar love-bird—which were recorded as common in the last century, have since become practically extinct. Residents are inclined to blame their disappearance, which, in the case of the guinea fowl, seems to have been fairly dramatic, on the frequent cyclones. They may, of course, be right, but one cannot help seeing something ominous in this observation, an indication that nature has a way of hitting back. Otto Kersten, a scientist attached to Baron von der Decken's African expedition, explored Réunion in the 1860s and thought that the destruction of the forests had brought about a definite deterioration of the climate. A few decades later, Keller made similar remarks with regard to Mauritius, stating that soil erosion was already lessening the fertility of the island. Over-population has done nothing to improve matters and, the way things are going, there is a possibility that the descendants of the present-day inhabitants of the Mascarenes could one day be faced with a situation quite as disastrous as the one that confronted the dodos and solitaires when their paradise was invaded by man. The last laugh may well be with the ghosts of the big, flightless birds!

Slaughter on the Prairies

'On the first day of the World, the Great Spirit planted a tree near the water,' so goes a legend of the Kiowa Indians. 'It grew up into the sky and formed a pathway, down which all the living creatures descended to Earth. The last to climb down were a man and a woman of the Kiowa. After having walked around and looked at all Creation, they returned to the tree, and there encountered the bison. At that moment the Great Spirit appeared to them and said: "Here are the bisons. They shall provide you with food and raiment. But on the day you see them perish and disappear from the face of the earth, you will know that the end of the Kiowa is near and that their Sun will soon go down for ever."'

It is thought that on that fateful morning of October 12th 1492, when Christopher Columbus watched the island of Guanahani taking shape in the dim light of early dawn, forty to sixty million bison were roaming over the North American wilderness, grazing, chewing the cud, wallowing; in short, doing everything that comes naturally to a large shaggy bovine. Their area of distribution extended from the Great Slave Lake to northern Mexico, eastwards into New York State, Maryland, Pennsylvania, Virginia, and Georgia, westwards into Oregon, Idaho and Colorado. The buffaloes—as they came to be called by many people, even though they are not closely related to the true buffaloes of Asia and Africa—were not equally abundant in all parts of this vast expanse of country. Comparatively rare in the forested regions of the east and among the mountains of the west they had their real stronghold on the grassy, treeless plains of the Mississippi Valley.

The summer and winter ranges of the herds were widely separated, and their migrations, extending over three to four hundred miles, must have been truly spectacular. In densely packed masses they moved along the same routes year after year, and nothing could stop them. They poured through passes with the irresistible force of an avalanche, they splashed through marshes and swam across rivers, hundreds of them getting bogged down or drowned in the process, but on they went. Packs of wolves followed them, they were plagued by clouds of flies, and the places where they wallowed in the dust, in order to get some protection from these winged pests, can be recognized in areas where there have been no bison for almost 100 years.

Travellers fortunate enough to visit the prairies when the bison were still numerous, have given us impressive accounts of what they saw. Thus John Kirk Townsend, the naturalist, found himself on top of a hill in the valley of the Platte River in the 1830s, overlooking a plain at least ten miles long and eight miles wide, the whole of it covered with bison and no stretch of ground visible anywhere—a sight, he thought, which should stir even the most unimaginative of minds.

On their grazing grounds, the bison spread out far and wide, forming innumerable parties and herds numbering from four or five to thirty or forty. These groups led a nomadic existence, staying in one place for only a few days and then moving on to new pastures five or ten miles away. There was consequently no overgrazing of the bison range, despite their fantastic numbers, and they even left enough herbage to feed large herds of pronghorn antelopes and a multitude of small mammals. These herbivores were preyed upon by wolves and coyotes, pumas, bobcats and, of course, by human hunters.

Man is a comparative newcomer on the American continent, probably having made his way across the Bering Strait, which then may have been a land bridge connecting Asia and Alaska, about 20,000 years ago. We do know for certain that there were people on the great plains at least 10,000 years ago, hunters and food-gatherers, who knew nothing of agriculture and had no domestic animals. At a place called Folsom their beautifully-shaped stone spearheads are found in association with the bones of gigantic, long-horned bison, which soon afterwards disappeared together with the mastodons, the mammoths, the wild horses, the long-necked camels and the giant sloths. Why North America should have lost three-quarters of her large herbivores between 10,000 and 6,000 years ago is a mystery that has not yet found a satisfactory explanation. Various theories have been advanced, but not one of them has met with universal acceptance. Whatever may have caused the extinction of all these animals, a new, though very much depleted grassland community had been in existence for many thousands of years by the time the White Man reached the American Continent.

The dry, elevated plains of the west formed the normal hunting grounds of the Indian tribes living along the Rocky Mountains, food-gatherers who had not progressed far beyond the stage attained by Folsom Man. At certain times of the year they ventured considerably farther out across the plains, in order to take their toll of the bison herds.

The inhabitants of the somewhat more humid south-eastern grasslands had developed a primitive

Winter hunting on the Missouri in 1832—painted by George Catlin

system of farming. They cultivated maize and had a tendency to spread westwards along the banks of the big rivers. Owing to periods of drought and to the ravages of locusts, such advances into the prairie often ended in disaster. Even in the marginal areas it was not possible for these farmers to depend entirely on their agricultural efforts. The communities could only survive if the men did a considerable amount of hunting, the bison naturally being their favourite quarry. The central parts of the plains were, however, only rarely visited, for these hunting expeditions, both from the east and from the west, had to be undertaken on foot, the American wild horse having become extinct long before the Indians had a chance to try their hand at domesticating it.

The Indians usually set out to surround a small herd and to shoot as many animals as possible with arrows. Sometimes they crept up to the game camouflaged in wolf skins. The bisons, used to the sight of these predators, simply bunched together, facing the presumed wolves, and thus gave the men

some easy shots at short distance. The bovines were also herded into corrals or lured into such traps by an Indian who covered himself with the skin of a young animal and bleated like a calf that had lost its mother. Prairie fires were started in order to move bison in a certain direction, and sometimes the hunters succeeded in stampeding a herd over a cliff. The Blackfeet called this method of getting a really plentiful supply of bison meat 'piskun', which means 'deep-blood kettle'. In the valley of the Yellowstone River there is a rock which still bears the name of 'Buffalo Jump'. The Chugwater, a river halfway between Cheyenne and Fort Laramie, was given the name 'chug' by the Indians, in onomatopoeic imitation of the sound made by bison hitting the water after falling down from the rim of a vertical 200 foot rock-face.

Meanwhile, the Spaniards had conquered Mexico and were approaching the prairies from the south. Towards the end of the 16th century, they established the first cattle ranches along the Rio Grande, the

Indians hunting bison with bows and arrows—painted by Karl Bodmer in 1833

large herds being guarded by vaqueros or cowboys, on horseback. As most of these herdsmen were Indians, it did not take long for some of the horses to fall into the hands of the independent tribes farther north—an event which, in a very short time, was to bring about a fundamental change in the existence of the grassland peoples. The Indians proved to be born horsemen, and they were quick to recognize the tremendous advantages the possession of horses conferred upon them. Within fifty years all the southern prairie tribes had taken to riding and were making the fullest use of the newly acquired mobility. It became possible not only to range much farther across the endless plains, but also to transport a lot more equipment and supplies. Where formerly the members of a hunting party had to carry all their belongings on their backs, except for what their dogs could drag along on little travois, a whole community could now wander from one hunting ground to another in utmost comfort, taking along the big conical tents, which were called tepees, and all the other goods and chattels. Many of the tribes gave up agriculture altogether and became horse-nomads, a transformation which was all the easier as they still had an old and deeply ingrained hunting tradition.

The change-over, which began in 1600, was completed about 1780. Among the last to change were the Cree of southern Canada, who adopted this new way of life only after 1750.

Some tribes, like the Pawnee, the Arikara and the Wichita, kept up a certain amount of farming right to the end. The western tribes, having hitherto lived as food-gatherers, hunted not only bison, but small game as well, besides doing a lot of fishing in the rivers, which came down from the Rocky Mountains. In its purest form, the bison-hunters' culture could be found among the Indians who, after acquiring horses, had moved to the central parts of the plains. Hunting had become so much easier, that their methods were rather more wasteful than they had been in ancient times. But this did not matter much, as the human populations remained low. The Comanche probably never numbered more than 7,000, while the strength of the Cheyenne tribe is said to have been around 3,500 in 1780. There were at that time about 4,000 Crows, who had at their disposal a hunting territory larger than the German Federal Republic. Among the biggest tribes were the Blackfeet and the Dakota, with 15,000 and 25,000 people respectively.

The bison provided the Plains' Indians with practically everything they needed. Meat they did not eat fresh was sundried or 'jerked', then pounded or shredded, mixed into a paste with melted fat, flavoured with acid berries and thus turned into the highly nourishing and very compact preparation known as 'pemmican' among the Cree. Skins with the hair left on—the buffalo robes—served as blankets or overcoats for the winter. Finely cured, soft and pliable, they were used for mocassins, leggings, dresses and shirts, besides furnishing the covering for the tepees. Out of rawhide were manufactured cooking pots, ropes, quivers and saddles, while circular shields were cut out of the thick hide on the bison bull's neck. Hoofs could be boiled down for glue, spoons and ladles were carved out of the horns, the ribs found a use as sledge runners, and sinews made excellent threads and bowstrings. The bison even had to play a part in the preservation of the tribal records, which took the shape of elaborate and very artistic picture stories painted on tanned hides, many of which are now highly valued museum exhibits.

Such utter dependence on one animal species could not but comprise serious dangers, for, whenever climatic or other reasons induced the bison herds to change their migration routes or the time-table of their wanderings, famine swept through the camps of the nomad hunters. Eventually, this dependence was to bring about their downfall.

Contemporary with the acquisition of the horse by the Plains' Indians, British settlers founded the colonies of Virginia and Massachusetts. Similar enterprises followed in quick succession, and the White Man began his advance, first to the foot of the Appalachian Mountains, and then into the vast virgin forests beyond. Wherever the pioneers appeared, the country resounded to the cracks of their rifles, and the game was decimated with frightful rapidity. At the beginning of the 19th century there were no bison left between the Appalachians and the Atlantic seaboard. Ten years later the big bovines became extinct east of the Mississippi and were being pushed back into Iowa and eastern Missouri. By 1850 their range was restricted to the western plains and mountains.

Most of the Indians had long since given up their lances and bows in favour of the guns sold to them

Sioux women dressing hides—a sketch by George Catlin, 1830's

by white traders along the Missouri and its tributaries. For the weapons, as well as for powder and lead, they paid in the one currency available to them, bison skins, and they were now slaughtering many more animals than they needed for their own use. Despite this, there were still some eight million bison in 1868.

But the final act was drawing near, and it may be said to have opened when the tracks of the Union Pacific Railway began their advance from Omaha to Cheyenne, cutting into and right through the centre of the bison range. Thousands of hunters fanned out north and south over the plains, first to shoot meat for the construction gangs, then to collect buffalo robes, which had become fashionable in the eastern states and could now be transported easily and cheaply by rail. The hunters got $1.25 apiece for a skin, and 25 cents for a tongue. The following figures will give an idea of the wholesale massacre that was in progress: four and a half million bison were killed in 1871, four million in 1873, and one million in 1874. Not a finger was lifted to stop the butchery. The bison hunters received, on the contrary, a considerable amount of official approval. As General Sheridan had said: 'Every buffalo dead is an Indian gone!'

The building of the Kansas Pacific Railway opened up the southern bison range to similar

Contemporary illustration of General Custer's men counting bison tongues

Soldiers cutting out the tongues to provide proof of the number of bison slaughtered

To deprive the Indian of his way of life, thousands of soldiers were instructed to kill bison

destruction, and it was there that Scout Cody earned himself the nickname of 'Buffalo Bill' for shooting, under contract to the railway company, 4,120 bison in 18 months. This was not even a record, for Billy Tilghman, who later became famous as the 'Last Frontier Marshal', bagged 3,300 bison in as little as seven months. When the Northern Pacific Railway was being pushed eastwards from Glendive, the bison of the nothern range came under fire, and one of the largest herds of that area, numbering about 10,000 animals, is said to have been wiped out within a few days by an army of hunters posted strategically at all available waterholes.

That was the end of the tragedy, and, at the turn of the century, apart from a few scattered herds protected in semi-captivity on private estates, a group of 20 animals in Yellowstone National Park were the only bison left in the United States. Those few survivors lived under a steady threat from poachers and it looked as if the species was doomed to share the fate of the dodo and Steller's sea cow.

'Never in the history of the whole animal kingdom has there been such another bloody and cruel carnage, or one that yielded so little in proportion of the total value involved', wrote William T. Hornaday, the distinguished American naturalist.

Hornaday started an intensive campaign to save the pitiful remnants and succeeded in rousing so much public interest that Colonel Charles J. Jones, who had for some time made experiments in breeding and domesticating bison, was not only enabled to safeguard the last Yellowstone survivors properly, but also to build up a second herd in the park with animals acquired from various sources. The Colonel has gone into history as 'Buffalo Jones'—not for slaughtering bison, but for saving them!

In 1905, the 'American Bison Society' was established under the leadership of Hornaday, with Theodore Roosevelt as honorary chairman, and from that moment the fortunes of the nearly extinct buffalo improved considerably. The situation was improved even more by the discovery that, near Lake Athabaska in Canada, a considerable herd of so-called wood-bison, somewhat larger and darker than the prairie animals, had escaped destruction. It was immediately given full protection by the Canadian Government.

Thus the big wild ox of America was saved, and 'dead as the bison' was not destined to be added to the English language as a figure of speech equivalent to 'dead as the dodo'. Today, there are 12,000 of them in the National Parks and National Refuges of the

Soil erosion can be caused by overgrazing of domestic stock. Without grass or other plant roots to bind the fertile top soil it is lifted from the land by wind and rain

United States and roughly the same number again in Canada.

The Indians, however, have gone from the plains. It came as the Kiowa legend had predicted. With the passing of the 'thundering herds' their sun had set. In their place came the farmers who brought cattle and sheep, wheat and corn to the prairies. The whole ecology of the grasslands was profoundly changed, and the consequences of this transformation did not fail to become only too apparent. As far back as 1908 Hornaday wrote with respect to the Sunday Creek region of Montana:

'In days gone by that was one of the finest buffalo ranges in all the West. After the buffalo days, this side of 1884, it was a fine cattle range, but the awful sheep herds have gone over it, like swarms of locusts, and now the earth looks scalped and bald and lifeless. Today it is almost as bare of cattle as of buffaloes, and it will be years in recovering from the fatal passage of sheep.'

What Hornaday saw was the shape of things to come. Over-grazing and root destruction by domestic stock have laid the soil open to erosion, and large tracts of valuable land have been turned into deserts. Dust bowls have brought distress and misery to numerous farmers, not to mention the enormous expense they have caused to the nation. Did the world at large at least learn a lesson? It does not look like it.

The story of the North American plains, of the bison and Indians, and of the arrival of the white settlers is of great interest, for it reflects, in miniature, the turbulent way in which the relationship between man and the animal world has evolved through time and space, and highlights the deadly impact of civilization on nature as a whole. It also shows what can be achieved by people determined to stem the tide of destruction and to salvage what can still be saved from the holocaust.

Plate I (top) George Catlin visited the upper Missouri regions early in the last century and his spirited paintings of Prairie Indian life are of great documentary value

Plate II Indians sometimes approached a herd of bison camouflaged in wolf skins—as painted here by George Catlin

Plate III Rock paintings in Markwe Cave, Rhodesia. Below the frieze of dancers there are representations of zebras and various antelopes of which two, a kudu bull and cow, have just been killed by hunters

Chapter 2   Man, the Hunter

The time has come to bury once and for all Jean-Jacques Rousseau's conception of man's original goodness. At the same time we might also dispense with the popular fantasy of man's ancestor being a benevolent ape leading a placid vegetarian existence among the fruit and nuts of a bountiful tropical jungle. Before he even fully emerged from the 'ape' stage, man turned against his erstwhile brethren, and stands revealed as being a predator and a ruthless killer for as long as he has existed.

Available evidence suggests that the cradle of humanity was located, not in Asia, as scientists once speculated, but on the highlands of eastern Africa and on the South African veld where, between one and three million years ago, hordes of hominid creatures prowled through savannahs and grasslands, resembling apes in many ways, but walking upright like modern man. There were several species of them, varying in size from the stature of a chimpanzee to that of an orang-utan. Their remains have come to light in quite a number of places, and anthropologists classify them as *Australopithecines*, which means 'southern apes', though 'southern ape man' would have been a more suitable designation. One little fellow has even had the perhaps rather doubtful honour of being considered worthy of inclusion with the genus '*Homo*', though most authorities consider him merely a somewhat more advanced australopithecine.

These hominids probably ate everything that could possibly be eaten and certainly did not reject vegetable matter such as melons, roots, bulbs, berries, seeds and pithy stalks. But if you do not happen to be a confirmed grazer or browser, savannahs and grasslands do not provide you with an abundance of vegetable food, and the australopithecines were, therefore, very largely dependent on animals, ranging from beetle larvae, termites, locusts, tortoises, lizards and rats to antelopes and perhaps on occasion even to larger game.

Proconsul, a primitive anthropoid ape, living in the Lake Victoria area some 20 million years ago and considered as standing close to the human family tree, may have had a similar diet. Chimpanzees consume large numbers of termites, and have been seen to kill and eat monkeys and young antelopes. There are reliable reports of full grown gazelles being attacked by baboons. It was therefore quite natural for the ape-man of the African veld to take to a mainly carnivorous diet.

They might not appear so well equipped for a predatory existence as the big cats and wild dogs, but their bipedal gait gave them manipulatory powers not possessed by four-footed animals. Chimpanzees, still very dependent on their forelimbs for locomotion, have been seen to throw small trees at a leopard with considerable force. It is certainly not fanciful to imagine even the most primitive australopithecines armed with sticks and large bones for offensive and defensive purposes. Evidence strongly suggests that they soon learned to make pebble tools.

Man has often been called the 'tool-maker' but, as Robert Ardrey quite rightly points out, he might just as well be referred to as a predator whose natural instinct is to kill with a weapon. There is no doubt that of all human activities, hunting has to be regarded as by far the most ancient, and out of it grew what was to become our culture and civilization.

Among the *pithecanthropines*, which followed the *Australopithecines* and spread to Asia and Europe half a million years ago, Java Man and Peking Man were not only very able hunters, using a considerable

Hunters of the Lower Palaeolithic—reconstruction of Swanscombe Man who lived in Kent about 200,000 years ago—painted by Maurice Wilson

assortment of stone and bone implements, but both are definitely known to have indulged in cannibalism. Where, one may ask, is the original goodness of man?

Even in our technological era there are people, scattered relics of our past, who subsist entirely on the proceeds of hunting and on what else they can gather from wild nature, such as the pygmies of the African rain forests, the Bushmen of the Kalahari Desert, the Veddahs of Ceylon, the Semang and Sakai of Malaya, the Negritoes of the Philippines, the Andamanese and the Australian aborigines. It is a great tragedy that the most primitive of them all, the Tasmanians, became extinct in 1877.

During an expedition through the north-eastern parts of the Congo Basin undertaken in 1954, I had an opportunity of spending some time with the Bambuti pygmies of the Ituri Forest and to get acquainted with their ways of hunting. Deep in that dense and sunless world of theirs I saw them use nets to catch small game and shoot at monkeys with their little bows. They also showed me how they

killed the small Congo elephants by literally crawling underneath an animal and forcing a spear upwards into its vitals. The elephant spears were slightly longer than the hunters themselves, and had a broad iron blade which made up about one third of the length of the weapon. When I asked the pygmies if such an audacious way of tackling elephants did not lead to a number of accidents, one of them grinned, pulled down his loincloth and revealed two big, ugly scars, one on each side of his belly. 'An elephant did this,' somebody said, and it was easy to see that the thin, downward pointing tusks of a forest elephant had been pushed deep into the little man's body. It seemed truly miraculous for him to have recovered from such terrible wounds—but here he stood, hale and hearty, and he was the one who, for hours on end, carried the heavy hunting net slung over his shoulders.

Right: *Bambuti pygmies holding their elephant spears*

Some years later, a lecture tour took me to the German town of Hanover, where I visited the State Museum of Lower Saxony. On the wall of one of the exhibition galleries there was a huge elephant skeleton cut out of cardboard, with a sharp pointed wooden pole, about 2·5 m. (8·15 ft.) long, mounted in such a way that it seemed to be entering the pachyderm from below.

'That is the way Neanderthalers hunted elephants during the warm period of the third Interglacial, 150,000 years ago,' the director of the museum explained. 'This spear was actually found inside the skeleton of a straight-tusked elephant at a place called Verden on the Aller. It is made of yew, and the point has been hardened by fire. Scattered around the skeleton were found numerous stone splinters, a sign that the successful hunters had chipped the knife blades they used to cut up their quarry from a nearby block of flint.'

A French doctor, who made a careful study of the bones of animals killed by Palaeolithic hunters, has come to the conclusion that these people were highly efficient butchers. Their flint knives were much more serviceable than might perhaps be expected, and with them a modern butcher can cut up a carcase as neatly and easily as with his own steel knives.

Because stone tools proved to be the most durable of ancient man's artefacts, a very long period of human development has become known as the Stone Age. The importance of stone tools to the prehistorian can be compared with that of 'time-marker' fossils to the geologist, for just as geological strata of far distant places can be correlated because they contain the same fossils, so the presence of stone tools of a certain type at an archaeological site will make it possible to assess its position within the Stone Age time scale.

Bone tools have also been found in large quantities, but we must not forget that Stone Age Man is certain to have made very full use of wood, though, for obvious reasons, very little actual evidence of this has been discovered. It may, however, be considered as significant that the Tasmanians made all their weapons of wood and used stones mainly as tools. Clubs and wooden spears must surely have been the arms most generally carried by Neanderthalers and other very ancient hunters.

People of the Old Stone Age or Palaeolithic are popularly referred to as Cave Men, and a lot of what we know about them has, in fact, been gathered from caves. But the regions where they could have found such an amazing number of caves as in the Dordogne and in the Pyrenees are few and far between, and a majority of them probably never sat inside a rock shelter. Branches may have been used for rigging up simple windbreaks, similar to the 'scherms' constructed by the Bushmen, and at a very early date these roving hunters learned to cover a few propped-up poles with some animal skins, thus obtaining something like a prototype of the Indian tepee. The skins were weighted down either with stones or with the heavy bones of elephants and mammoths.

Stone rings indicating the emplacements of tents were found in 1952 near Salzgitter, a town to the south of Brunswick. A municipal building project led to the discovery of prehistoric animal bones and soon a team of archaeologists took temporary possession of the site. The scientists came to the conclusion that the bones had accumulated in what had been a pond 100,000 years ago, and some very astute detective work led them to the spot where the Neanderthal hunters had pitched their camp.

We have to imagine this camp in surroundings very different from the site of Verden on the Aller when the straight-tusked elephant was speared. The 50,000 years that had gone by since then were marked by a dramatic deterioration of climate which eventually led to the formation of an ice-cap over Scandinavia and northern Germany. The country around Salzgitter must therefore have been a bleak, sandy tundra, covered with grass, Arctic willows, dwarf birch and perhaps a few scraggy conifers.

The fauna of Central Europe had changed almost as much as the vegetation. Gone were the straight-tusked elephants, Merck's rhinoceros and other animals associated with the third Interglacial. Out of the pond, filled in ages ago, on the banks of which the hunters sat gorging themselves and throwing the gnawed bones into the water, the archaeologists extracted the remains of 80 reindeer, 16 mammoths, six or seven bison, four to six wild horses and two woolly-haired rhinoceroses. At the camp site itself they found not only an enormous amount of stone artefacts, but also bone implements, such as daggers shaped out of mammoth ribs and clubs made from reindeer antlers. There were bone points which had obviously been fixed to spears, one of them with a barb, a refinement thought to have been invented much later. All the evidence pointed to the site having been occupied for a couple of seasons by a horde of 50 or 60 people.

During the warm spell of the third Interglacial, Neanderthalers penetrated the Alpine valleys and climbed up to altitudes between 5,000 and 8,200 feet

Kalahari Bushmen's huts—called scherms—are probably similar to those used by Palaeolithic man

in order to hunt the gigantic cave bear. They sometimes smoked the formidable beasts out of their caves and dropped big stones on them from above the cave entrances, but there is no reason why Neanderthalers, armed with spears should not have attacked bears in the same way Indians and Eskimos did before they had rifles.

Quite a number of caves are known to have been used by bears and bear-hunting Neanderthalers in turn, among the best known being the Drachenhöhle ('Dragon's Cave') at Mixnitz in Styria, and the cave of Krapina in Croatia. At Krapina the majority of bones were from bears, with the remains of some rhinoceroses, aurochs and wild boar thrown in, but the excavators also found over 300 fragments of human bones, cracked, scorched and burnt, lying among charcoal and ashes, and representing about 20 individuals of both sexes and of ages ranging from around six to very old. It would be difficult to interpret this gruesome find in any other way than as the left-overs of a cannibalistic feast.

Of course, the Neanderthalers had no knowledge of agriculture in any form, nor did they own domestic animals. Even the dog had not yet made its bow to the world as 'Man's best Friend'. The women probably gathered what berries, wild fruit and fungi there were to be found, but it can safely be said that survival depended entirely on the skill of the hunters. This also applies to the people of true *Homo sapiens* stock, who gradually began to displace the Neanderthalers all over Europe. It is not known whether they simply killed them off, or whether the more primitive hordes were at least partly absorbed by the invaders—we can only register the fact that the crude Mousterian implements and the massive prognathous skulls vanish towards the middle of the Würm Glaciation, giving way to more sophisticated tools and to skulls and skeletons hardly distinguishable from modern man. Culturally, the men of the European Upper Palaeolithic are classified as Aurignacians, Solutreans and Magdalenians.

The woolly mammoth was one of the favourite game animals of the Aurignacians. One of their camps was situated at the foot of a steep and overhanging cliff near Predmost in Moravia, well sheltered from the wind, and excavations, which have been going on from 1894 to the present day, have brought to light the skeletal remains of over 1,000 mammoths, besides the bones of reindeer, elk, musk ox, chamois, Arctic hares, lemmings, wolverines, Arctic foxes, bears, wolves, and lions. Scattered through this fantastic accumulation were over 100,000 stone tools, as well as an abundance of implements made of bone and mammoth ivory. We must assume that the mammoth herds performed seasonal migrations. The Aurignacians obviously had certain favourite localities, where year after year they waylaid the wandering herds, just as the Plains' Indians intercepted the bison. Such hunting stations were in use for hundreds, perhaps thousands of years, and they can be found right across Central and eastern Europe, from Lang-Mannersdorf and Willendorf in Austria, via Lower Wisternitz and Predmost in Moravia to the vicinity of Kiev.

The station of Lang-Mannersdorf seems to have been provided with every Palaeolithic comfort. A regular cooking place has been uncovered close to a number of flat sandstone rocks which served as tables and could seat eight to ten diners at a time. If roasting did not render the steaks tender enough, mammoth molars served for pounding and shredding the meat. The excavators found refuse pits, and workshops where the champion stonechippers of the horde manufactured a wide variety of tools. One of

these craftsmen had dug himself a hole, in which he could crouch and work protected from the cold wind, using a mammoth tusk as an anvil.

The Aurignacians not only had skin tents like the Neanderthalers of Salzgitter, but in some parts of Europe they built what amounted to proper huts, encasing the outside of the tepees with sticks and poles to give them added protection. Such dwellings contained a hearth and a smoke vent. Like the present day Eskimo they wore clothes made of animal skins, carefully sewn together. Wooden needles have been found, as well as the bone boxes in which these were carried around.

The Aurignacians probably dug rows of pitfalls across the tracks used regularly by the shaggy elephants. The herds were then made to move in the direction of these carefully camouflaged pits, either by a line of yelling and gesticulating beaters, or, if the wind was favourable, by setting the grass on fire, while strategically placed hunters saw to it that the animals did not break out on one side or another. If the

Rock shelter home of Magdalenian man

The Hottentots' method of using pitfalls for hunting elephants can be traced back to Aurignacian times (mid-eighteenth century drawing)

operation went off without a major hitch, a few of the stampeding pachyderms were sure to get themselves caught. Occasionally a few mammoths may also have been driven over a cliff.

The classic example of what the Blackfoot Indians called the 'deep-blood kettle' belongs to the next cultural level of the Old Stone Age, in which the place of the mammoth as man's favourite object of the chase had been taken by the wild horse. It is known as Solutrean, the name coming from Solutré, a small town not far from the famous vine-growing centre of Mâcon, in the valley of the Saône. There, at the foot of a 1,000 ft. high rock wall, which forms the edge of a sloping plateau, prehistorians have come across a deposit of wild horses' bones 4,000 sq. m. (4,784 sq. yds.) in extent and varying from 20 cm. (7.9 in.) to 2.3 m. (7.55 ft.) in depth. Conservative estimates speak of it representing the remnants of 10,000 to 40,000 animals, but there are those who say that it is in reality the tomb of about 100,000 horses which plunged to their deaths after having been driven up the slow incline of the plateau. Solutré is the greatest

and most important hunting station yet found, and it is thought to have been in operation for from ten to fifteen generations.

Where there were no convenient cliffs to facilitate the slaughter of horses, the Solutreans manoeuvred whole herds into enclosures or brought single animals down by using lassoos, bolas, slings, javelins propelled by spear-throwers—the implements known as 'woomera' in Australia—and, at least in certain areas, also bows and arrows.

The next and upper-most culture of the Palaeolithic, named Magdalenian after the cave of La Madeleine in the Dordogne, might just as well be called the Reindeer Age. In the two famous Magdalenian caves of Kesslersloch and Schweizersbild in Switzerland, about 75% to 80% of the bones found came from this species. People were as dependent on the reindeer as the Ihalmiut, the Eskimo inhabiting the Barren Grounds of Canada, have up to our time been dependent on the American reindeer or caribou.

The economy of the Barren Ground Eskimo is based entirely on the *tuktu*, as they call the caribou, and it provides them with food, clothing, tents, tools and, not so long ago, also with weapons. Their whole life is regulated by its migratory movements. The introduction of firearms has now led to overshooting of the herds with disastrous results to the Eskimo. Finds made during excavations in the mid-thirties at Meiendorf and Stellmoor, near Hamburg, revealed a way of life very similar to that of the Barren Ground Eskimos. They also led to the discovery of the most ancient bows that have, so far, been unearthed. From cave paintings and arrow tips found at many Stone Age sites it was known that bows had been in use prior to Mesolithic times. Artifacts at Meiendorf and Stellmoor belong to Palaeolithic and Mesolithic times, but it was amongst the Palaeolithic finds that bow-like pieces of wood were recovered. The bows had a length of about $1\frac{1}{2}$ m. (4·9 ft.) and were made of pine wood. Reindeer guts most probably served as bow-strings. The arrows were 20 to 75 cm. long (7·8 to 29·5 in), 0·5 to 1 cm. thick (0·2 to 0·4 in.) and tipped off with points made of flint, bone or horn. There were also axes made of reindeer antlers.

Of the bones recovered from Meiendorf and from the lower Stellmoor level, 90% came from reindeer, the rest from hares, wolverines, foxes, badgers, and from a good number of wildfowl, such as ptarmigans, swans, geese, ducks and moorhens.

There is one very important difference between the culture of the North German reindeer hunters and the Eskimo; the latter have their invaluable huskies to draw sledges for them and to help with the hunting, while there is absolutely no evidence of domestic dogs at either Meiendorf or Stellmoor.

We have now followed Man the Hunter through very many millennia, during which he has drawn practically all his sustenance from the animal king-dom. His entire existence was based on hunting, and the beasts that shared the world with him represented by far the most important factor affecting his survival. They therefore filled his thoughts and were the objects of all planning and endeavour. If he succeeded in outwitting them, he and his family could eat, could even gorge themselves to repletion—if his skill failed him, if the herds moved away from his vicinity, never to return again, there was starvation and death. No wonder that in his mind animals took on a very special significance, and became the focal point of magic rites and elaborate cults.

It is impossible to say at what stage in human prehistory this way of looking at the beasts of the chase originated; it was certainly present at the time of Neanderthal Man, as Emil Bächler was the first to

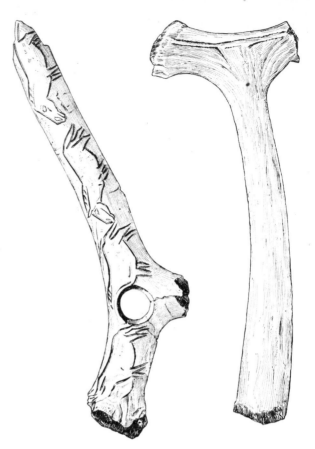

Left: *Magdalenian decorated reindeer antler (after Mortillet)*
Right: *Magdalenian antler hammer (after Absolom)*

prove. During his excavations in the Drachenloch Cave in the Swiss Alps he came upon a rectangular chest with walls made out of flat stones, the top covered by a heavy stone lid. This was itself a thrilling discovery, for the chest could be considered as the most ancient stone construction ever found. Things became even more exciting when two of Bächler's labourers carefully lifted off the lid revealing seven cave bear skulls, neatly packed into the chest and all facing towards the cave entrance. Ranged along the inside of the walls were three tibias, two ulnas and a broken humerus. As work progressed, several more chests were uncovered, each containing at least two or three, sometimes five or more skulls.

Bächler realized at once that he was confronted with one of the earliest manifestations of man's spiritual life. He had no doubts about the ritual significance of these skulls, so carefully packed away, and prehistorians the world over agreed with him. Perhaps the skulls were sacrifices or the cult might have been addressed to the bears themselves. Professor Meuli of Basel regards the storing of the skulls as a burial in ritual form, undertaken with due ceremony in order to reconcile the animals with the sad fact that they had to be deprived of their lives, so that the humans might live. Rites of exactly the same nature are, in fact, widely distributed among Siberian tribes and North American Indians, and they have often been described in great detail.

Primitive man does not think of himself as something unique, fundamentally different from the rest of the animal world. Even though he kills with all the ruthlessness of a predator, he has nevertheless an inborn feeling of close friendship, and even kinship, with the beasts that form his quarry, a feeling that highly anthropomorphic religions and philosophies have tried hard to eradicate in civilized man. Anthropologists working in northern Asia and North America have collected numerous myths and legends referring to a common ancestry with certain animals, especially with bears, and many an Eskimo tale begins with the words: 'It happened when one was half man, half animal . . .' Killing an animal cousin is not a thing to be undertaken lightly and special rites become necessary, not only to appease the feelings of the injured beast's *manes,* but also to clear the hunter of the blood guilt with which he has covered himself.

We do not know whether the Neanderthalers tried to cast spells over the animals in order to get them into their power, but it can be considered as certain that magic rites played a very important part in Aurignacian and Magdalenian times. The hunters of the Upper Palaeolithic tried to achieve this spiritual domination of their quarry by creating animal effigies which could have the form of engravings, of paintings or of plastic figures. Ice Age magic thus led to man's first venture into the world of creative art, hesitant and awkward in the Lower Aurignacian, but finally rising to that splendour and magnificence which we can admire in Altamira, Trois Frères, Lascaux, Rouffignac and many other famous caves.

Bison, wild horses, reindeer and mammoth are among the animals most often represented; red deer appear less often. Aurochs, rhino, musk ox, ibex, chamois, wild ass, wild boar, saiga antelope, elk and bear, they all turn up in those Ice Age art galleries. Arctic hares, marmots and lemmings are rare, and so are birds such as ptarmigan, cranes, swans, wild geese, duck, eagles and owls. Lions and other felines were depicted occasionally, possibly in connection with some protective magic, which was to keep these dangerous predators out of the way.

Many of the Magdalenian drawings and paintings are of a very high quality. The artist was, after all, not just drawing pretty pictures of bison and wild horses for his own edification, but he attempted to conjure the animals themselves on to the cave walls and to capture some of their life force, so that they would become vulnerable to magic influence.

After what has been said, it is easy to understand why animal representations make up four-fifths of Palaeolithic art. Human figures are much less numerous and, with few notable exceptions, less artistically perfect. Hunting scenes, showing man and game, are exceptional and almost entirely restricted to Spanish caves. One of the few hunting

A shaman disguised as a bison is casting a spell over a bison and a reindeer (after Bégouen and Breuil)

Cave drawing from Niaux showing bison wounded by arrows (Magdalenian)

pictures found in France is of a man, armed with a javelin and camouflaged in an animal skin, crawling up to an aurochs and it brings to mind George Catlin's famous water colour of two Plains' Indians, disguised as wolves, stalking a herd of bison.

Though the hunters themselves make only a rare appearance in this magical art, their hunting equipment can be seen all the more often, for animals are very frequently shown as being pierced by javelins, harpoons, and arrows, or being caught in traps and snares. In the Cave of Montespan there are several big clay figures of animals, most of them destroyed beyond recognition by humidity, though one is still in a good state of preservation and can be recognized as the headless statue of a bear. Between the forepaws lay a bear's skull and the clay body is pit-marked all over, clear evidence that it was prodded with spears, javelins or harpoons. It is safe to assume that on the occasion of a ceremony taking place the skull was fixed to the stump of the neck, and a bear skin may possibly have been spread over the figure, to give it an even more lifelike appearance.

It was in the interests of the Palaeolithic hunters that the animals they pursued should always remain plentiful, and they must have had magic spells which were supposed to act on the fertility of their quarry. Paintings and drawings are often of bulls following cows, of stags running after hinds. The two magnificent and very well preserved clay bison in the cave of Tue d'Audubert, which display no signs of having been stabbed at, are also thought to have been connected with fertility rites.

Some writers refuse to accept the view, held by the majority of prehistorians and ethnographers, that Palaeolithic art arose to serve the purposes of hunting and fertility rites. Their arguments, based mainly on statistical considerations, are however not convincing. They do not explain why the paintings are so often found in the remotest and darkest recesses of caves, or in passages to which access is very difficult. Moreover, they seem to ignore the fact that hunting magic of a very similar kind to that so obviously practised by the Aurignacians and Magdalenians is still alive today.

Leo Frobentus, the anthropologist, observed hunting magic being practised among the African pygmy tribes and Australian aborigines have been seen standing around the outline of a kangaroo sketched in the sand, poking the drawing with their spears. The Ice Age hunters stabbing at the bear effigy of Monte-

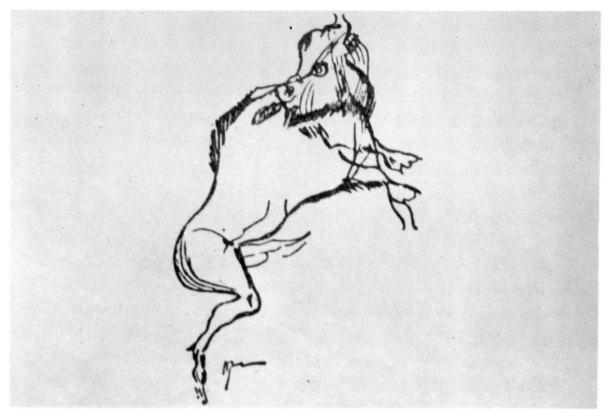

Shaman wearing a wild boar mask, from Grotte des Trois Frères

span, also brings to mind those practitioners of witchcraft and voodoo who, even in these supposedly enlightened days, seek to harm or even destroy an enemy by sticking pins into a wax doll! It can surely be said that beliefs and customs which have become ingrained in man from ancient times are exceedingly slow to die.

Even the earliest hunters may have danced around a fallen animal, in exuberant celebration of a success and in pleasant anticipation of the feast in store for them. In due course dances probably became an integral part of the rites which were performed in the mysterious depths of many a cavern, with lamps made of hollowed-out stones filled with fat casting a dim, flickering light over the painted animals on the walls, making them look truly alive and moving. Some members of the horde, who thought that they had a more than average ability to exert power over the game herds, soon began to take a leading part in the rites, assuming the role that is still played by the witch doctor, by the Shaman among some of the Siberian peoples and the Angekok of the Eskimo. To strengthen their mystic powers, they dressed up in skins and masks, imitating the gait and movements of the beasts over which they were trying to cast a

spell. Of this we have direct evidence in the form of cave paintings of masked dancers. The oldest representation of this kind from the Abri Megè in the Dordogne, shows three men wearing the heads and skins of chamois. The most famous is, of course, the 'sorcier' of the Grotte des Trois Frères, prancing around clad in a deer skin, with a horse's tail hanging behind and a pair of antlers sticking up from his head. In the same cave, another magician can be seen doing a lively dance dressed up as a wild boar, while a third one, wearing a bison's head on his shoulders, is exorcising a bison and a reindeer. The last scene recalls the bison dance of the now extinct Mandan Indians, recorded in masterly fashion by Karl Bodmer, the able Swiss artist who accompanied Prince Maximilian von Wied on his scientific expedition across the American prairies.

The elaborate hunting magic of the Aurignacians and Magdalenians, to which we owe humanity's first and by no means least experiment in artistic expression, does not seem to have been connected with sacrificial offerings until almost the close of the Reindeer Age. At Meiendorf and Stellmoor, a considerable number of complete and undamaged skeletons of young female reindeer were dug up, each

Karl Bodmer's painting of the buffalo dance of the Mandan Indians

with one or several stones enclosed in its rib cage. In one of them a shoulder blade was perforated by an arrow, a sign that it was an animal killed by hunters and not one that had simply been picked up dead. The undamaged state of the skeleton proved that the reindeer in question had not been eaten. They had, in fact, been thrown into a pond, weighted with stones, so that they would immediately sink to the bottom and remain there for ever.

A new element had thus entered Magdalenian hunting magic. The Shamans may have learned from bitter experience that their efforts to control the movements of game herds by direct magical influence were not as effective as they should have been, that they were in fact, very much hit and miss affairs. To prevent the blame for frequent blunders falling entirely on their own shoulders, they had the idea of inventing an unseen power, a 'Reindeer God' or a 'Great Spirit', that could be made responsible for unaccountable failures in finding game. In addition to performing their usual magic, the Shamans now had to intercede with the 'Great Spirit' and get his approval for every hunting enterprise. There was unfortunately always the possibility of the unseen power turning a deaf ear to their entreaties, be it out of sheer caprice or for having been offended by a member of the horde. The next step consisted in buying the 'Reindeer God's' or 'Great Spirit's' goodwill by offering a sacrifice before setting out to hunt, not forgetting to express one's gratitude in the same way after a successful season. Sacrifices of exactly the same type as those discovered at Meiendorf and Stellmoor took place during the Bronze Age, a good 10,000 years later.

A pole with the skull of a female reindeer stuck on top, which was found at Stellmoor, may also have had some cultic significance. The people who left such ample evidence of their presence in the upper Stellmoor level, were the last Ice Age hunters in Germany, perhaps in all of western and Central Europe. The edge of the Scandinavian ice shield had retreated far to the north and forests were already beginning to invade the European tundra. The reindeer still formed the main quarry of the Stellmoor hunters, as it had several thousand years earlier, but elk and beaver were also killed. The landscape was not that of the Barren Grounds any

Right: *The famous 'sorcier', clad in deer skin, from the Grotte des Trois Frères*

longer, but rather of Canada's subarctic forests, and the people must have lived more like the Chipewyan Indians than the Ihalmiut.

With the forests increasing in density, and oak trees making their first appearance, the reindeer herds moved northwards and the hordes or tribes whose economy was entirely based on these animals may have followed them. The Mesolithic hunters of the Azilian culture level—named after the Cave of Maz d'Azil—turned to the red deer for their main sustenance. When a stag was brought to bay, the forest now resounded not only to excited shouts, but also to eager barking, for man had at long last domesticated the dog, and thus won his first servant and helper from among the animal kingdom.

While there can hardly be any doubt about the dog being the first animal to have been domesticated in the true sense of the word, there is a definite possibility that some of the reindeer herds at the end of the Magdalenian might have been at least semi-domesticated, and we can be fairly certain that an economy based on tame reindeer, as it can still be found among the Samoyeds and other northern peoples, came into being at a very early date.

Living on a desolate tundra swept by chill winds coming off the northern ice shield and the glacier-covered mountain ranges, the hunters of the Upper Palaeolithic had no possibility for agricultural

experiments of any kind. There simply was nothing for them to grow, nor were the inhabitants of the subarctic forests, which later spread over the tundra, any better off. The Magdalenians succeeded splendidly in making the most of a difficult and often hostile environment, at the same time developing a culture of an amazing height and versatility. For them, and for their immediate successors, there was no other choice than the existence of the hunter, and as this meant a considerable amount of moving about, there was no inducement for the building of solid houses or for congregating in large communities. It was essential to remain mobile, to range as far and wide as did the game animals on which the economy depended. The semi-domestication of reindeer, which may have taken place in certain areas could not have brought about any fundamental changes, for whatever their status, the herds must still have been migratory.

Conditions were, however, very different in the mild lands between the Mediterranean, the Persian Gulf and the delta of the Nile, in the semi-circle around the Arabian Desert, which, at that time, fully deserved the name of 'Fertile Crescent'. It was there that primitive farming originated around 10,000 B.C. Sowing selected seeds and protecting the resulting shoots from the competition of other plants by means of careful weeding, gave man his start along the road which was to lead him to undisputed mastery of the world. He lived in sedentary communities for the first time in his existence, and, having settled down, he found the necessary leisure to experiment not only with a considerable number of plants, but with some animals as well. From 9000 to 6000 B.C. sheep, goats, and oxen became domesticated. The horse joined the ranks of man's slaves at a somewhat later date.

The change-over from a food-gathering to a food-producing economy brought about a steady increase in population density, and 9,000 years ago there was already a place which might have been called a town on the site of present-day Jericho. Agriculture spread east, west, south and, with the gradual improvement of the climate, also northwards into Europe. In areas of special fertility, such as the Nile Valley, Mesopotamia and the Valley of the Indus, populations were able to increase to a point where the formation of highly civilized communities became a possibility; but north of the Alps and the Pyrenees life was still far from easy. Even though the sombre coniferous forests of the immediate post-glacial age had now largely been replaced by deciduous trees, there were still the cold, snowy winters and the prospective farmer and animal husbandman found himself confronted with problems and difficulties quite unknown to the inhabitants of Mesopotamia, Egypt and Sind. Human ingenuity, however, came through triumphant, agricultural methods were adapted to adverse circumstances, and by 2500 B.C. we find the Lake-dwellers of Switzerland and Southern Germany living in villages consisting of comfortable wooden houses—not, according to most recent opinions, built on platforms over the water, but on the flat shores of the lakes which, at that period, had a level considerably lower than today—breeding cattle, goats, sheep and pigs, as well as planting millet, barley, spelt, wheat, flax, poppies, peas and lentils. Armed with bows and arrows, and accompanied by their pomeranian-like dogs, the men went hunting in the forests and killed large numbers of red deer. These animals were needed not so much for their meat but for their skins, and especially for their antlers, of which a great variety of useful tools and implements could be fashioned.

From excavations of the lowest culture level at the Lake-dwellers' site of St. Aubin in Switzerland it is thought that hunting furnished only about one fifth of the meat consumed by the inhabitants.

The effect that the transition to a producing economy was having on the population of Europe is well illustrated by the fact that the 2,000 years of the Neolithic Age produced a thousand times more human skeletal remains than the 200,000 Palaeolithic years preceding them!

In the earliest and most densely populated centres of civilization, agriculture and animal husbandry were now bringing forth considerably more food than was needed to feed the producing family units. This meant that large numbers of people could turn away from farming and devote themselves to various crafts, to pottery and weaving, to manufacturing tools and weapons, first exchanging their goods against food, later against money, with which food could be bought. Wealth began to be accumulated, and it soon grew into an instrument of power. As the communities became ever more closely knit, leaders arose, and kingdoms came into being. The wild animals, which had provided man with food over hundreds of thousands of years, were still around, but far from being the focal point around which all life revolved, they were now regarded as obnoxious pests. They were vermin preying upon his herds, ravaging his fields and he protected his property by killing them whenever he could. There was, of course, absolutely no necessity for kings, princes and their courtiers to demean themselves by going out into the

A reconstruction of a Neolithic household scene in Jericho by Maurice Wilson

wastelands surrounding the cultivated areas, in order to kill wild beasts. The animals could do them no harm, nor would hunting provide them with anything that they could not get in some very much easier way.

What, then, must we think of the hieroglyphic inscription on the scarab of Amenhotep III, in which the Pharaoh expresses his pride at having killed 110 fierce lions in Syria, and of having hunted wild oxen in the district of Queneh in Egypt? How can we interpret the boast of Tuthmosis III, that he slaughtered 120 elephants? And what about King Ashur-nasir-pal, who had it put on record that he slew 30 elephants, 257 aurochs and 370 lions. What about Tiglat-pileser I with his bag of 4 aurochs, 10 bull elephants and nearly 1,000 lions? The Assyrian kings went so far as to have their triumphs in the hunting field faithfully depicted on magnificently executed friezes, which show that they even bred lions in captivity and had them released in order to kill them.

Sculpture in bas relief of wounded lioness—from the hunting scenes of Ashur-bani-pal, King of Assyria, 668—630 B.C.

Untold millennia had left their indelible mark, and people who had absolutely no need to hunt went out, and battled with lions, elephants and wild oxen, enjoying every moment of it. Hunting, once a necessity on which human survival depended, had become a sport.

This very same development was to take place wherever man succeeded in attaining civilized status. In Persia, where King Cyrus established well-stocked game parks, hunting was declared as an excellent training for war.

The Greeks and Romans were enthusiastic sportsmen. Hunting wild boars stood in special favour among them, and they dedicated numerous temples to Diana—or Artemis—the Goddess of the Chase.

In western and Central Europe, where the Neolithic had now given way, first to the Bronze Age, and finally to the Iron Age, it was amongst the Celtic tribes of southern Germany, Switzerland and France that hunting acquired the character of sport at a very early date. The Celts had brought agriculture and animal husbandry to a level which was greatly admired even by the sophisticated Greeks and Romans. They were the inventors of the wheeled plough and of a simple harvesting machine. Agriculture was already making deep inroads into the European forest belt, and it can be assumed that at the beginning of our era there were no truly virgin forests, completely untouched by man, left in the densely populated country of the Helvetians, which today we know as Switzerland.

From the 'Cynegeticus' of Arrianus, the Greek author, we learn that hunting enjoyed a tremendous popularity. Bows and arrows served for shooting wild fowl, but javelins and spears must be considered as the Celtic sportsman's favourite weapons. He had at his disposal various types of dogs, such as bloodhounds, greyhounds and bassets, and the different breeds were often used together as a pack. There was an annual hunting festival, during which the devotees of the chase gave thanks for their successes by offering the Goddess of Hunting—whose name has not been recorded—payment for every head of game bagged during the past year. That hunting did not count as an economic factor any more was shown in a very striking way by the excavations at the site of a Celtic town near Manching in Germany, where of 276,428

Plate IV Hidden among the rocks of a kloof, Bushmen are shooting poisoned arrows into a mixed herd of black wildebeest, quagga, blesbok and springbok stampeded by other members of the tribe. Thomas Baines painted this beautiful canvas in 1849—a mere 34 years before the very last quagga died in a European zoo

Plate V William Cornwallis Harris, who hunted in the areas of the Orange River shortly before they were settled by the Boer trekkers, has left us a faithful pictorial record of the wildlife that could be found in the provinces now known as Orange Freestate and Transvaal

King Darius of Persia shooting a lion from his chariot—from a cylinder seal 500 B.C.

animal bones the great majority came from pigs, cattle, goats and sheep. Only 563 bones were from wild animals, mostly from red deer and roe deer.

Celtic hunting customs reveal the first stirrings of a somewhat more ethical attitude towards the quarry, the beginning of what nowadays might be called good sportsmanship. We are less well informed with regards to the hunting customs of the Teutonic peoples whose lands lay to the north of the Celts, though we have Caesar's testimony that their lives revolved around hunting and war. Swords and spears were the arms they used most often, while it took some time for the bow to become widely adopted. Their attitude to game seems to have been similar to that of the Celts, and it was mainly due to peoples of Teutonic descent, both in continental Europe and in the British Isles, that an ethical code of fair hunting became established, which has, with some setbacks, survived to the present day.

When large parts of Europe came under Teutonic domination after the fall of the Roman Empire, hunting was at first open without restriction to every free-man. More and more land came under cultivation and had to be protected against the ravages of game animals. Due to the cutting down of the forests that went with this intensification of agricultural activities, the habitat of the larger mammals became seriously reduced. Aurochs, bison, elk and wild horse declined in numbers, and even became extinct in certain parts of their range. All four species are known to have disappeared from Switzerland between the years A.D. 500 and 1200. In the old centres of civilization around the Mediterranean most of the game had long ago been eradicated through unrestricted hunting, and perhaps even more through habitat destruction. Now the same thing seemed to be happening all over western and central Europe.

Paradoxical as it may seem, the game survived due to the unbridled passion for sport which began to manifest itself among the masters of post-Roman Europe. The first unit to emerge from near-chaos was the Frankish kingdom, and its rulers were quick to abrogate to themselves the hunting rights which had hitherto been open to all. They claimed certain forests as their own private hunting grounds and this set an example that was to survive the splitting up of Charlemagne's empire and has found innumerable imitators to very recent times. The exhilarating sport of the chase became a jealously guarded privilege of nobility, and from the 10th to the 12th century increasing numbers of farmers were forced to give up the right to kill game on their own lands to their feudal overlords, who often used those rights to reward devoted courtiers or successful military leaders. Louis XI of France went to the extreme of declaring hunting the sole prerogative of the crown, denied even to the members of the nobility, except with the king's most gracious permission. In the cantons of the Swiss Confederacy dominated by wealthy towns, such as Berne, Zürich and Lucerne, hunting rights were firmly in the hands of the ruling burgher families, while in the rural cantons control was exerted by the local parliament, or by the dignitaries of the church. But, whoever was privileged to hunt, be he king, prince or baron, bishop, abbot or burgher, woe to the farmer bold enough to shoot an arrow at a deer feeding on his wheat! He would probably be hanged out of hand, and in medieval times the mere scaring away of game was regarded as an offence punishable, at least, by severe imprisonment. From the 15th century onwards farmers were allowed to chase deer off their fields, but they had to do this without wounding any of the animals.

One can, of course, sympathize with the wretched peasants, yet had the feudal sportsmen been less harsh in the exertion of their rights, the game would most certainly have been wiped out. As it is, we have to register the almost miraculous fact that since the beginning of our era, densely populated Europe with her highly developed agriculture has lost only one species and three subspecies of large mammals— aurochs, Caucasian bison (a victim of the Russian Revolution), Portuguese ibex and wild horse. While the aurochs were certainly exterminated through hunting and through the destruction of the forest habitat, the wild horse, as an animal of the open plains, may already have become rare when forests invaded most of the continent shortly after the Ice Age. The scattered herds which adapted themselves to life in a completely different environment probably vanished as much through interbreeding with domestic horses as through actual hunting pressure. In the steppes of southern Russia the European wild horse or tarpan survived until the last century. The subspecies known as Przewalski's horse can be found in Mongolia even today.

Medieval followers of the chase were mainly armed with spear and sword. From the 13th century onwards a new and fairly accurate weapon became available in· the form of the crossbow, and in the 16th century firearms reached a stage of development which made them adaptable to hunting purposes, sportsmen thus gaining another tremendous advantage over their quarry.

The noble art of falconry, which originated on the plains of Asia long before medieval times, stood in high favour, not only among the nobility, but also among the clergy. It is said that some priests could not be parted from their falcons even at Mass and set them down on the altar!

Under Louis XIV royal hunts grew into occasions of lavish display, and soon every prince and princeling in Europe was bent on imitating the 'Roi Soleil', much to the detriment of the more sporty aspects of the entertainment. Large numbers of animals were sometimes driven into enclosures and shot down by the ruler, his courtiers and his guests from a luxuriously appointed stand, to the accompaniment of prodigious feasting and drinking. Some gentlemen were disinclined to let anybody else have a shot, preferring to give a solo performance of mass slaughter to an admiring and fawning audience. During the first half of the 18th century a Bishop of Würzburg thus bagged 43 stags, 94 hinds, 32 fawns, 2 roe deer and 10 wild boar in the course of just one day. In 1769 Karl Eugen, Duke of Würtemberg, shot 200 rutting stags in less than a month, having them driven up to his gun one by one by a whole army of hunters and foresters. Despite frequent excesses of this kind, the animals continued to flourish, until the revolutions at the end of the 18th century and during the first half of the 19th century very nearly swept Europe's game from the face of the earth. In 1848 large areas of Germany were completely shot out within a few weeks, and only in some of the larger state forests and in a few remote mountain regions were some red deer, roe deer and wild boar able to survive.

Fortunately these orgies of ruthless destruction did not last very long. Order was restored, reasonable hunting laws were drafted, and the game recovered in a truly amazing way. Venerable customs and traditions which had been lost sight of during the period of luxurious court massacres, were revived and great stress was laid on an attitude of fair play. Game management became increasingly important, at first within the framework of forestry, but eventually as a fully-fledged and very important science in its own right.

The atavistic urge to hunt, to outwit a quarry, is still with us, and shooting as a sport has lost

After being driven into the water by beaters the luckless game faced certain death as easy targets from the courtiers' guns

A more common method was to release the animals into an arena—they soon faced death as they passed the ruler's stand. If they avoided the bullets it wasn't long before they were round again

none of its popularity. This chapter is not meant as an apology for what some people call blood-sports, nor is it supposed to contain a condemnation of the chase in all its various forms. A considerable array of honest and sincere arguments can, of course, be brought forward in opposition to hunting and as an animal lover, one feels emotionally constrained to agree with them. Yet it has to be remembered that so often it was the sportsmen who preserved the game from extermination, and one wonders what measures would have to be taken in the absence of hunting to keep the numbers of game animals within reasonable bounds. Control—and this means killing—surely is inevitable, so it might just as well be done in the form of controlled hunting, subject to strict game laws and to the rules of good game management.

There are, of course, the game hogs, the unprincipled killers, who have no hesitation in breaking the laws if they can do so with impunity. Others have no real interest in the sport and only shoot because it happens to be the fashionable thing to do. But many of those who hold hunting licences or rent shooting blocks must be respected as true sportsmen, who play the game according to the rules and try conscientiously to live up to the ethics of fair hunting. They get pleasure and recreation from wandering over fields and through forests with a gun, and not a few of them are genuine nature lovers. The interest in the spoils of the chase may be a mainly culinary one, and, where the sale of game to shops and restaurants is permitted, there often is some financial gain as well though this is usually kept to a fairly modest scale by the limits the law imposes upon the bag. There are also the hunters who rate the trophy higher than anything else.

Trophy hunting as we know it is of a fairly recent origin. The primitive hunter killed for meat, to make clothes from the skins and useful tools from bones and horns. If he kept some part of his quarry without making any practical use of it, then he did this for ritual purposes. We know that Ice Age hunters threaded bears' teeth upon strings and wore them around their necks. This has sometimes been considered as an early display of a trophy—but the teeth could just as well have been worn as some kind of an amulet.

William Cornwallis Harris was a big-game hunter with a love for natural history. When he went on an expedition to South Africa in the 1830s he painted the animals he encountered

In European castles, however, we find a good number of real trophies, mostly stags' antlers of unusual size and beauty, mounted on heads carved of wood. The advances made in the art of taxidermy during the 18th and early 19th centuries were responsible for the fashion of mounting the whole head of one's quarry. Sportsmen, who travelled abroad to North America, South Africa and India, brought back representative collections of the animals they encountered and had them mounted in this way. Right from the start they were, of course, keen to get specimens with especially fine horns, but it was only when a great number of trophies had been measured, and books like Rowland Ward's 'Records of Big Game' became available, that the hunters were given a definite scale and knew what they had to look for, so far as quality was concerned. Nowadays the judging of trophies has become something of a fine art and is done according to complicated formulae which take into account various measurements as well as the general shape and beauty of the horns.

Strangely enough, it is the trophy hunter who has come in for special censure on the part of people opposed to hunting. To kill an animal in order to eat it—even if there is absolutely no necessity to do so —may be forgiven; the sale of the hunter's spoils can be tolerated—perhaps because the critics like to buy an occasional pheasant or to eat jugged hare in a restaurant. But to hang the mounted head of a prize specimen on one's wall—that is an action which brings forth scorn and derision! There is, of course, not a single human activity where abuses and excesses do not occur, and anybody living in Africa can see more than enough 'trophy hunting' for sheer snobbery's sake. But serious hunting for really good specimens is certainly much less damaging than any other kind of shooting. The sportsman who is out to collect a near-record by fair means has to work hard for it, and when he finally bags his trophy, it is probably an old male, more or less past his prime so far as reproductive activity is concerned.

What did the few bison killed so that their heads could grace an ancestral hall in Britain or a baronial castle in Germany or in the Austro-Hungarian Empire weigh in comparison with the millions that were slaughtered for the sale of meat and skins?

Camera hunting in Nairobi National Park can be very easy

Chapter 3

Man, the Master

For most of the time he has existed, man has killed animals out of sheer necessity, his own survival depending on his skill as a hunter. It cannot be denied that he has had considerable advantages over his victims. The fortuitous evolutionary accident of some savannah-inhabiting African ape taking to moving about on its hind legs gave him the free use of his hands, enabling him to arm himself with weapons and thus to make up for the lack of the acute scent, sharp teeth and speed of wild dogs, the tremendous muscular coordination, the agility and the tearing claws of lion and leopard, or even the sheer brute force of the bear. Becoming acquainted with the use of fire at a very early stage, he was able to protect himself effectively against his fellow predators. The development of his brain gave him the power to reason, to plan, to remember the past and to assess the future, making him capable of outwitting the swiftest ungulate and the largest pachyderm.

Hunting was nevertheless a strenuous, exacting and often highly dangerous business. Man had to struggle hard to keep his place on earth, and there must have been very many setbacks. But we need not imagine Palaeolithic life as entirely grim and without cheer. It may actually have been quite a happy kind of existence, with the hunters thoroughly enjoying the thrills of the chase, the excitement of combat, the pitting of their wits against the more highly developed senses and the superior strength of their quarry. The successes were doubtlessly celebrated boisterously, in time of plenty there was feasting, good fellowship, and general merrymaking. When hard times came along, one gritted one's teeth and tried to survive as best as one could, perhaps getting a boost to flagging morale from the mysterious ceremonies performed in the deepest recesses of the caves, the impressive rites of which were fully expected to bring about a change for the better. The Eskimo live under conditions not very dissimilar to those during the last glaciation, and they are by no means an unhappy people!

A careful assessment of the evidence accumulated by prehistorians, explorers and anthropologists working among the primitive peoples of today, makes it quite evident that Palaeolithic hunters did not despise the beasts they pursued. They met them as worthy opponents, as equals, whom they were forced to slay, but for whom they nevertheless had a deep respect.

All this was radically changed when man made himself independent of hunting by producing food crops from the soil and when, soon afterwards, he succeeded in bringing a number of animals under his control. He gave them protection and either fed them or provided them with the possibility of feeding themselves under his direct care and guidance. In return they had to serve him, to carry both him and his baggage, to draw his vehicles; they had to provide him with wool, milk and eggs, and they had to die for him, so that he could consume their meat and make use of their skins.

The first to throw in his lot with man was the dog. Even though its presence in a domesticated form cannot be proved farther back than the Mesolithic Azilian and Maglemosian cultures, we can safely assume that experiments in bringing up dog-like animals took place a very long time ago, and in many different places. From time to time a man brought back some wolf cubs or a litter of young jackals, to amuse the women and children or with an idea of

Right: *Bambuti pygmy with prey*

eating them later on. Growing up in camp, the cubs soon began to look upon the humans as members of their own pack and to follow them about. They were seen to chase and bring down animals, and it cannot have taken long for somebody to assess the potentialities of these swift, determined but nevertheless sociable, and easily-tamed predators. In this way a partnership between hunters of equal standing was born, and it is significant that the dog has often been considerably more of a friend and associate than a mere servant.

The present state of our knowledge makes it very likely that, with the doubtful exception of the reindeer, the sheep can be considered as the first ungulate to have come under man's domination. While excavating the site of an agricultural settlement dating back to about 9000 B.C. at Zawi Chemi Shanidar among the rugged mountains of Kurdistan, an American expedition came across skeletal remains of sheep, which zoologist Charles A. Reed pronounced sufficiently different from those of the ancestral oriental mouflon, *Ovis orientalis*, as to be considered a primitive domestic form.

The animals were kept exclusively for meat, wool-producing sheep making their first appearance very much later, during the 4th millennium. Anatolia seems to be their most likely place of origin, and they spread to Egypt early in the 2nd millennium.

The oldest known skull of a domestic goat comes from the cave of El Khiam in Palestine and belongs to the 8th or 7th millennium, when the surrounding country was inhabited by Mesolithic farmers who built proper houses and planted rye and wheat. It differs considerably from that of the wild goat, *Capra hircus*, which today ranges from Sind through Persia, Caucasia and Asia Minor to Crete and some of the Aegean Islands, and this points to domestication having taken place long before, perhaps in northern Syria, Anatolia or western Persia. During the 5th millennium there were people in Mesopotamia who lived in tents and had large herds of goats, though they apparently also grew corn. In many areas not well suited for agricultural pursuits, in deserts and semi-deserts, wandering nomads were soon to base their economy exclusively on their herds of sheep, goats, and cattle.

Why the pig, present in the Near East some 5000 to 6000 years ago, and at times considered as a sacred animal, should suddenly have been declared unclean among the Hebrews has given rise to a lot of speculation. Hygienic reasons were favoured by many authorities, but it has also been pointed out

that managing a large number of pigs is far more difficult for nomadic peoples than driving herds of other live-stock. The domestic pig's ancestor is the wild boar, *Sus scrofa*, of Europe, North Africa, western, south-western and central Asia.

The various breeds of cattle are descendants of the mighty aurochs, *Bos primigenius*, which as we know from the 'game books' of Tuthmosis, Ashur-nasir-pal and Tiglat-pileser, occurred not only in Europe, but throughout the Near East as well, ranging from the Caucasus through Syria, Mesopotamia and Palestine to Egypt. Domestication must have taken place during the 7th and 6th millennium, very probably in many different places and over quite a long period.

No efforts whatever seem to have been made to domesticate the European bison. The high tablelands of inner Asia contributed the yak, *Bos grunniens*, which, however, did not spread very far beyond its original range. The Asiatic buffalo, *Bubalus bubalus*, with an area of distribution that once extended from Burma to the Nile Delta, probably entered man's service at the time of the Indus Valley Civilization. Within the Fertile Crescent it appeared in domesticated form about 3,000 years ago. The wild buffaloes vanished from Egypt during the 3rd millennium, but their tame descendants can still be seen wallowing in the irrigation channels along the Nile.

It was soon realized that cattle were not only excellent providers of milk and meat, but could be made to draw ploughs and carts, to turn water wheels and even to carry people on their backs. Representations of oxen being ridden have been found both in Mesopotamia and in Egypt, and riding oxen are still in use in certain parts of Africa.

Of the equines, the ass, *Equus asinus*, was the first to be domesticated. This must have happened in North Africa, where it occurred in a wild state, probably during the 4th millennium. In ancient Egypt it was for a long time the most common beast of burden, much admired for its strength, endurance and virility, and we hear of desert caravans consisting of 300 asses. The now extinct Syrian wild ass, not a true ass at all, but an onager, *Equus hemionus*, entered the ranks of domestic animals for a time, but was eventually ousted by the horse, which proved a stronger, faster and generally more serviceable beast.

The domestic horse came into use on the plains of central Asia and possibly southern Russia at about 4000 B.C., and there is no reason why both Przewalski's horse and the tarpan *(Equus caballus przewalski* and *E.c. gmelini)* should not have figured in its ancestry. It reached the Nile Valley at the time of the Hyksos

Cattle boats on the Nile—VIth Dynasty

invasion, early in the 2nd millennium, and became known as 'ketri', meaning 'the yoked', to the ancient Egyptians. The horse was, in fact, made to draw chariots long before it was ridden, the harness being of the same type as that used for an ox. This gave it no chance to make full use of its strength, but thousands of years were to pass before a harness which really fitted its build, and turned it into a first-class draught animal, was eventually designed. Horses were first ridden bareback or with saddle-cloths and it took an astonishingly long time for the saddle to be invented.

The one-humped camel or dromedary, which was to enable man to penetrate the farthest corners of the Arabian and North African deserts, seems to have lost its freedom during the 4th millennium. Its subjugation was so total that nothing whatever is known of its wild ancestors, which presumably must have existed somewhere in Arabia. Wild Bactrian camels, however, were discovered in the Kum-tagh Desert of Chinese Turkestan, by General Przewalski, the Russian explorer.

Considering the important part the dromedary was to play in the Sahara Desert, the Sudan and even as far south as the Somali peninsula, it may seem amazing that this animal became properly established in Egypt only in Graeco-Roman times. There is evidence that odd specimens reached the country very much earlier—a camel hair rope about 2,500

years old has, for instance, been found at Fayum.

The 'domestic' cat, is usually stated to have originated in Egypt about 2,000 to 2,500 years before the Christian era. While it is true that it made its appearance in the country of the pyramids at about that time and promptly managed to acquire sacred status, there were, in fact, tabbies roaming the streets of Jericho in the late 6th and early 5th millennium. The archaeological site of Hacilar in Asia Minor, which dates back to the middle of the 6th millennium, has produced several small statues representing women playing with cats.

Rock pigeons appear to have been the first birds to become associated with man, most likely being attracted to his villages and towns fairly soon after his settling down to an agricultural life. Representations of pigeons from the 4th millennium have been found in northern Mesopotamia and in Palestine.

Domestic geese, descended from the familiar greylags, have been with us for almost as long as pigeons, while chickens began laying eggs for man's benefit in the valley of the Indus during the 3rd or early in the 2nd millennium.

Compared with the mammals and birds we have dealt with so far, the rabbit is quite a newcomer. It is supposed to have been domesticated by the Romans in Spain, but in most parts of Europe it only became established during the Middle Ages.

I have not yet mentioned the Indian elephant, and

I do not know if I should do so for, though it has served man in various ways since the 3rd millennium, stocks have mainly been replenished by bringing in more and more wild-caught animals, and only to a very small degree by actual breeding. It is questionable, therefore, whether we can consider it as a case of real domestication.

The New World brought forth few additions to the list of man's servants; only three of them, the turkey, the muscovy duck and the guinea pig, have become generally accepted. The two animals that can be considered as the greatest American triumph in animal domestication, the load-carrying llama and the wool-producing alpaca, remained restricted to their Andean homelands.

To have made so many beasts and birds his servants and slaves was undoubtedly one of man's greatest cultural achievements, but it seems also to have filled him with an inordinate sense of superiority with regard to the animal kingdom as a whole. Gone was his respect, his feeling of close kinship. He became Man the Master, Man the Unique, and it is surely significant that all the religions which have emerged from the East are built on highly anthropocentric foundations, setting man far apart from the rest of creation and fully supporting his claim to absolute dominance over all living things. Christianity, for instance, gave man an immortal soul, but denied it to animals, leaving them soulless so that they could be ignored as unworthy of any consideration. Buddhism, so often acclaimed as a religion friendly to animals, is, if possible, even more anthropocentric than the others. Animals do receive a certain amount of at least theoretical consideration, but only because they are regarded as the receptacles of human souls which, after a life more or less misspent, have to descend to a lower sphere. The accent is on 'lower' sphere, and man towers far above the animal world.

The trend started by the great religions has been pursued assiduously by a host of philosophers and, even today, over a hundred years after Darwin's *Origin of Species*, some philosophizing scientists are performing the most amazing antics in postulating the uniqueness of man, even if only on the spiritual level.

All this has left the animal kingdom wide open to unlimited and ruthless exploitation, by no means only on behalf of human survival but just as much in the interest of luxury, pleasure and entertainment. The utter failure of religious leaders and philosophers to provide any sort of ethical guidance in these matters has, all too often, been interpreted as a licence for the perpetration of the most unspeakable cruelties in the normal course of everyday life.

The primitive farmer of the Fertile Crescent was often forced to take up arms in order to protect his crops and livestock from the ravages of wild beasts. If he could not spare the time, or did not feel skilled or courageous enough to cope with lions, leopards, wolves, wild pigs and wild oxen, he had to look for help. There were, after all, many who found it impossible to go without the deeply ingrained exhilaration of the chase and those who could not afford to kill for sport thus had a chance to make hunting their profession. This must have been the first step towards 'commercial exploitation of wild animal resources'.

Man might now have his sheep, goats and cattle, but venison was still eaten, and some came to regard it as a welcome change from beef and mutton. In civilized society there was a rapidly growing demand for leather, which could, in part, be satisfied by the sale of wild animal skins. Some beasts had beautiful pelts, and these were appreciated and highly prized by the wealthy.

For a long time, man had been dependent on animal skins to clothe himself. Now that he had learned to manufacture textiles out of the flax he grew and from the wool of his sheep and long-haired goats, the coats of certain wild animals became associated with luxury and the Near-Eastern hunter must have found it easy to get rid of cheetah and leopard skins.

The best and most precious pelts, however, were found in the cold regions of the north, far away from the ancient centres of civilization. It seems probable that many Magdalenian women trimmed their reindeer clothes with the furs of martens, ermines and foxes, as Eskimo girls do to this day. We definitely know that the Teutonic peoples of the Bronze Age wore furs for adornment. But this was still a more or less incidental use of pelts, and it needed the demand generated by a high level of civilization to turn furs into a valuable commodity.

The fur-trade is possibly the oldest large scale commercial exploitation of a group of animals for a purpose that had nothing to do with the pressing needs of everyday life. As early as the 7th century B.C. furs from the countries between the Ural Mountains and the River Yennisei found their way to the Mediterranean markets.

Around the year A.D. 800 several important fur-marts were in full operation right across what was later to become Russia, from Bolghar on the Volga to Cherdyn (Perm) and to Kholmogory on the

Sable furs as they were worn in 15th century Novgorod

Dvina, near present-day Arkhangelsk. The most important of these trading centres, however, was located on the River Volkov, near its entry into Lake Ilmen. It had been founded by the Varangians, the eastern branch of the Vikings, who named it Holmgard. Rurik, the Norse adventurer, who carved himself a kingdom out of these Slavic lands, made it his capital and it can thus be considered as the first capital of Russia. The Slavs called the place Novgorod, the New Town, and under this name it grew into a very wealthy medieval merchant city.

The fur traders of Novgorod opened up the northern basin of the River Dvina, reached the White Sea and are known to have hunted on Novaya Zemlya in the 11th century. In the 14th century they also sent expeditions over the Urals into Siberia. There were very close links with the town of Wisby on the Island of Gotland, and especially with the Hanseatic ports. The Hanseatic League established an agency in Novgorod, which was known as the 'German Court'. Trade was brisk, for in the early parts of the Middle Ages fur clothing reached a peak of popularity in central and western Europe.

With Novgorod placed astride the waterway from the Baltic to the Black Sea, its merchants also had direct communications with Constantinople and with places even much farther away, precious furs being appreciated at that time quite as much by oriental potentates and courtiers as by the nobility and the burghers of Germany. The fur fairs, which took place in mid-winter, when travel was easy on the frozen rivers and lakes and there were no mosquitoes and gnats to make life miserable, counted merchants from Arab countries among their regular visitors, and one Ibn Fadhlan, an emissary of Caliph Muktedi of Baghdad, has left an account of his adventures among Russian snows, where people travelled, as he put it, 'on small dog-carts without wheels'. He also described the skis, which, he said, gave the hunter such speed that he 'conquers the birds in flight or greyhounds in running, even the reindeer, which is twice as fast as a stag.'

In the late Middle Ages, the European demand for furs was still considerable, even though pelts were used more as an inside lining or in trimming certain articles of attire, than for manufacturing whole garments. By that time Novgorod had already gone into decline. After its conquest by Ivan III in

1494, the 'German Court' was closed, and in 1570 the town received the death blow at the hands of Ivan the Terrible, who sacked and plundered it, killing 60,000 people in the process.

Russian penetration of Siberia, hitherto restricted to occasional trading ventures, really got into its stride in 1580, when the Cossack leader Yermak, supported by Prince Stroganov, crossed the Urals with a force of 1636 men and conquered the Tartars. Yermak was drowned in the River Yrtisch in 1584, and his followers returned to Russia, but the road had been opened, and numerous bands of adventurers and hunters began pouring into that immense and very sparingly inhabited country. In 1628 the Russians reached the Lena and founded the town of Yakutsk, and two years later they established themselves on the Sea of Okhotsk. Furs were the lure that brought about this rapid advance, and led to the subjugation of the Yakuts, the Tungus and other Siberian peoples who had hitherto lived a primitive and peaceful existence as hunters and reindeer nomads. The vast forests constituted an untouched treasure house, swarming with beautiful squirrels, with lynxes, foxes, otters and ermines. Above all, they were the home of that prince of Old World fur-bearers, the sable!

The sable, *Martes zibellina*, resembles the European pine marten, *Martes martes*, but its fur is longer and finer, darker in colour, and with a throat patch more orange than yellow. This wonderful fur meant as much to the Russian invaders of Siberia as the Inca's gold to the Spanish conquerors of Peru.

A very able Russian naturalist, S. P. Krasheninnikow, who was Steller's companion and assistant in the far-eastern forests, wrote: 'Before the conquest of Kamchatka there was so great a plenty of sables that one hunter would kill 70 or 80 in a year; and that not for the sake of the fur, but the flesh, which they esteem very delicious. The inhabitants at that time willingly agreed to pay tribute in sables; and were glad to receive a knife for 8, and an axe for 18. Some merchants have gained in one year by furs only, more than 30,000 roubles. The sable are still in much greater

The sable—Martes zibellina

plenty here than in any other country. . . .'

Many of the Siberian pelts went to Irbit, where great fairs had been held since 1643, and to Nizhni, (Lower) Novgorod (at present called Gorki), a place on the confluence of the Rivers Volga and Oka, which had gradually taken Novgorod's place as the great emporium of the fur trade. Early in the 19th century, the merchants of that town also began to organize annual fairs, which soon attained great fame. About 75% of the furs passing through Nyzhni Novgorod are said to have gone on to Leipzig.

A considerable part of the precious harvest, however, did not flow west to Europe, but south into China, where furs had been objects of great luxury for a very long time. It is understandable that this double drain on the Siberian resources of fur-bearing animals would soon make itself felt, and as early as the 1740s, Krasheninnikow found himself obliged to write:

'Before Siberia was conquered by the Russians, it abounded with sables; but at present, wherever the Russians are settled, none can be caught; for sables retire at a distance from all inhabited places and live in desolate woods and mountains.'

A work of reference, published in 1911, had this to say:

'The sable, which formerly constituted the wealth of Siberia, is now exceedingly rare.'

While the Russian fur traders advanced from west to east across Siberia, a similar penetration took place in an east-westerly direction in North America, halfway across the world from the endless forests of the Lena and the Yenissey.

The Canadian forests were not very different from those of Siberia. If anything, they harboured an even greater profusion of fur-bearing animals. There were foxes of many colours, raccoons, ermines, badgers and bears. In place of the sable could be found the American marten, *Martes americana*, and the magnificent pekan, *Martes pennanti*. The network of rivers and streams, on which one could travel by canoe from Quebec to the foot of the Rocky

Fur auction in Alaska: A combined fur market and carnival is held every year at Anchorage—thousands of dollars worth of furs are sold during the weekend fur rendezvous

Mountains, was teeming with otters, mink, muskrats and more especially, with beavers. To this interesting rodent fell the part the sable had played in the conquest of Siberia. As A. Radcliffe Dugmore, naturalist and pioneer animal photographer, put it in his excellent and informative book: *The Romance of the Beaver*: 'In reading the earlier history of Canada, we find that from the beginning, its development was inextricably interwoven with the life, I should say, the death of the beaver. It lived on the beaver.'

The forest Indians hunted the beaver assiduously, eating it, applying its fat as a skin ointment and using the pelts for making caps and for adorning their buckskin clothes; but it was also the subject of innumerable myths and legends, and some tribes even claimed descent from it.

The French colonization of the St. Lawrence was the beginning of a long period of ruthless exploitation of the beaver. Beaver waistcoats were soon worn in Paris; a way of manufacturing a very fine felt from beaver pelt was discovered and this led to a wide-spread and long-lasting fashion for beaver hats. Beavers became big business and lured an army of French trappers—'coureurs de bois' as they were called—into the Canadian wilderness. Two of them, Pierre Radisson and Jean Baptiste Groseillers, pioneered the overland route from the St. Lawrence River to Hudson's Bay and later quarrelled with Governor d'Argensons, who wanted to deprive them of the greater part of their profit. They sailed to London and managed to interest Charles II and Prince Rupert in beaver pelts, thus becoming instrumental in the setting up, under Royal Charter, of an organization that had a beaver in its coat of arms and bore the rather ponderous official designation of 'The Governor and Company of Adventurers of England Trading into Hudson Bay'. After 300 years it is still the biggest trading company in America, though now known as the 'Hudson's Bay Company'.

In 1759 the whole of Canada became a British possession, and almost immediately two new fur companies sprang up in Montreal. There was bitter

The Plain's Indians were masters at making fur and skin adornments. On the right is a beaver pelt

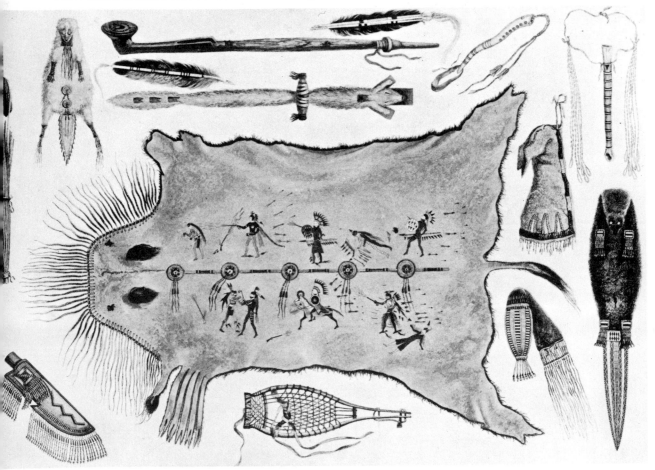

The beaver played an important part in Canadian history

rivalry, but the threat from the powerful Hudson's Bay Company eventually brought the Montreal traders to their senses, and the latter joined forces under the name of the North West Company.

Between the North West Company and the Hudson's Bay Company something akin to a state of war existed for a good many years, and acts of violence were by no means unheard of. From the side of the newly established United States, a German immigrant by the name of John Jacob Astor joined in the fray, sent his own expeditions to the still unclaimed territory known as Oregon and laid the foundation of the fabulous Astor fortune.

It must not be thought, however, that the virtual rule of the fur companies over large parts of Canada only led to vicious quarrels, for a great deal of effort went into exploration, and the tremendous pioneering journeys of Samuel Hearne, Alexander Mackenzie, and David Thompson were all undertaken in the interests of the fur trade. In 1821, the two big companies finally buried the hatchet and amalgamated under the name of the Hudson's Bay Company.

From the meticulous records of the fur companies we can get an excellent idea of the rate at which the fur-bearing animals of the North American forests, and, more particularly the beavers, have been destroyed. In 1742, for instance, two parties of Indians arrived at the Hudson Bay post of Fort Prince of Wales, bringing in 50,000 beaver pelts and 9,000 martens. Towards the end of the 18th century, the North West Company handled an annual total of 106,000 beavers, 32,000 martens, 11,800 minks, 10,000 muskrats and 17,000 other skins. At the trading posts, 10 to 12 beaver pelts would buy a gun, six pelts a red Hudson Bay blanket, a braided coat (what an atrocity to sell to an Indian brave!) or a laced woman's dress. Half a pound of powder, four pounds of lead, an axe, six knives, and a pound of tobacco cost one pelt each item. For a comb and a mirror two pelts had to be put on the counter.

This was, of course, the kind of exploitation that inevitably kills the goose laying the golden eggs. During the 19th century this fact must have become painfully apparent at the Hudson's Bay Company's headquarters. From 1853 to 1877 an annual average of something like 118,615 beaver pelts were sold on the London market. Sales dropped to 50,000 in 1897, to 46,000 in 1902, and it is doubtful whether more than 30,000 skins were taken over the entire range of the species in the years just before and after 1910. Beaver hats had, of course, long since gone out of fashion, but there were still plenty of uses for the furs. Now, by good fortune, the demand began to dwindle rapidly, and it was this decline in interest that saved the beaver and gave it a good chance of recovery. To-day, it is doing well in many parts of North America and has been reintroduced in a number of regions where it had been trapped out a long time ago.

While the North West Company struggled for supremacy with the Hudson's Bay Company, and had its precarious hold over Oregon challenged by the American Fur Company, the Russians gained a foothold in Alaska, on the coast discovered by Bering in 1741, and touched by Chirikov, another member of the 'Great Northern Expedition', shortly afterwards.

Steller's reports brought a tremendous influx of 'promishlenkis', as the Russian fur traders were called, into the northern Pacific, and while the French 'coureurs de bois', the agents of the Hudson's Bay Company and the Scottish Canadian traders had always tried to keep on friendly terms with the Indians—who, after all, provided them with most of the pelts—the Siberian adventurers displayed no inhibitions and indulged in bloody massacres and wholesale robbery. The animals which caused this outbreak of general mayhem were principally the sea otter and the northern fur seal, or sea bear. The extermination of Steller's sea cow was just one minor incident of this violent and sanguinary epoch.

The sea otter, *Enhydra lutris*, is a most striking animal, about 4 ft. to 4 ft. 6 in. in total length, with

Seals of the Bering Sea as figured by Steller

Sea otter—Enhydra lutris

a 1 ft. tail. The head is roundish, the ears are small, hardly visible above the fur, the eyes black and beady, and the white whiskers resemble those of a cat. The species can be found along rocky mainland coasts and island shores, mostly in schools, which may number over a hundred individuals.

This engaging creature differs from other marine mammals by not having a subcutaneous layer of fat. Its protection against the cold comes entirely from the air trapped in its fur, the pelt therefore being quite exceptionally dense, soft and silky. It has been the sea otter's misfortune to carry just about the finest fur in the world, and because of this it has had to suffer 170 years of relentless and indiscriminate persecution.

Around the northern Pacific there is no coast, no bay, no fjord or inlet, no island, sound or strait that was not searched and searched again for what became known to the fur traders as 'Kamchatka Beaver', and by 1910 the sea otter had been practically exterminated. When the species was given protection on an international basis, it was not definitely known whether it still existed. There certainly was no profit in going to look for any survivors, and this may have been the reason why no one objected to the proposed conservation measures.

There had been some survivors, however, and in 1938 zoologists and conservationists were amazed and thrilled by the news that a school of sea otters had been sighted off Bixby Creek on the coast of California. The rangers of the Wildlife Service of Alaska then discovered small colonies of otters in no less than five different bays. Since that time, the species has steadily increased in numbers both on the American and the Asiatic side of the Pacific, but, after over fifty years of strict protection, not more than about one fifth of its former range has been regained.

Steller had found both the sea otter and the fur seals on Bering Island, and the Komandorskie Group therefore became the 'promishlenkis" first object. After having wiped out most of the seals both on Bering Island and Copper Island, they moved on to the Aleutians, establishing their headquarters on Unalaska, and one Captain Pribilov set sail for some reported seal islands far to the north. After a long search he turned up in 1787 at the Siberian port of Okhotsk with no less than 40,000 seal skins. The Captain had found the islands and they bear his name to this day.

A year later 20 ships visited the Pribilov Islands and it is said that one crew managed to kill and skin 4,000 seals in one single day.

News travelled slowly in those days, but when reports of the 'promishlenkis' doings began to reach St. Petersburg, the Russian Government took steps to establish law and order and formed a semi-official trading organization, the Russian-American Company, with Alexander Baranov as its resident director. No less than 280,000 sea bears reached Russia in

1803, and a lot more were sold to American and British traders on what might be called the 'black market'. The number of sea bears declined rapidly and Baranov finally had to introduce a closed season for the Pribilov Islands.

In 1867 the United States bought the Russian American possessions for 7,200,000 dollars. The Pribilov Islands' seal population had increased to about 20,000,000 animals, and exploitation was leased to a private company. This step brought about a tremendous amount of poaching, and the Bering Sea became the stage for an epoch of lawlessness, which rivalled the early days of the 'promishlenkis'. The fur seal herds dwindled away and by 1894 there were only 600,000 left. At this point the Government of the United States stepped in and introduced an excellent game management scheme, while the massacres at sea were stopped by international treaty. The much depleted Pribilov herds made a total recovery, and today 30,000 skins can be harvested annually. Fur seals have also returned to the Komandorskie Islands and to other places where they could formerly be found.

The story of the Pribilov Islands shows that commercial exploitation need not be an unmitigated evil. The animal lover may not like the actual killing involved, but if this is done under strict control and on the basis of sound scientific data, it will not be fatal to the species as a whole. In a world in which the balance of nature has been thoroughly upset almost everywhere, controlled exploitation may sometimes even be desirable to keep populations within reasonable bounds and to prevent them from suffering heavy losses through lack of food, overcrowding and disease. It is, however, an unfortunate fact that exploitation as practised on the Pribilovs still has to be considered the exception rather than the rule, and blind greed, not sound reasoning, is more often the driving force, as it was in the early days of sealing in the Bering Sea.

Beside the sea bear, *Callorhinus ursinus*, of the northern Pacific, there are several other species of

Licensed sealing: seals being clubbed to death on one of the Pribilov Islands

fur seals. They can be found on Guadalupe Island off Lower California (*Arctocephalus phillipsi townsendi*), on the coasts and islands of South America (*A. australis*), and South Africa (*A. pusillus*), around the southern tip of New Zealand and on adjacent islands (*A. forsteri*) and on many sub-Antarctic islands of the southern Indian and Atlantic Oceans (*A. tropicalis*). It is sad to record that in all of these places they have fared extremely badly at the hands of man. After James Cook's pioneer explorations of the Antarctic seas had revealed the presence of great numbers of seals on many of the islands discovered by the great navigator, sealing captains began to sail south, using his charts and searching for other islands. The fur seals of St. Paul and Amsterdam Islands had gone by 1808, and about 320,000 animals were killed on the South Shetland Islands from 1821 to 1822. The crew of one ship alone massacred 9,000 seals in three weeks, while two ships manned by 60 sailors brought home a season's catch of 45,000 skins. According to Bailey and Sorenson, the New Zealand species was just about extinct by 1840.

When indiscriminate persecution ceased, the various species of southern fur seals began to recover, but they have by no means regained all the lost ground. On Kerguelen, where they were once common, P. Paulian, a French zoologist, who recently investigated the fauna of that island, was able to find just one specimen. In some other areas strict protection has brought about considerable increases, and the world population is at present assessed at between 430,000 and 900,000 animals.

The actual killing of seals has nothing whatsoever in common with real hunting. The animals can usually be clubbed to death with the greatest of ease, and one wonders how many women would wear a sealskin coat, if they were present to see the wretched creatures having their skulls bashed in, and the skins ripped off their bloody, twitching carcases. The present world-wide outcry against the revolting butchery of baby harp seals, *Phoca groenlandica*, along the coast of Labrador and in St. Lawrence Gulf, has been very encouraging to animal lovers and conservationists alike, and it is to be hoped that the pressure will be kept up and, if necessary, increased.

Public opinion has, after all, been successful in putting an end to the shocking slaughter of koalas. Yes, incredible and shameful as it may appear today, these delightful 'teddy bears' of the Australian eucalyptus forests have also been victims of the fur trade! In 1927 about 600,000 were killed in just one month, and that year's export amounted to over a

Top: *Baby harp seal—after clubbing*
Above: *Mother seal over the carcase of her cub*

million skins. Numbers soon dropped to a point where the survival of the species became a matter of utmost concern. Under strong pressure from the public, the koala was protected just in time, and it now shows satisfactory signs of recovery.

It has been the same all over the world—wherever an animal was unfortunate enough to have a nice, soft fur, it was killed off mercilessly for the sake of human vanity. That lovely creature, the chinchilla, once extremely common, is now extinct in Peru, and very rare in Chile. The magnificent black and white colobus monkeys, too, are still being slaughtered relentlessly. In the far interior of South America, the splendid giant otter, *Pteronura brasiliensis*, is at present being hunted on such a scale that it will soon be on the verge of extinction.

Why does the modern woman crave to be dressed up in animal skins as if she were living in the Stone Age? In Palaeolithic times there was nothing else to wear. During the Middle Ages, houses and even castles must have been miserably cold and draughty, and it can be understood that there was a great and very general demand for furs. Heating has long ago ceased to be a problem, and present-day technology can produce textiles of every possible kind, including artificial furs with all the qualities of the real thing and with greater durability—so, at least, the advertisements tell us. But no, blood must flow to clothe her ladyship, and what does she care if five million ranch minks and a further million wild ones have to give their lives and skins every year to satisfy her capricious whims.

So far as species survival is concerned, we can derive some consolation from the fact that it has become possible to breed quite a number of fur-bearers in captivity. The mink is an outstanding example, and the Russians have had excellent successes with ranching sable. The chinchilla, too, is firmly established in captivity. But madam must always have something new, something out of the ordinary, and one of the most deplorable developments of recent years is the urge that has come over playgirls, so-called models, film stars and other assorted females of the human species to display themselves in garments made of skins rightfully belonging to leopards, jaguars, ocelots, clouded leopards and snow leopards. Tens of thousands of these beautiful spotted cats have been trapped and killed, and their skins have become valuable enough to encourage large-scale poaching and smuggling in countries where the animals in question enjoy a certain degree of legal protection. Some people may try to shrug the whole matter off by pointing out that the victims are, after all, predators. But so are the creatures who strut around in their stolen skins, and in these enlightened days it seems rather pointless to kill one predator simply in order to clothe another one—quite apart from the fact that a leopard, for instance, is doing a useful job keeping down baboons, wild pigs and small buck.

It would be so easy for civilized governments to prohibit the import and sale of these skins and thus to stop the senseless killing. President Hoover stopped the importation of koala skins into the United States—is there no statesman of his calibre around today?

Mammals bearing soft furs or handsomely marked skins are by no means the only animals that have had to pay a heavy tribute to human vanity. Looking through the files of illustrated magazines published about 60 years ago, we find the ladies of the time not trying to look like panthers or outsize teddy bears, but imitating peacocks and fantail pigeons, carrying on their heads weird and monumental contraptions bristling with feathers and plumes.

The use of feathers for personal adornment is, of course, a very ancient custom and has played an important part among many primitive peoples.

Ostrich plumes were popular in Europe for a long time, waving from knights' helmets and German mercenaries' caps, from the hats of noble ladies at 17th and 18th century courts, and from the elaborate efforts of the milliner's art worn by 19th century society beauties. In the Sudan and in Arabia ostrich hunting was, therefore, a very profitable occupation until the practical South Africans began breeding the birds in captivity.

Not satisfied with what could now be obtained fairly easily and without doing any harm, the dictators of fashion had to look round for something more spectacular. They came up with the wretched idea of propagating the use of the magnificent plumes which adorn the males of many of the birds of paradise. Malay plume hunters invaded the forests of New Guinea and the Aru Islands and the beautiful birds were killed in tens of thousands, so that their ornamental feathers might grace women's headpieces in Paris, London and New York. At one single London sale of 12,500 bird skins collected for millinery purposes, no less than 2,000 were birds of paradise.

Equally scandalous was the fashion of decorating hats with the delicate white plumes worn by egrets at breeding time. To obtain them, the 'hunters' slaughtered the parent birds at their nests and left the young to starve. Wherever there were breeding colonies of these lovely birds, from the Delta of the Danube to the remotest marshes of the Gran Chaco, the plume hunters sought them out, leaving death and desolation in their wake. Lawless gangs raided the colonies of egrets in the Everglades of Florida, which were under the protection of the Audubon Society, and eight rangers had to be appointed to keep these pirates out. One of them, Guy Bradley, was foully murdered while guarding the birds entrusted to his care. In the great centres of civilization, society beauties meanwhile postured at parties, in theatres and on promenades, displaying the

Kee-o-nuk warrior in ceremonial feathers

1908: Ladies in fashionable feather hats

plumes that had been gained by acts of barbarous cruelty. They were, however, truly shaken when Queen Alexandra of England made it quite clear that she did not want to see any lady at court wearing a hat with egret plumes. It can be said, without exaggeration, that this courageous and highly commendable decree did as much for the egrets as did President Hoover's ban on koala pelts for the koala bear.

Feathers and plumes have been out of fashion for a considerable time, yet conservationists will be well advised to keep a watchful eye on those who have made vanity their business.

Fashion constitutes a grave threat to many reptiles. The skins of iguanas and monitor lizards are used in hundreds of thousands for making ladies' shoes, while crocodiles and alligators are slaughtered on a world-wide scale mostly for the sake of handbags. The disappearance of the much-hated crocodile over large parts of Africa has revealed the interesting fact that these saurians do not live first and foremost off unsuspecting African women drawing water along the rivers, as some writers and film producers would

like us to believe, but that they mainly feed on large predatory fish. With the crocodiles gone, these fish quickly increase in numbers and destroy the smaller fish valued for human consumption. In Kenya serious thought is now being given to the possibility of bringing the crocodiles of certain regions under game management schemes, which would exploit them, while nevertheless ensuring their survival.

The fashionable woman of 1908, who wore a hat decorated with egret plumes, probably had on her dressing table a hand mirror and a set of combs and brushes with ivory handles. Queen Cleopatra may have been in possession of very similar toilet utensils, for ivory has for a very long time been one of the main adjuncts of luxury. The suitability of this material for artistic expression was recognized as far back as Aurignacian times, and many a hunter carved figurines out of mammoth ivory or scratched drawings on to a tusk.

Throughout historical times ivory has been a highly valued commodity. The Greeks erected monumental statues to the gods, which were covered with ivory and gold. In Rome, too, ivory figures were popular, and there was much utilization of the material in the production of furniture and musical instruments. From the 6th century Byzantium became the world centre of ivory carving, with the art reaching an extremely high development in the 11th and 12th centuries. There are many other examples. Ivory is, of course, also used in great quantities for making piano keys and billiard balls.

Even after such a brief summary one's mind boggles at the number of elephants that must have been killed for their tusks. Some ivory did come from southern Asia, but the main supplier was always the African elephant. Merchants from Dieppe visited that part of the African west coast which is still known as the Ivory Coast as early as the 14th century. The Portuguese later established trading posts or 'factories' and their example was soon followed by the French, the Dutch, the English and several other nations. In East Africa the Arabs found a convenient way of combining the trade of white and black ivory by having the newly acquired slaves carry the tusks obtained by their native hunters from the interior to the coast.

Professional ivory hunting by Europeans began when the Dutch settled at the Cape of Good Hope and went on all through the 19th and into the 20th century, coming to an end between the two wars in Ubangi, when game laws finally reached even that remote French colony.

The introduction of firearms brought about the extermination of elephants in vast areas of southern and western Africa. It seems amazing that any of the pachyderms managed to survive at all, but the African elephant is a very intelligent and adaptable creature, and he will respond exceedingly well to the slightest amount of protection.

The tusks of walruses, narwhals and hippos are considered as ivory for commercial purposes, and all of these species have had to suffer accordingly. Ivory carving among the Eskimos of Alaska, with an eye on the tourist trade has, in fact, developed into a major threat to the walrus herds.

Besides encouraging the use of soft furs, waving plumes and smooth ivory in an appeal to visual and tactile perception, luxurious living has also developed ways and means to stimulate the sense of smell. The

An ivory caravan in 19th century East Africa

70

An Alaskan craftsman drilling a walrus tusk, an old art preserved mainly for the tourist trade

great majority of natural perfumes have been derived from the vegetable kingdom. Animal scents are very limited in number, fortunately, one is inclined to add! One of them is civet, obtained from the anal glands of the African and Indian civet cats. Similar to it is castoreum, a glandular secretion of the beaver. Quite a number of animals, such as the musk rat, the musk rat kangaroo, the musk duck (*Biziura lobata*) of Australia, the European musk beetle and the alligator, emit a musky smell. The main source of the substance known as musk, is, however, the musk deer, *Moschus moschiferus*, a small hoofed animal found in Siberia, Korea, on the Island of Sakhalin, in China and in the Himalayas. The secretion extracted from the glands or 'pods' of this animal provides a scent more penetrating and persistent than that of any other substance known to occur in nature, and it has therefore played a highly important part in perfumery. The powerful and enduring odour gives strength and permanence to vegetable essences, and musk was until recently used as an ingredient in many perfumes. A synthetic equivalent has now been developed.

Musk deer were already hunted for the contents of their scent glands when Marco Polo visited China. The unfortunate animals have been under relentless pressure ever since. In Kansu there are professional musk deer hunters, and between the two world wars 10,000 to 15,000 of these little deer were killed in China each year. No wonder that the Chinese sub-species (*sifanicus*) is extinct in many parts of the country and threatened everywhere else. The status of the Manchurian and Sakhalin subspecies (*parvipes* and *sachaliniensis*) must be regarded as equally precarious. The two Siberian and the Himalayan subspecies (*arcticus*, *turowi* and *moschiferus*), even though much reduced in numbers, seem to be somewhat better off.

A substance of the greatest value in perfumery is ambergris, waxy to the touch, of a fatty consistency and inflammable. In alcoholic solution it can be used, in minute quantities, to give a floral fragrance to washes, soaps and similar cosmetic preparations. The stuff is occasionally found floating in the sea or washed up on tropical shores, and because of this oceanic origin, the dull grey or blackish lumps have been compared with the yellow amber of the Baltic, receiving the name of 'grey amber'. Ambergris is, in actual fact, a biliary concretion from the intestine of the sperm whale, *Physeter macrocephalus*, and whalers sometimes take it out of this animal's abdomen in quantities weighing from half an ounce to 100 or more pounds.

Sperm whales are, of course, not hunted just for ambergris alone, but mainly for their blubber, and for the spermaceti or sperm oil, carried in the head. Spermaceti was formerly used for making candles; now it is considered as the best lubricant for scientific instruments. Oil from whale blubber was widely used in lamps up to the beginning of the 19th century.

Early 19th century method of harpooning a whale

The value of whales must have been realized early in human history; it seems probable that the Phoenicians hunted them.

Whaling on a properly organized basis was begun, however, in the 12th and 13th centuries by Basque sailors from Bayonne and Biarritz, their quarry being the Nordkaper or North Atlantic right whale, *Eubalaena glacialis*. When it became rare in the southern parts of its range, they followed it to the coasts of north-western Europe and right up to Norway. In due course northern whaling fell to the Dutch, the English and the Norwegians, who, for several hundred years, hunted the Greenland right whale, *Balaena mysticetus* in Spitzbergen and Greenland waters. The first voyages of discovery in Antarctic seas induced many captains to turn their backs on the sadly depleted northern hunting grounds and to go south, where they could combine whaling with the killing of fur seals. All along the pack ice they found whales aplenty, but most of them were not 'right' whales, which could be caught with hand harpoons, floating on the surface after having been lanced to death, but huge rorquals—fin whales and blue whales—dangerous monsters to tackle and so heavy that even if a crew succeeded in killing one, it sank and was lost. So the whalers left the giants severely alone, and only searched out the southern right whales, *Eubalaena australis*.

In the 18th century, the Americans began to take a very prominent part in whaling, and early in the 19th century, whole fleets of New England ships went to the Indian and Pacific Oceans for sperm whales, and hunted North Pacific right whales, *Eubalaena sieboldii*, along the coast of Alaska.

Some experiments were made with harpoon canons and harpoon guns. One early 'improvement', the bomb-lance, eventually came into general use, and it made the actual killing of a harpooned whale very much easier. All the right whales were now rapidly being decimated, and by the end of the 19th century had become so scarce that looking for them was no longer profitable.

In 1867, however, a Norwegian by the name of Svend Foyn had designed and tested a canon which was able to throw a bomb harpoon. With this weapon mounted at the bow end of a small and fast chaser, it became possible to attack the whales which, hitherto, had not been 'right', and the hunt was on for the rorquals—the fin whale, *Balaenoptera physalus*, the blue whale, *Balaenoptera musculus*, and the humpback, *Megaptera novaeangliae*. With a range of action severely limited by their small size, the chasers could not operate independently like the old time whaling ships, but had to work out of shore stations. Until the turn of the century, modern whaling therefore remained restricted to the northern hemisphere.

Someone then remembered the immense numbers of rorquals reported by Antarctic explorers and whalers and a Captain Larsen went south to have a look. The rorquals were certainly there; and the

Cutting up a whale; early 19th century

A method often used today is to 'shoot' the whales then haul them all in together for processing

rest was inevitable. A close examination of the Antarctic and sub-Antarctic islands revealed many a deep, safe harbour where a whaling station could be established. In the vastness of the southern oceans the limited range of the chasers soon began to appear as an even greater handicap than it had been on the northern hunting grounds, but this was eventually overcome by the construction of floating factories, which could cruise far and wide, each one taking in and processing the whales caught by its fleet of chasers. The assault on the Antarctic whales thus entered its final phase. Attempts were made to limit the catches, but they proved quite inadequate, and a good indication of the scale of whaling operations can be gained from the fact that the value of the oil taken from the southern seas during the past 50 years exceeds the sum of 700 million pounds sterling!

Public opinion has been rather apathetic with regard to the slaughter of whales. They are little known to most people and do not have the immediate appeal of baby seals or koalas. But recent experiments have shown that porpoises—closely related to whales—have an intelligence at least at the ape-level and a sophisticated vocal communication system. Can we be sure that whales are not similarly endowed?

To kill a porpoise is nowadays regarded as an act not far removed from murder. A war of extermination is still being waged, against the whales, however, in which even spotter planes and radar play their part. There is not the slightest doubt about it being a true war of extermination; the people involved in the slaughter are fully aware of it. In 1931/2, the blue whale—with a length of 100 ft. and a weight of 120 tons the biggest of them all—constituted 82.1% of the total catches. Today it figures with only 5%, and in 1961/62 the entire world population was reliably assessed as somewhere between 930 and 2,790 animals! The fin whale, 80 ft. long and weighing up to 80 tons, has not yet been reduced to such a low level, but 32,400 were killed during the 1963/64 season, and their extinction must be near.

A great deal of research has been done with reference to Antarctic whales, especially by the scientists connected with the British 'Discovery' investigations. Enough data were accumulated to

Flensers cutting up a sperm whale

make possible a management scheme on an international basis to safeguard the survival of the rorquals for an indefinite period. The facts have long been submitted to all those representing whaling interests, and some nations would have been very willing to listen to expert advice. Others, and certain wealthy shipping magnates with whaling fleets under 'flags of convenience', were very uncooperative to say the least, and only after the catastrophic decline of the last few years did they grudgingly agree to further limitations of the catches. But these limitations are very far from what scientists regard as essential; greed still ploughs the Antarctic seas and reddens their waters with the blood of the last specimens of the biggest animals the world has ever known. Monstrous murder is being done to satisfy certain national aspirations, to fill the pockets of directors and shareholders. Soon, very soon, it will all be over! The day is rapidly approaching when it will not be profitable any longer to send the huge and costly killer fleets into the empty wastes surrounding the Antarctic Continent. Whaling will be a thing of the past, killed by the whaling interests themselves.

In this, of course, there may be a certain hope for the whales, for a few scattered survivors might conceivably be able to start breeding again. Before their numbers could be of a magnitude to make hunting profitable, the whaling fleets will have rusted away, the men willing to spend six months out of every year in the stormy southern seas will be old or gone, and humanity as a whole will have had to find substitutes for the raw materials hitherto derived from whales.

The sea otter made a come-back after hunting became unprofitable. The Greenland right whale, thought to be extinct a few decades ago, has re-appeared and seems to be increasing. The southern right whales, at one time reduced almost to extinction level, have been seen in the waters of Tristan da Cunha and South Georgia. Near extermination could possibly bring salvation to the rorquals.

The Oceans have long been regarded as immensely bountiful and absolutely inexhaustible, but they, too, can be over-exploited, and the shameful destruction of the whales is only one example of this. The manatees and dugongs are declining everywhere, with the exception of the Queensland coast and, perhaps, Florida, and the status of the marine turtles is rapidly becoming very precarious. Worst of all, statistics published by fisheries experts make increasingly grim reading.

The North Sea, for instance, has been one of the world's most prolific fishing grounds for centuries. It is, however, generally admitted that in the years before the first world war its yield declined tremendously. While humans turned away from fishing and applied their ingenuity to kill each other, the fishes had a chance to recover, and when trawlers could operate again, fishing was as good as ever. But not for long! During the 1920s the catches dwindled rapidly, the average size of the fish entangled in the nets became smaller. The second world war brought another enforced closed season. There was a further spectacular recovery—only to be followed by what has been called an 'appalling' decline in the catches brought into Yarmouth and Lowestoft during 1955 and 1956. As Sir Alister Hardy, one of the very great marine biologists of our time, has said: 'Certainly no one can deny that over-fishing exists; we must find a way to remedy it.' Scientists of Sir Alister's type will most assuredly come up with an answer— with all the data provided by excellent fisheries research organizations they probably have it already— but will their advice be taken? Or will greed triumph, as it has triumphed in the case of the whales?

Ambergris from the intestine of the sperm whale is not only used in perfumery, but has been found to be of some pharmaceutical value as a stimulant. On the other hand many animals have had medical properties attributed to various parts of their anatomy which quite definitely come under the heading of superstition. In medieval Europe, and even considerably later, almost every organ of the Alpine ibex was thought to have some specific healing qualities and this led to the animal being hunted assiduously by poachers. It was exterminated over most of its range, surviving only in the Gran Paradiso region of the Italian Alps, where it was eventually given effective protection by King Victor Emanuel II, who was a keen sportsman. From the Gran Paradiso reserve, now a national park, the mountains of Austria, Switzerland, Germany and France have been re-stocked with ibex.

The giant armadillo, *Piodontes giganteus*, of South America, is becoming increasingly rare, magical powers being ascribed to its claws, while the status of the maned wolf, *Chrysocyon brachyurus*, of the pampas gives cause for grave concern, because a concoction of its shaved bones is supposed to ease delivery in pregnant women. The rare imperial woodpecker *Campophilus imperialis*, of the Sierra Madre in Mexico, the largest member of the woodpecker family, is killed for its supposed medicinal properties. Deer antlers, the bones and the blood of tigers, and the fur of the very rare snubnosed monkey, *Rhinopithecus roxellana*, are objects of Chinese superstition.

The most harrowing story is that of the rhinoceroses. Superstition has brought the Asian species to near extinction and is now threatening the African rhinos as well. In many parts of southern Asia, rhino blood is said to speed departing souls safely on their way, the urine is considered as an excellent disinfectant, and the hide, bones, intestines and the stomach contents all have their place in eastern quackery. For thousands of years rhino horns were thought to have the power of detecting poison. But even more harm was done through the Chinese belief in the aphrodisiac qualities of the horn substance, the chemical composition of which, incidentally, does not differ in any way from that of human hair or nails. It need hardly be stressed that biochemistry has not been able to detect even the slightest evidence of the miraculous properties imputed to powdered rhino horn in the Far East. But with a horn almost worth its weight in gold, the rhinos have been tracked down relentlessly, and today the Javan species, *Rhinoceros sondaicus*, is nearly extinct, only very few surviving in the Udjung Kulon Reserve in western Java, and of the Sumatra rhinoceros, *Dicerorhinus sumatrensis*, not more than about 150 are now in existence. The very last figures given for the Indian rhinoceros, *Rhinoceros unicornis*, assess the total population at 740 animals, and this is encouraging in so far as it indicates a slight increase under strict protection. There is still a great demand for rhino horns, and persecution has long ago extended to the two African species, which will need very careful conservation if they are not to go the way of their Asiatic cousins.

Man has thus enslaved animals, and he has hunted them for sport, he has killed them wholesale for their meat, for furs and feathers, for ivory, for their glandular secretions, for the industrial raw materials he is able to extract from their carcases, even for superstitious reasons. I should again like to emphasize that exploitation need not necessarily be fatal —there have been many examples of highly successful management of wildlife resources—but it very frequently is, for where animals are concerned, man's

Rhino horns—confiscated from poachers

greed usually knows no bounds. Apart from direct exploitation, human domination over the world of living things has, however, been asserted in a great many other ways. Man has, for instance, not only carried his domestic stock all over the world, but he has indulged in transplanting numerous wild animals as well, for the sake of sport or exploitation, in generally very ill-conceived efforts to combat local 'pests' or even for sentimental reasons. Thus rabbits and foxes were brought to Australia, mongooses to the West Indies and to Hawaii, muskrats to Europe, starlings, sparrows and pheasants to North America, American grey squirrels to the British Isles. New Zealand probably had to endure by far the widest range of introductions, its fauna being 'enriched' by, among others, red deer, wapiti, sambhar, fallow deer, Japanese deer, moose, tahr, chamois, ferret, rabbit, hare, hedgehog, blacktailed wallaby, flying phalanger, blackbird, sparrow, starling, chaffinch, mynah, turkey, pheasant, peacock, black swan, wood pigeon and little owl. It is hardly necessary to state that many—if not most—of these transplantations have done irreparable harm to that country's ecology.

The primitive hunter and food gatherer is himself an integral part of the ecological system to which he belongs, leaving hardly more marks of his presence than any of the other predators, and certainly having less of an impact on the habitat than animals such as elephants, beavers and termites. From the time of the Neanderthalers to that of the reindeer hunters of the upper Magdalenian, all the changes in the European landscape were entirely due to climatic and geological factors. Man accepted his environment as he found it and did not try to effect any changes. Weeding a plot and planting a crop, however, meant a transformation of a part of the environment and a fundamental change in its ecology. By becoming a farmer and a stockbreeder, man began to change the world to suit his own purposes, and as time went by, these changes became ever more far-reaching. Age-old habitats were radically destroyed and replaced by environments of man's choosing. The Fertile Crescent and the entire Mediterranean region lost most of their forests very early in history. The European forest belt was decimated and might have disappeared altogether, if it had not been for the game-preserving nobility. The old-established plant associations of grassland tracts had to give way to just a few cultivated species.

Habitat destruction and transformation gained momentum with the industrial revolution and spread to the farthest corners of the earth with European colonization. To the animal world, this process has been at least as fatal as direct exploitation. Just try

The top photograph shows badly eroded farmland—the whole area (lower photograph) was reconstructed by agricultural engineers and restored to something like its original fertility

to imagine how many small mammals, birds and insects are deprived of their homes when a hedge is being cut down. Their numbers mount enormously if a copse or a small wood has to give way to 'development'. What, then, of the ruthless destruction that overtook the wonderful deciduous forests which only a couple of hundred years ago covered a large part of the eastern United States? Only 25% of this 'undulating surface of impenetrable forest' is still woodland; a mere one tenth of one per cent can be considered as having retained something of the pristine state in which the pioneers found it. The effect on the fauna of that immense area was, of course, utterly devastating. Wheat conquered the western prairies of America, maize the high veld of South Africa; Hawaiian forests gave way to pineapple plantations; Malayan jungles to well regimented rows of rubber trees; Assam and Ceylon were invaded by tea, the Brazilian wilderness by coffee, the East African bush by sisal. From large areas of the globe the natural vegetation disappeared, and with it went most of the animal life. Only the species dependent on the few crop plants selected by man did well. They suddenly found their food supply increasing beyond bounds and multiplied accordingly, becoming 'pests', against which difficult and costly campaigns had to be waged.

The enormous technological advances of the last few decades, coupled with what has come to be called the 'population explosion', have increased man's destructive powers to super-juggernaut proportions. There is now no place on earth he cannot reach, where he cannot create living conditions to suit his requirements. He settles down in the midst of the most arid deserts, which a short time ago even the wandering nomads rarely visited; he has established himself on the icy high plateau of the South Pole, and is erecting dwelling places on the bottom of the sea. There is practically no feature on earth which he cannot change if he wants to, nothing he cannot destroy if it suits his plans to do so. Not only is he himself breeding more and more rapidly, multiplying at a rate which is beginning to outstrip that of many of the more prolific animals, but the same also applies to the beasts that have become his servants. Today's world population of cattle, not counting the domestic Asiatic buffaloes, is around 800 million head, of which 30% are to be found on the American continent, where the ancestral aurochs was never found. There are about 950 million sheep, with approximately 113 million in Australia, far outside the original range of the genus *Ovis*. The populations of goats and pigs are assessed at 450 and over 300 million respectively, and the domestic fowl with an estimated population of 3 billion must be considered as by far the most abundant bird on

With an estimated 3 billion population, domestic fowl must be the most abundant bird on earth

this earth. Wild animals need not necessarily attack man's livestock directly to arouse his ire—simply to compete with his servants for food is quite sufficient for a species to be destroyed with the utmost ruthlessness.

Despite the fact that he has monopolized vast regions for his crops and overcrowded the earth with domestic animals, man, who calls himself *sapiens*, the Wise One, cannot manage to keep his own increase in balance with food production; so, at least, we are told. The uncommitted observer cannot help feeling that in many parts of the world there is a tremendous amount of waste and inefficiency in dealing with what has been produced. This situation unfortunately plays into the hands of that unmitigated evil, the person who hunts—or poaches—professionally and indiscriminately, with modern arms, perhaps even equipped with modern transport, in a country not civilized enough to have good game laws, or not orderly enough to give its laws proper enforcement. He is the greatest curse to wildlife the world has ever known, and the most mild-mannered of animal lovers feels that he would gladly take out a licence, if it were for hunting down this utterly unscrupulous and merciless type of predator.

Homo sapiens has reached a state of mastery, of domination over nature as a whole, which even he could not have foreseen a short while ago. Just as he has always tended to over-exploit what nature offered, he now grossly abuses his all-powerful position. Overgrazing, which in many parts of the world has been a problem for centuries, is becoming more widespread and more serious. De-forestation has taken on truly terrifying proportions, magnificent stands of timber being cut down not only for building purposes, but in order to produce more and more cheap-quality paper on which to print more and more sensational stories and political hypocrisies. There

Deforestation in the south-eastern coastal region of Alaska. A major part of the State's economy is based on lumbering and the stands of virgin timber are rapidly being destroyed. If they are not speedily replanted soil erosion will set in as has happened in many other parts of the world

Plate VI (top) This river is being gradually choked up by refuse from a nearby tip

Plate VII Soil erosion in Lesotho, due to overgrazing

Plate VIII (top) Slaughter on the Arctic ice : a sealer ripping the skin off a baby seal that has been beaten to death

Plate IX (below) Larger seals are sometimes shot and then hauled on board for skinning

Dead fish—killed by de-oxygenation of the water following silage pollution

are far too many newspapers as it is, but not enough forests! Urbanization and industrialization are growing at so fast a rate that it is becoming increasingly difficult to deal adequately with the gigantic amount of waste products. Streams, rivers and lakes are, therefore, being hopelessly polluted, and the very air the city dweller has to breathe is infested. Economists and planners are running wild in gigantic orgies of 'development', vying with each other in their efforts to transform the world beyond recognition. Valley after valley is being drowned to generate hydro-electric power. Rivers are canalized, re-routed, even drained of their waters. Marshes disappear, pools and ponds are filled in. Whole mountainsides are turned into scenes of devastation for the sake of the minerals they contain.

The recently invented insecticides and herbicides are applied with boundless enthusiasm, poison raining down on crops and forests year after year, destroying not only the pests they are supposed to kill, but millions of harmless and beautiful creatures as well. It has been established beyond any doubt that they are now causing havoc among many species of birds.

It will only be a matter of time until we all begin to feel the effects of the indiscriminate application of chemicals. Traces of insecticide have recently been found in a variety of foodstuffs and many people must be wondering how much of it they are assimilating into their system, day in, day out.

Truly, compared with the 'fatal impact' of modern 'development', the efforts of the fur traders, the market hunters, the plume hunters, the sealers and even the whalers might seem almost puny!

But there arises one question: How long can man continue?

Chapter 4

Extinction

Life is thought to have existed on earth for something like 2,000 million years. We have no direct evidence of what took place during the first 1,500 million years or so, the most ancient organisms to leave traces of their presence being 600 million years old. About 425 million years ago, ancestors of the modern lampreys crawled over the mud deposited at the bottom of primaeval seas, creatures of such a complex organization that they must have been the product of a very long period of evolution.

The records preserved in sedimentary rocks give irrefutable proof that innumerable species, genera and families of animals have come into being playing their part for a shorter or longer duration, only to disappear again, swallowed up in the inexorable passage of time. There was the Age of Fishes, with its strange arthrodires and placoderms. After that, the amphibians took the centre of the stage, their rule culminating in the ponderous stegocephalians. They were followed by a fantastic array of reptilian monsters, such as the dinosaurs, the ichthyosaurs, and the pterodactyls. The first primitive mammals, small, shrew-like creatures, scuttled out of the way in the undergrowth when *Tyrannosaurus*, the biggest terrestrial carnivore the world has ever known, attacked the heavily armed *Triceratops*. The Age of Reptiles lasted from the Permian to the end of the Cretaceous—and then the saurians unaccountably perished and made way for the mammals, which reached great preponderance during the Tertiary. A stroll through a large museum's exhibition gallery devoted to mammalian palaeontology gives us, clear evidence however, that, of the beasts which inherited the earth from the reptiles, only very few are with us today, most of them having already followed *Tyrannosaurus* and *Brontosaurus* into oblivion.

Untold species have thus become extinct long before a man-ape ever picked up a club or shaped a pebble-tool. A careful study of fossils will even show that from time to time whole faunas vanished into the limbo of extinction, and early palaeontologists such as Georges Cuvier and his disciples, found no other way to explain such puzzling occurrences than by postulating tremendous catastrophes which periodically swept the earth bare of all existing life, to be followed by completely new bursts of creation. Thanks to Lamarck's theorizing, groping and inadequate as it was, and to the genius of Charles Darwin, we now know that life on earth has been continuous, steadily advancing from the simple to the more complex, and the idea of recurring, world-embracing cataclysms has itself become as extinct as the prehistoric animals to whose fossilized bones it owed its conception.

Biologically, a species is doomed to extinction as soon as the ratio of its reproduction drops below its mortality rate. With more individuals dying off or being destroyed than young being born, a decline sets in which must eventually be fatal. Such an excessive mortality rate can be due to a great many causes. Numbers of species must have disappeared because they simply became obsolete, finding themselves unable to compete successfully with closely related forms, with their own descendants, so to speak who, through the mechanism of mutation, had been awarded a definite advantage in the struggle for existence that enabled them to oust the unchanged ancestral line from its niche and to usurp its role in the ecological pattern.

Land bridges, created either by geological upheavals or by the lowering of the sea-level, often gave animals of a more highly evolved type the opportunity to invade areas populated by primitive faunas, with disastrous results to the original inhabitants both through competition and through direct predation. Far-reaching climatic changes brought on ice ages, caused the spread of deserts or furthered the advance of dense forests, and thus caused the extermination of very many species, the main sufferers being the animals which had become so thoroughly adapted to a certain type of habitat that they found it impossible to cope with changed conditions or even to move away. Finally, we must surely take into account the fact that species, as well as families, genera and orders, go through a period of youthful development to maturity and finally to senile decline. The odd-toed ungulates—Perissodactyla—for instance, reached their highest peak during the Eocene and Oligocene periods of the Tertiary, which might with some justification be called the 'Age of Perissodactyls'. Very many genera came into existence at that time, half of which became extinct before the end of the Oligocene. At present the Perissodactyla are represented only by the three genera of rhinoceroses, one genus of horses, and one genus of tapirs. While the

Artiodactyla, the even-toed ungulates, were never more numerous and more varied than they are today, the odd-toed ungulates appear to have long ago gone into a steady decline, and the species still with us seem, as a whole, rather less able to hold out against human pressure than many of the even-toed ungulates. If the horse and the ass had not become servants of man, they would most certainly be on the way out. The wild horses of America disappeared mysteriously long before Columbus set sail, and of the Old World wild horses, once found all over Europe and in large parts of Asia, there are only very few left alive in Mongolia.

Both the African and Asian wild asses have become extinct in large parts of their original area of distribution, and the surviving herds are considered endangered. One zebra, the quagga, is extinct, while the mountain zebra has been reduced to a dangerously low level. Five species of tapirs are still lurking in dense jungles, retreating rapidly wherever man invades their habitat. The precarious status of the rhinoceros has been mentioned in the foregoing chapter.

One of the last remaining quaggas was kept at the London Zoo—it died in 1872

Phylogenetic senescence probably lowers the reproduction rate of a species, thus initiating both a population decline and gradual shrinking of the area occupied by the species. Many animals which we list as 'rare' may, in fact, be in an advanced stage of senile decline, and such species would of course be especially vulnerable. The slightest adverse changes in their environment are sure to accentuate the downward trend and to speed up extinction.

Phylogenetic senescence could well have been at least partly responsible for bringing the Age of Reptiles to a close, an evolutionary event for which nobody has yet given a really convincing explanation. Of one thing we can, of course, be certain—man had nothing to do with this holocaust, for very many millions of years were to go by before he made his first appearance. He was, however, present when a considerable part of the Pleistocene fauna of both the Old and the New World became extinct at the end of the last glaciation. As has been mentioned already, giant bison, wild horses, long-necked camels, ground sloths, mammoths and mastodons vanished from the American plains about 6,000 to 10,000 years ago. In Eurasia, the same fate overtook the mammoth, the woolly rhinoceros, the Irish elk and the cave bear. We know definitely that these animals were hunted intensively, and it is quite permissible to ask the question: 'Was man responsible for their extermination?' There are a good number of experts who think that he actually did wipe out these species or at least played a very major part in their extermination. We must, however, keep in mind that during Upper Palaeolithic and Mesolithic times man was undoubtedly a fairly rare creature, spread over vast areas in small, roving bands. His weapons were still of a very primitive type, and it is difficult to imagine him as being able to completely destroy large and vigorous animal populations. The natives of tropical Africa and southern Asia, even though more numerous and better armed than the post-glacial hunters, failed to make a real impact on the big game of their homelands before they acquired fire-arms. What enabled the Clovis and Folsom people of North America to slaughter a rich and varied mammalian fauna, when the Red Indians of later times cannot be said to have noticeably reduced the bison herds even after they had obtained possession of horses?

Mesolithic hunters could, of course, have contributed materially to the decline of Pleistocene animals, if the species involved were already on the way out, their decline being due to phylogenetic senescence or to changes in their habitat. Human predation would then have been enough of an adverse factor to speed up the natural processes of extinction. The climatic revolutions which brought about the final shrinking of the glaciers and ice-caps, may also have contributed to the wholesale destruction. Habitat changes are sure to have forced certain species into long migrations, in the course of which they may have lost a lot of their former vigour. The old-world mammoths, for instance, had to withdraw north-eastwards into Siberia, where, according to Russian scientists, they hung on more and more precariously until a few thousand years ago.

The great majority of animals that we can safely assume to have been exterminated by primitively armed hunters were inhabitants of islands. On Hispaniola and Puerto Rico, for instance, remains of ground sloths belonging to the genera *Parocnus* and *Ancratocnus* have been discovered in association with human bones and pottery, and it is believed that they may have become extinct during the last 2,000 years, very probably through human predation. They were much smaller than the famous giant sloths, weighing only 45 to 70 kg. (100–154 lb.) but there is some evidence that one of the big species of the American continent, *Mylodon listai*, also survived until fairly recent times. When several pieces of mylodon skin were found in a Patagonian cave, together with human artefacts and shreds of guanaco skin, it looked as if some giant ground sloths might still be wandering through the unexplored forests of southernmost America. A number of expeditions went in search of the animals, but nothing was ever found. We can, however, be certain that the mylodon was at one time hunted by the Patagonians, and if the species was already on the decline, as there is reason to believe, man must at least have hastened its extinction.

The first Polynesians to reach New Zealand about A.D. 950 found several kinds of big, flightless birds in the forests and grasslands of both islands. The largest stood between 8 and 10 feet high, the smallest were as large as turkeys, while some medium-sized species carried their heads about level with a man's shoulder. The human invaders must have been delighted with this plentiful supply of easily obtainable meat, and they massacred the larger species at such a rate that some of them were exterminated within a fairly short period. Archaeologists call these earliest settlers of New Zealand the 'Moa Hunters', though the name 'moa' for the birds that formed their prey, really comes from the language of the Maori, who landed between 1150 and 1350. The newcomers conquered

Right: Dinornis maximus—*the moa*

84

and exterminated the Moa Hunters and then proceeded to slaughter what was left of the moas. But when did these birds really become extinct?

In 1892 an excavator found a moa skeleton surrounded by rusty metal, broken pipes and pieces of glass, objects which the Maori could only have obtained from Europeans. This was considered as proof that a few moas were still lurking in the forests when European settlement began. The authenticity of the finds was, however, not generally accepted, and the extinction date of the last surviving species of moa remained a subject of controversy. While it was admitted that some forest moas of the genera *Megalapteryx* and *Anomalapteryx* did manage to evade their final doom for quite a long time, most authorities nevertheless thought that they had disappeared long before the arrival of the white settlers. In 1949 a Maori camp site containing not only skeletal remains of *Megalapteryx didinus*, but well preserved feathers as well, was discovered at the foot of a cliff in Takahe Valley, and carbon dating has since established that it was occupied at some time between 1660 and 1780. It is thus more than likely that there was at least one species of moa in existence when the 'Endeavour' sailed along the New Zealand coast in 1769 and 1770, and one can only regret that Banks and Solander, who accompanied Cook as naturalists, never caught sight of one of these birds!

There can be no doubt about the moas having been exterminated by primitive hunters, but there is a certain amount of evidence which suggests that the genera *Dinornis*, *Pachyornis* and *Emcus* were on the decline even before the Moa Hunters made their appearance. This may have been due to climatic changes which brought about a shortage of food and, according to some authorities, made it impossible for the big birds to let their eggs be hatched out by the heat of the sun. We have absolutely no proof that moas did, in fact, merely expose their eggs to the sun. They may well have done so, but we shall never know for certain. Whatever the cause of their decline, the moas were unable to hold out against human predation in its most primitive form.

When travelling from China to Persia, Marco Polo heard of the island of Madagascar, which, so his informants told him, was inhabited by an extraordinary bird known as rukh or roc. 'In form it is said to resemble an eagle, but it is incomparably greater in size', the adventurous Venetian later said, 'being so large and strong as to seize an elephant with its talons and to lift it into the air, from where it lets it fall to the ground, in order that when dead it may

prey upon the carcase.' Marco Polo suspected that the creature may be no other than the griffon, which he had so often seen represented in paint and sculpture.

In 1642 the French established a settlement on Madagascar, and Etienne Flacour, who was sent out to govern the small and struggling colony, soon picked up some native tales about a gigantic bird. 'Vouron-patra', the Malagasy called it, and they said that it lived in isolated places and laid enormous eggs. Here, then was Marco Polo's rukh—though it was described, not as an elephant-eating eagle, but as looking rather like an ostrich and being unable to fly. No European has ever seen a 'vouron-patra', but when explorers later penetrated the southern parts of the island they soon came across gigantic bird bones, and the natives showed them where the huge eggs, up to 14 inches long and almost 9 inches wide, could be dug out of the sand. Studying the skeletal remains of those nightmare-ostriches, which became known as elephant birds, palaeontologists were able to distinguish two genera, *Aepyornis* and *Mullerornis*, and several species, the largest of which, *Aepyornis titan*, must have been just over 10 feet in height. The elephant birds were built very massively, and the fact that most of them had four toes on each foot is a good indication that they were not fast runners like the two-toed ostriches of the African mainland. Their movements must have been clumsy, but they lived on an island where there were no large predators to harry them and thus enjoyed complete safety until the fatal moment when man set his foot on Madagascar soil, an event that probably took place not very long before the beginning of our era. The slow and ponderous elephant birds fell an easy prey to the invaders and must have gone into a very rapid decline. We do not know with any certainty when the last elephant bird succumbed to Malagassy hunters, but native traditions and Flacour's account make it appear likely that at least one species survived until about 1640.

Some West Indian rodents—the narrow-toothed hutia, three spiny rats and the Puerto Rico isolobodon—are known only from skeletal remains found on old village sites and in kitchen middens. They are thought to have become extinct shortly before or immediately after the arrival of the Spaniards, and it seems reasonable to assume that they were exterminated by the Caribs, who killed them for food. The extermination of the emu of King Island in the

---

Right: Aepyornis maximus—*the elephant bird*

Bass Strait was quite definitely brought about by primitive hunters some time before the arrival of the Europeans, but this insular subspecies of the Australian emu can never have been very numerous.

While we have no way of assessing how much—or how little—the Stone-Age people of Eurasia and America contributed to the extinction of a considerable number of Pleistocene animals, there can be no doubt about modern man being a highly destructive factor, particularly if we examine his activities during the last 400 years or so. For that period, infinitesimal if compared with the span of time that had elapsed since the appearance of Neanderthal man, or even since the end of the Pleistocene, I have been able to find records of 49 species of mammals and 87 species of birds which are known—or presumed—to have become extinct within the last 370 years owing to human activities of one kind or another. Several more have not been heard of for a long time, and may also be lost to us. We also have to deplore the disappearance of a great number of sub-species or 'races' of still surviving species.

The most immediate impact is, of course, caused through direct human persecution, such as hunting, trapping, poisoning and egg collecting. Steller's sea cow was overhunted in this way for its meat and also for its skin. In South Africa, unrestricted hunting led to the loss of the blue-buck *Hippotragus leucophaeus*, and the quagga, *Equus quagga*. The first of these two was a beautiful antelope, related to the roan, but smaller and having a coat of velvety bluish-grey. It occurred only in the vicinity of Swellendam, in an area which probably did not measure more than a hundred miles across, and was already becoming rare in 1774. In 1781 François Levaillant, the French naturalist, found a small number left alive in the valley of the Soete Melk River, and when Henry Lichtenstein passed through Swellendam in 1803, he could only record that the last 'blaauwbok' had been killed in 1800. Mounted specimens can be seen in the museums of Paris, Leyden, Vienna, Stockholm and Uppsala.

The quagga, a brownish zebra, striped only on the head, neck and forepart of the body, roamed in numerous herds over the eastern parts of the Cape Colony, west to about Prince Albert and Swellendam, north into Griqualand-West and Orange Free State, ranging as far as the Vaal River. Quaggas were shot by farmers to feed their native workers, later also for their hides, which the Free State Boers either used for making grain sacks, or exported to the coast in wagon loads. Nobody seems to know exactly when the last quagga fell to a bullet, but this may well have happened before 1860. The very last survivors died in the zoos of Berlin and Amsterdam, in 1875 and 1883 respectively. Twenty-two skins, a few complete skeletons and some odd skulls are all that is left to us of this interesting species.

The Falkland island dog, *Dusicyon australis*, and the Japanese wolf, *Canis hodophilax*, were exterminated as vermin, as was a bird of prey, the Guadalupe caracara, *Polyborus lutosus*.

I have already mentioned the spectacled cormorant of the Bering Sea, wiped out through hunting and egg collecting. A similar fate befell the famous great auk, *Pinguinus impennis*, of the North Atlantic. This flightless bird, standing about 50 in. high, nested on rocky islands off Newfoundland and Iceland. It may at one time have bred on the Faroes, the Orkneys and the Hebrides.

The great auk was killed as easily as the dodo, and the American breeding colonies were devastated by sailors and fishermen, who slaughtered the birds for food and for use as bait. Jacques Cartier, the discoverer of the St. Lawrence River, reported that his men killed thousands of 'penguins', as he called them, on the Isle of Birds, now known as Funk Island. When the Norwegian naturalist, Stuwitz, visited Funk Island in 1841, he found only piles of bones and a few mummified carcases. There was not a single auk left alive.

The biggest of the Icelandic colonies, and the one to survive longest, was situated on Gyrfuglasker, a tiny island off Cape Reykianes, where landing was usually very hazardous. This last stronghold of the great auk was, however, destroyed by volcanic activity in 1830, the surviving birds taking shelter on neighbouring Eldey Island. As soon as museums and private collectors became aware of the impending extinction of the species, they offered large sums for specimens, thus encouraging a ruthless trade in eggs and skins. Three men who went ashore on Eldey, in June 1844, found only one pair of great auks which they killed forthwith. A single egg was picked up, and thrown away, the shell being cracked. The two birds were sold to a museum in Copenhagen and that was the end of another sad story. No great auk has been seen since.

The Labrador duck, or pied duck, *Camptorhynchus labradoricus*, bred around the mouth of the St. Lawrence River, as well as on the coast of Labrador. In winter it moved south to the shores of Nova Scotia, New Brunswick and New England, where it had to run the gauntlet of innumerable guns. Even

The extinct blue-buck, Hippotragus leucophaeus

more disastrous must have been the depredations caused on the nesting grounds by the notorious 'eggers' of Labrador.

In the course of an expedition to Labrador in 1833, Audubon recorded the pied duck in the vicinity of the sealing establishment at Bras d'Or. The season was too far advanced for finding the nests, but he was told that the birds bred on the top of low bushes. Ten years later the wildfowlers in Fundy Bay, on Long Island and along the New Jersey coast began to comment on the decrease of the species. Only a few Labrador ducks were seen between 1860 and 1870, and in 1875 the very last one was shot on Long Island. Forty-eight specimens have been preserved, but there is no egg of the species in any museum or private collection.

Audubon's writings about the passenger pigeon, *Ectopistes migratorius*, and its mass migrations are well known. Even though they were massacred on a truly tremendous scale all through the first half of the last century, the pigeons did not seem to decline in numbers and it needed an astute observer like Audubon to foresee what would eventually happen. Referring to the horrifying slaughter at the roosting places, he remarked:

'Persons unacquainted with these birds might naturally conclude that such dreadful havoc would soon put an end to the species. But I have satisfied myself by long observation that nothing but the gradual diminution of our forests can accomplish their decrease, as they not infrequently quadruple their number yearly, and always at least double it.'

Intensive hunting alone would probably not have been sufficient to effect the complete eradication of the passenger pigeon but the wholesale destruction of the enormous American forests deprived the birds of their habitat, of their roosts, and of the places where they were able to nest in large colonies. They could only exist in these enormous flocks and found it impossible to split up into smaller groups which would have been able to make the most of the remaining patches of woodland. When the decline eventually set in, it was a very rapid one. In 1879, one firm alone was still able to sell a thousand barrels of salted pigeons—but a mere twenty years later, in September 1899, the last passenger pigeon ever to be seen in the wild was shot near Babcock, Wisconsin. Some specimens survived in captivity, the species becoming finally extinct on September 1st 1914, when a pigeon died in the Cincinnati Zoo.

If Audubon, though aware of the threat hanging over the species, was not able to observe any notice-able reduction in the multitudes of passenger pigeons in the course of his lifetime, he did, on the other hand, record the alarming decline of the Carolina parakeet, *Conuropsis carolinensis*.

Farmers killed the parakeets because they damaged their apples and tore the wheatears to pieces. But again it was the destruction of the forests that did most of the harm, for the birds formed nesting colonies in big old trees full of holes, while outside the breeding season they congregated in large flocks and roosted in hollow trunks. With their nesting and roosting places gone, they were unable to adapt themselves to changed conditions. By 1870, Carolina parakeets had become very rare, but there were still a good number of them in captivity, and as they bred fairly well, there might perhaps have been a chance to preserve the species. But the time for such a co-ordinated attempt was not yet ripe, and the last

Passenger pigeon, Ectopistes migratorius

parakeet died in 1914—the same year that also saw the final passing of the passenger pigeon.

Habitat destruction has accounted for a good many species and brought a lot of others to the verge of extinction. The magnificent ivory-billed woodpecker, *Campephilus p. principalis* was quite common during the first half of the last century in Texas, the lower parts of the Carolinas, in Georgia, Alabama, Louisiana and Mississippi. Audubon encountered it often when traversing the 'deep morasses, overshadowed by millions of gigantic dark cypresses', and it forms the subject of one of his liveliest paintings. The present status of the species is given in the 'Red Data Book', published by the I.U.C.N. in 1966, as:

'Extremely rare and must be very near extinction.'

In 1961 a specimen was seen in South Carolina, and five were said to be still surviving in eastern Texas. There has obviously been no improvement during the last few years, for so far as numbers are concerned, the 'Red Data Book' is unable to give any more definite information than:

'Not known and no estimation possible.'

The ivory-billed woodpecker requires extensive forest areas with large, dead trees, and its decline began just as soon as logging operations were extended to the cypress swamps which formed its habitat. Numbers diminished very rapidly from 1885 to 1900, when logging activities reached a peak, in 1915 the species was already restricted to only a dozen localities. The Cuban subspecies, *C.p. bairdii*, is listed as 'barely surviving, may even be extinct', due to exactly the same factors.

Of the aye-aye, *Daubentonia madagascariensis*, the strangest of Madagascar's fascinating lemurs, C. Keller wrote in 1901 that it could be met with rather frequently on the east coast, the natives now and then bringing specimens into the town of Tamatave. Raymond Decary recorded its occurrence from the northernmost extremity of the island to Majunga in the west and to Matitanana, about 750 miles down the coastline, in the east. He reported the nocturnal creature as inhabiting dense forests, spending the daylight hours rolled up into a furry ball inside a nest constructed of leaves and twigs. Large parts of the Madagascar forests have now been cut down, and with them went the inoffensive aye-aye. Today it is one of the rarest and most endangered mammals on earth, the number of surviving individuals being estimated at possibly not more than 50!

The aye-aye formerly had quite an extensive area of distribution, and only habitat destruction on a very vast scale could bring it to its present, precarious

A 19th century illustration of the aye-aye, Daubentonia madagascariensis

status. There are, however, many animals with an exceedingly limited range, confined, perhaps, to only a few square miles or even less. Such species must be considered as being in very great danger. An interesting West Indian rodent, the dwarf hutia, *Capromys nana*, and a wren, *Ferminia cerverasi*, are both known only from the Zapata Swamp on the Island of Cuba. Should this piece of marshland ever be drained and reclaimed for agriculture, the two species would inevitably be doomed to quick extinction. This is, in fact, exactly what happened to the slender-billed grackle, *Cassidix palustris*, of Mexico's Lerma Valley, which has not been seen for such a long time that it must be considered as extinct. Kirtland's warbler, *Dendroica kirtlandi*, occurs only in a small area of jackpine thickets in central Michigan, and the whole population may consist of less than a thousand individuals. Destruction of the thickets which form its home would mean the end of the species. The Mangare Island parakeet, *Cyanoramphus auriceps forbesi*, inhabits two or three acres of tall vegetation on Mangare Island. Its habitat could be utterly annihilated in a few days.

The blue-buck was, as we have seen, to be found only in a very small area, and the quagga, too, had a somewhat restricted range. The early loss of both species is highly significant, and similarly localized species, such as the Abyssinian ibex, the mountain nyala and Hunter's hartebeest, will need careful watching if they are to remain with us.

When somebody had the unfortunate idea to release rabbits on Laysan, a Hawaiian island declared a bird sanctuary by Theodore Roosevelt early in this century, most of the available vegetation was destroyed in a very short time. This brought about the near-extinction of the Laysan finchbill, *Psittirostra c. cantans*, and the Laysan teal, *Anas laysanensis*.

The finchbill population dropped to about 1,000 individuals in 1938. The rabbits were then eradicated, and the birds immediately began to recover. In 1958 their numbers were estimated at around 10,000, and the species can be considered as having been saved in the nick of time. The Laysan teal, which some ornithologists consider as a dwarf race of the mallard, was down to just over 30 individuals in 1950, but it is now making a slow comeback and has already climbed up to the four- to six-hundred mark. The extermination of rabbits came too late, however, to save the Laysan reedwarbler, *Acrocephalus f. familiaris*, which has not been seen since 1925. The Laysan rail, *Porzanula palmeri*, also became extinct. Its decline was noted in good time, and some specimens were transferred to Midway

The Laysan teal which nearly faced extinction a few decades ago

Island, in order to give the species a better chance of survival. They did well in their new home, and outlived the Laysan population, only to become the victims of introduced rats in 1944 or 1945.

The introduction of animals, accidental or on purpose, has done immeasurable damage to indigenous faunas throughout the world. The story of the Stephen Island wren, *Xenicus lyalli*, may perhaps be quoted as a classic example of what can so easily happen: in 1894 the whole population was wiped out by the lighthouse-keeper's cat!

Cats are thought to have destroyed the Bonin wood pigeon, *Columba versicolor*, collected on Nakondo Shima Island in 1889 and never seen again, the crested Choiseul pigeon, *Microgoura meeki*, from Choiseul Island in the Solomon Group, which vanished shortly after its discovery in 1904, the Macquarie Island parakeet, *Cyanoramphus novae-zelandiae erythrotis*, and they are certainly responsible for eradicating a shrew, *Crocidura fuliginosa trichure*, and two interesting rats, *Rattus macleari*, and *Rattus nativitatis*, on Christmas Island, situated south of Java in the Indian Ocean.

Rats invading Lord Howe Island from a ship wrecked in 1918 took only a few years to exterminate the Lord Howe whiteye, *Zosterops strenua*, a thrush, *Turdus poliocephalus vinitinctus*, a flycatcher, *Gergyone igiat insularis*, a fantail, *Rhipidura fuliginosa cervina*, and the Lord Howe mountain starling, *Aplonis fuscus hullianus*. In addition, these aggressive and highly adaptable rodents may have played a major part in the extermination of the Kusaie Island crake, *Aphanolimnas monasa*, the Kusaie starling, *Aplonis corvina*, and the Chatham Island race of the New Zealand bell-bird, *Anthornis melanura melanocephala*.

Cats and rats probably joined forces in eradicating the red-billed rail, *Rallus ecaudatus*, of Tahiti, the Chatham Island rail, *Rallus modestus*, the Chatham Island banded rail, *Rallus dieffenbachii*, of which only two museum specimens are in existence, the Samoan wood rail, *Pareudiastes pacificus*, the Iwo Jima rail, *Poliolimnas cinereus breviceps*, the Raiatea thrush, *Turdus ulietensis*, and Kittlitz's thrush, *Zoothera terrestris*, of Peel Island in the Bonin Group.

Pigs and rats accounted for the Tahiti sandpiper, *Prosobonia leucoptera*, while dogs are said to have exterminated the flightless rail of Tristan da Cunha, *Porphyriornis n. nesiotis*.

Mongooses have been introduced in many of the Caribbean Islands, as well as in Hawaii and Fiji. These introductions were well meant, for mongooses have a great reputation as destroyers of rats and snakes, but in every single case, they quickly turned into unmitigated pests, killing domestic fowl and creating havoc among the indigenous animals. The bar-winged rail of Fiji, *Nesoclopeus poecilopterus* and the Hawaiian rail, *Pennula sandwichensis*, are among the victims of these efficient little predators. In the West Indies, mongooses wiped out the burrowing owls of Antigua and Guadeloupe, *Speotyto cunnicularia amaura* and *guadeloupensis*, the Jamaican least pauraque, *Siphonorhis a. americana*, the wrens of Guadeloupe and Martinique, *Troglodytes aëdon guadeloupensis* and *martinicensis*, and brought the Puerto Rico whip-poor-will, *Caprimulgus noctitherus*, to the verge of extinction. They may have played a considerable part in exterminating at least some of the very little known West Indian shrews of the genus *Nesophontes*.

Soon after vervet monkeys were released on the island of St. Christopher, the local subspecies of the Puerto Rico finch, *Loxigilla portoricensis grandis* ceased to exist.

There could hardly have been a need for African monkeys to be established on a small West Indian island, and it is even more difficult to understand why anybody should have thought it necessary to introduce European foxes into Australia. If it was thought that reynard would be of some help in dealing with the equally introduced rabbits, such hopes were doomed to disappointment. So far as the Australian fauna was concerned, the consequences were, however, disastrous. The foxes killed off the Toolach wallaby, *Wallabia greyi*, and they must, together with cats, be held responsible for the loss of the eastern barred bandicoot, *Parameles fasciata*, Gaimard's rat kangaroo, *Bettongia gaimardi*, and the broad faced rat kangaroo, *Potorous platyops*. Many other marsupials had their numbers diminished to such an extent by foxes and cats that they are now on the danger list.

Extinction can result not only from direct predation on the part of an introduced species, but also through mere competition for the available food supplies. The decline of the Hawaiian nukupuu, *Hemignathus wilsoni*, is thought to be at least partly due to competition from the introduced Japanese whiteye, *Zosterops japonicus*, while barn owls, released on the Seychelles, seem gradually to be ousting the Seychelles owl, *Otus insularis*, and the Seychelles kestrel, *Falco araca*.

It was, of course, inevitable that cats, dogs, pigs, and other domestic animals should follow man to the farthest corners of the world, and nothing could have been done with regard to the rats, which came along as stowaways. Many transplantations of animals were, however, unnecessary and even highly irresponsible. The resulting damage, can in most cases, not be undone, but it is to be hoped that the lesson has finally sunk in and that the hazards of such experiments have at last been fully realized. When the transplantation of a species becomes really necessary, for instance in order to save it from complete extinction, due precautions must be taken to prevent things from getting out of hand. There was, of course, no danger in moving a few white rhinoceroses from the west bank of the Nile, where they are approaching extinction, into the safety of the Murchison Falls National Park on the other side of the river, nor in transferring some of the last surviving Arabian oryx into a game paddock in Arizona. But let us forget neither the damage rabbits and foxes did in Australia, nor the fact that red deer have become a real pest in New Zealand!

More often than not, the extinction of a species cannot simply be put down to one reason alone, but has to be regarded as due to the cumulative effects of a variety of factors. Thus, in the case of the passenger pigeon, the destruction of forests had to be added to excessive hunting pressure in order to cause the downfall of this highly prolific species. The introduction of predators or competitors is sure to make itself felt all the more, if the impact is additional to the distress caused by habitat destruction. There can hardly be anything more devastating than hunting pressure, habitat destruction and the ravages caused by introduced predators all working in conjunction, and many a unique and interesting fauna has been sadly depleted by such a combination of destructive forces.

When James Cook discovered the Sandwich Islands, Hawaiian chiefs were seen wearing magnificent state robes and casques covered all over with the feathers of small birds. Such an outfit was brought back by John Webber, the Swiss artist of Cook's third voyage, and it is now one of the most highly prized possessions of the Historic and Ethnographic Museum in Berne. As a schoolboy I often went to look at it. I had, of course, been told of its rarity and intrinsic value, but what fascinated me even more was its association with the great navigator-explorer, who ranked very high among my heroes. The feathers were yellow and red in colour, and I can remember wondering how many birds must have been killed in order to make up these regalia.

The birds, which had to provide the plumage

decorating the famous cloaks, belonged to the family of Hawaiian honey-creepers or *Drepanididae*. Like Darwin's finches, the Hawaiian honeycreepers may have come from a finch or bunting-like species, and have gone through a very similar phase of adaptive radiation. Their bills, for instance, show a truly remarkable variety of shape and development, some serving for sipping nectar, others for probing cracks in the bark of trees, for eating seeds and even for breaking nuts. A few have beaks closely resembling those considered as characteristic of the parrot family. Had H.M.S. *Beagle* paid a visit to the Sandwich Islands, Charles Darwin would have been utterly delighted with the nine genera and 22 species of honeycreepers!

The rich, yellow feathers favoured by Hawaiian chiefs were taken from the mamo, *Drepanis pacifica*, and from the four species of oo, the red ones from the scarlet creeper, *Vestiaria coccinea*. The mamo was already quite rare around the middle of the last century, and it has not been seen since 1898. The Oahu oo, *Moho apicalis*, vanished as early as 1837, the Molokai oo, *Moho bishopi*, became extinct between 1904 and 1915, the Hawaii oo, *Moho nobilis*, in 1934, while the Kauai oo, *Moho braccata*, is only just surviving, not more than 12 individuals having been recorded in 1962. Altogether, two genera and a dozen species of honeycreepers must now be regarded as lost. The scarlet creeper is, strangely enough, still fairly common, which gives us a good indication that persecution by the Hawaiians, intense as it must have been for at least some of the species, was by no means the only or even the most important factor in causing the extermination of these lovely and, from an evolutionary point of view, so highly important birds. Considerably more harm was probably done by the cutting of the forests and by the introduction of various predators. Bird diseases, which were accidentally brought into the islands, may have contributed to their decimation. It can be considered as highly significant, however, that the three species most common today are also the least specialized ones.

A high degree of specialization can be quite as fatal as restriction to a very limited area of distribution. While giving a species considerable advantages as long as conditions remain stable, it also makes it extremely vulnerable with regard to any changes that might occur in its environment. On islands practically free of predators, a variety of birds have gradually dispensed with the power of flight. In certain cases this trend may have been definitely

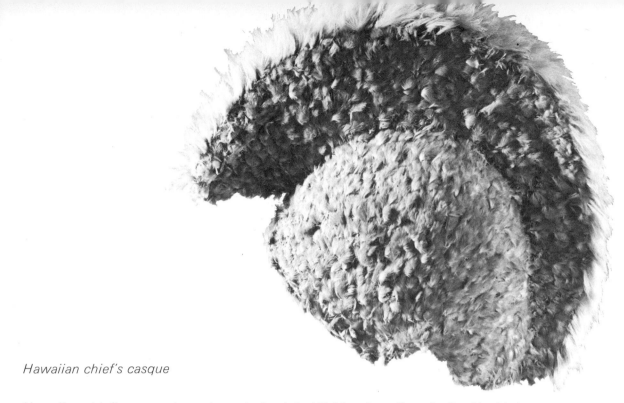

Hawaiian chief's casque

Hawaiian chief's state robe as brought back by Webber from Captain Cook's third voyage

advantageous, as it prevented individuals from being blown out to sea by gales and storms; in others, the ability to fly simply became superfluous. Living in an environment without enemies and finding its food on the ground, a species would not have its prospects of survival diminished by a mutational reduction in the size of its wings. Some birds, like the moas, the elephant birds and the dodo, went so far as to become slow and clumsy. The kiwis and many members of the rail family developed into agile runners, and took to darting around in dense undergrowth. And there were those that became flightless because they found their food in the sea and nested on remote, uninhabited islands or coasts.

The invasion of their insular habitat by man and his attendant predators has spelled disaster for many of these flightless birds. The moas, the elephant birds, the dodo and the solitaires have become extinct, and so have quite a number of flightless rails, such as van den Broeck's red rail of Mauritius, the blue rail of Rodriguez, the Laysan Island rail, the rail of Tristan da Cunha, and a mysterious species which was recorded on Ascension Island in 1656, but which nobody has ever seen again. Among the victims of an evolutionary development induced by a life in too safe and peaceful an environment must be numbered

the night heron of Rodriguez, the great auk, and the Stephen Island wren, which was never seen to fly before that wretched cat wiped out the whole population. The spectacled cormorant of the Komandorskie Islands was almost flightless. The Galapagos cormorant, *Nannopterum harrisii*, which is quite incapable of flight, still survives, but its numbers have dropped from between 3–5,000 in 1962 to about 1,000 in 1965. The takahé, *Notornis mantelli*, of New Zealand is so rare that it was long considered as extinct, and, of the flightless owl parrot or kakapo, *Strigops habroptilus*, less than 100 individuals are thought to be in existence. The flightless teals of the Auckland and Campbell Islands, *Anas a. aucklandia* and *nesiotis*, are both very rare. The Campbell Island subspecies may even be extinct, only a dozen specimens ever having been seen. The kagu, *Rhynochetos jubatus*, of New Caledonia, a bird related to both the rails and the cranes, is precariously surviving in a few densely forested mountain areas. On the list of endangered species we also find the flightless Titicaca grebe, *Rollandia micropterus*, and two almost flightless Australian parrots, the ground parrot, *Pezoporus wallicus*, and the night parrot, *Geopsittacus occidentalis*. It is pleasant to report that among so many flightless birds which have succumbed, or are

Stephen Island wren, Xenicus lyally

Kagu, Rhynochetos jubatus

Plate X (opposite page 96) The grey-headed kingfisher, *Halcyon leucocephala adeon,* was painted by J. R. Forster on Captain Cook's second voyage

Plate XI (below) One of the ground finches, or Darwin's finches, of the Galapagos Islands. The striking adaptations to various ecological niches displayed by these birds set Charles Darwin on the trail that finally led to the publication of 'The Origin of Species'

about to succumb, to the catastrophic changes which have overtaken them, the kiwis, at least, are holding their own. Even though much reduced in numbers through forest destruction, they are at present in no danger of extermination.

Of the New Zealand wattle birds, both the kokakos, *Callaeus c. cinerea* and *wilsoni,* and the saddlebacks, *Creadion c. carunculatus* and *rufisater,* are now very rare and restricted to a few localities. They move about in hops and leaps, using their wings more for balancing than for actual flight. The huia, *Heteralocha acustirostris,* once fairly common in certain parts of North Island, seems to have been an equally weak flyer. It became extinct around 1907, in which year the last two specimens, both of them males, were seen. The loss of any species is a deplorable event, but the passing of the huia must surely cause very special regret. The beaks of the two sexes were so different that John Gould, the famous ornithologist, first described male and female as separate species. The beak of the hen is long and gracefully curved, that of the cock much shorter, straight and chisel-like. It has been reliably reported that the pair collaborated in extracting beetle larvae and wingless tree crickets, called 'wetas' in New Zealand, from decaying wood. The male chiselled away at bark and wood until an insect tunnel was laid open, whereupon the female took over and withdrew the juicy morsel from its hiding place. What would we give for a movie picture illustrating this intriguing phase of behaviour—but, alas, nobody will ever see a pair of huias perform again. Among the Maoris, the black tail feathers were in great demand for adornment, and Gould wrote that the native hunters were very clever at luring the birds away from cover by whistling to them. Once they had them out in the open, they beat them to death with sticks. What the Maori began, was probably finished by the predators introduced with European colonization.

The reason for the decline of one of the huia's cousins, the North Island kokako, is given in the 'Red Data Book' as: 'Human predation on a confiding species'. This is by no means the only instance of an entirely misplaced trust in the human species. Mammals, birds and reptiles living on remote islands have, at first acquaintance with man, only too often displayed a most amazing confidence, and some seem never really to have learned any better. The tameness of sea cows wallowing in the kelp off Bering Island has been mentioned, and the reader may also remember the doves and parrots of Mauritius, which let themselves be knocked down with sticks. The

Huia, Heteralocha acustirostris. *Male bird in front of picture, female at rear*

classic remarks on the subject come from Charles Darwin, who witnessed the phenomenon in especially striking form on the Galapagos Islands.

'Before concluding my account of the Zoology of these islands', he wrote in his celebrated account of the voyage of H.M.S. *Beagle,* 'I must describe more in detail the tameness of the birds. This disposition is common to all the terrestrial species; namely to the mocking-birds, the finches, sylvicolae, tyrant-flycatchers, doves and hawks. There is not one which will not approach sufficiently close to be killed with a switch, and sometimes, as I have myself tried, with a cap or hat. A gun is here almost superfluous, for with the muzzle of one I pushed a hawk off a branch of a tree. . . .'

It is hardly surprising that of the terrestrial birds Darwin found so tame, one, the large ground finch, *Geospiza m. magnisostris,* became extinct shortly after the *Beagle* had visited the islands, while two others, the Galapagos hawk, *Buteo galapagoensis,* and the Charles Island mocking bird, *Nesomimus t. trifasciatus,* are on the danger list.

In course of the last few hundred years, insular faunas have proved to be especially vulnerable, suffering much heavier losses than those of the various continents. This is strikingly evident when arranged in a table listing the numbers of extinct species and subspecies of mammals and birds, according to the various continental and oceanic regions.

While all the continents have, so far as we know, only lost eight species and four subspecies of birds, 41 species and 30 subspecies have become extinct on the islands of the Pacific, New Zealand included. The bird fauna of Africa is still intact, but the islands of São Tomé and Principe, off the coast of West Africa, have lost one species and one subspecies respectively. The mammalian fauna of the Caribbean Islands has been depleted by no less than 34 species and two subspecies.

Animals inhabiting small islands have evidently been much more vulnerable than those of the larger ones. Assuming that *Aepyornis maximus* did survive until about 1640, Madagascar has, during the last 400 years or so suffered the loss of two species of birds, while the number of birds having become extinct on the neighbouring Mascarenes stands at 19 species, possibly at over 20.

Location	Mammals		Birds	
	Species	Sub-Species	Species	Sub-Species
South and Central America including Mexico, but without the Caribbean Islands	—	—	1	—
North America	1	9	3	1
Europe	1	3	—	—
Africa	2	7	—	—
Continental Asia	1	2	4	1
Asian Islands: Malay Archipelago, Ceylon, Phillipines, Japan, Kommandorski Islands	1	—	2	—
Australia and Tasmania	5	4	—	2
New Zealand and adjoining islands	—	—	7	6
Hawaiian Islands	—	—	14	9
New Caledonia and Lord Howe	—	—	3	7
Iwo Jima	—	—	—	1
Line Islands	—	—	—	2
Bonin Islands	—	—	3	—
New Hebrides	—	—	1	—
Carolinas	—	—	2	—
Fiji	—	—	1	—
Society Islands	—	—	4	1
Samoa	—	—	1	—
Wake	—	—	1	—
Choiseul	—	—	1	—
Galapagos	1	—	—	1
Guadalupe	—	—	2	3
Pacific, without exact locality	—	—	1	—
Caribbean Islands	34	2	9	10
Atlantic Islands (including São Tomé, Principe, Falklands)	1	—	4	2
Madagascar	—	—	2	—
Indian Ocean: Mascarenes, Assumption Seychelles, Christmas Island	2	1	20	4

Some of the figures given opposite will very probably be out-of-date by the time this book is printed. This is unavoidable for new information becomes available all the time. Very many species of mammals and birds are in great danger, and some of them are certain to become extinct in the very near future. There are, in fact, a number of borderline cases; species of which nobody can say definitely whether they still exist. Sclater's monal *Lophophorus sclateri*, a bird of the pheasant tribe, has not been heard of since 1938. Its original area of distribution extended from the Abor and Mishmi Hills to Yunnan and North Burma. All of this is very rugged country and has always been difficult of access. Today it is even more so for political reasons. So far as we know, the species has never been common. It used to be hunted and trapped by the natives and it probably still is, provided it has not been wiped out. We simply do not know, and there seems to be no immediate possibility of finding out. Another bird related to the pheasants of which no news has been received for a long time, is the western tragopan, *Tragopan melanocephalus*, of the north-western Himalayas. All that can be said is that years ago it was already considered as extremely rare and declining. It may well have become extinct in the meantime. The pigmy hog, *Sus salvanius*, used to be fairly common in southern

Nepal, as well as in Sikkim, Bhutan, and north-western Assam, but seems to have succumbed to hunting and habitat destruction. In his authoritative book of Indian wildlife, published in 1964, E. P. Gee reports some sportsmen as having encountered the species ten or twelve years before, both east and west of the Manas Game Sanctuary. Nothing further seems to have been heard of it, and the pigmy hog is now generally thought to be extinct.

When European settlers established themselves on the island of Tasmania, their sheep and fowl very quickly attracted the attention of a predatory animal that became known as the marsupial tiger, *Thylacinus cynocephalus*. Apart from having a striped coat, the creature has no similarity with a tiger, nor is it even remotely related to the cat family. Its outward appearance is more reminiscent of a dog, and it is now more commonly called the Tasmanian wolf. It is, in fact, the largest of the carnivorous marsupials. At one time, long before the advent of the Europeans, it also occurred on the Australian continent, where its extinction may well have been due to the competition offered to it by the dingo, the wild dog, said to have been introduced by the aborigines. In Tasmania, its depredation soon made it the object of a relentless war of extermination, the government at times paying a bounty of one pound for an adult, and ten shillings for

Thylacinus cynocephalus—*the only photograph existing of this animal in its habitat*

a young one. No less than 2,268 are known to have been killed during the period from 1888 to 1914.

In the time between the two world wars the Tasmanians suddenly realized that their campaign had succeeded beyond expectation, and that the 'tiger' had just about become extinct. Great interest was suddenly taken in the animal, and efforts were made to learn more about it. In 1933 a specimen trapped in Florentine Valley, where quite a number had been caught in the past, was taken to the Hobart Zoo. It was the last one to be exhibited in captivity. A few years later, Michael Sharland, a leading Tasmanian naturalist, stated that the species was now 'rarely seen', but thought that it might survive. He took a much more gloomy view in 1962, when he wrote: 'Maybe the last tiger has not yet gone. Therefore reports of its supposed occurrence justify official investigation; but one would be bold to say that Tasmanians will enjoy the excitement of seeing one alive again. Whether this belief is proved incorrect or otherwise, there is little we can do about it. The tiger has reached the point of no return, and the best of intentions will not save it.'

The *IUCN Red Data Book* strikes a somewhat more optimistic note: 'Reasonably reliable sightings have been made in widely scattered localities, such as the Cardigan River on the Queenstown Highway, the far north-west coast, the Tooms Lake region, and the Cradle Mountain—Lake St. Clair National Park (520 sq. miles). They may also occur in Frenchman's Cap National Park.'

Provided that it is not already extinct, the species will perhaps be able to get a toehold in the Tasmanian national parks. One thing is certain: its story strongly reflects the inconsistency of human nature! Many modern Tasmanians would consider it as the biggest thrill of their lives if they could just catch one fleeting glimpse of an animal which their grandfathers invariably saluted with a blast from a shotgun, and their government is doing everything possible to preserve a species for which a bounty was paid only half a century ago! Surely, there is a lesson in this, which should be taken to heart in every country on earth.

All too often, naturalists have had the sad duty to report the extinction of yet another species. But occasionally things do happen the other way round, and an animal thought to have been lost long ago causes jubilation among nature lovers and conservationists the world over by suddenly reappearing. A classic story of this kind was the rediscovery of the takahé, *Notornis mantelli*, the flightless, gallinule-like

rail of New Zealand. This bird first became known to scientists from bones that had been dug up on the North Island, and it was naturally assumed to have become extinct some time before the first European landings. In the 1840s Gideon A. Mantell, the English naturalist, received news that a bird existed on South Island, which could well be identical with the fossil, or rather sub-fossil species from North Island. After some disappointments, he managed to acquire and send to the British Museum two skins which had come from Resolution Island and Secretary Island, both on the south-western coast of South Island. A specimen collected near Lake Manapouri in 1879 went to the Dresden Museum, and in 1898 the Otago Museum came into possession of a takahé that had been caught by a dog near Lake Te Anau. That seemed to be the end, so far as the takahé was concerned. Nothing more was heard of this flightless rail with the beautiful blue plumage and red beak for many decades, in fact, until a New Zealand ornithologist, Dr. G. B. Orbell, thought it worthwhile to explore the Murchison Mountains near Lake Te Anau in 1948, hoping against hope

Takahé Notornis mantelli

that he might come across a few surviving takahés. The initial search brought no conclusive results, but Orbell heard some unidentifiable bird calls and saw strange, half-obliterated footprints. Within seven months, he was back among the Murchison Mountains and this time he found what he was looking for. The takahé still existed, and Dr. Orbell's discovery caused something of a sensation. The birds have been under almost constant observation ever since, and great efforts are made to ensure their well-being. There seem to be about 200 or 300 of them, living in small, scattered groups, and no significant population changes have come to notice during the past 18 or 19 years. Some authorities consider the takahé as a senile species, for it only lays up to four eggs a year, and of these many are infertile. Having lost its power of flight, it is, of course, highly vulnerable, but its decline, which obviously set in a long time ago, may thus be at least partly due to natural causes.

J. R. Forster and Andrew Sparrman, the naturalists accompanying James Cook on the second of his famous voyages, brought back specimens and drawings of six birds which vanished immediately afterwards and were not collected again by the scientific voyagers who followed in Cook's wake. They were the whitewinged sandpiper, *Prosobonia leucoptera*, of Tahiti, the sharp-billed sandpiper, *Aechmorhynchus cancellatus*, the Tanna ground dove, *Gallicolumba ferruginea*, the Raiatea parakeet, *Cyanoramphus ulietansus*, the 'mysterious starling', *Aplonis movornata*, of which we do not know where it was obtained, the Tahiti flycatcher, *Pomarea nigra*, and the Tongatabu flycatcher, *Pomarea n. tabuensis*. Surprisingly enough, the Tahiti flycatcher was found again in 1931 by members of the American Museum Whitney Expedition, which made a very thorough ornithological survey of the Pacific, while the Raiatea parakeet, not seen since Cook sailed away from Raiatea Island, was rediscovered quite recently.

A petrel once common around the Bermudas Islands and known as cahow, *Pterodroma cahow*, vanished during the 17th century, only to reappear again in 1916. The Seychelles owl, already mentioned as suffering from the competition of the introduced barn owl, was not heard of from 1906 until 1959, and the noisy scrub bird, *Atrichornis clamosus*, of south-

*The white-winged sandpiper—*Prosobonia *leucoptera, painted by J. R. Forster on Captain Cook's second voyage, and dated 1773. The bird was never seen again*

western Australia, last collected in 1889 and long believed extinct, is now known to survive as a rare and localized species. Another Australian bird, the almost flightless night parrot, was listed as extinct in 1935, but has been rediscovered in 1961. The Auckland Island rail, *Rallus pectoralis muelleri*, a subspecies of an Australian rail, and the Molokai creeper, *Loxops maculata flammea*, are two more species which have recently given the lie to premature reports of their extinction.

The scientific description of the Puerto Rico whip-poor-will, *Caprimulgus noctitherus*, published in 1919, was based on a few bones discovered in a cave. Rummaging through some old museum specimens, somebody came across the skin of an unnamed nightjar, that had lain unnoticed in a drawer for years, and realized that this was quite obviously the bird to go with the bones from Puerto Rico. Attempts to obtain more specimens in the island's jungles failed, and the nightjar was thought to have vanished, probably wiped out by mongooses, before its existence had even been formally recognized by science. In 1963, an ornithologist, following up unmistakable whip-poor-will calls, proved the species to be still in existence, collecting one specimen out of the half dozen or so he encountered.

Burramys parvus—thought to be extinct— was 're-discovered' in 1966

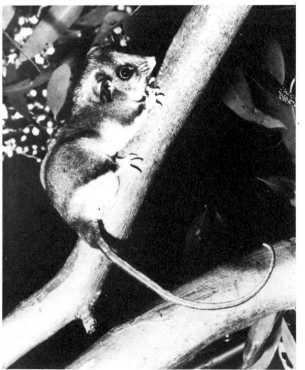

Nor are surprises of this kind restricted to birds. The dwarf hutia of Cuba, described from bones in 1917, was regarded as extinct until the small colony already mentioned was discovered in Zapata Swamp. The West Indian shrews of the genus *Nesophontes* are known only from skulls and bones taken from owl pellets which were collected in various caves. Most of them showed every sign of being very old, but in 1930 somebody extracted the remains of one of these shrews from fairly fresh-looking pellets, and there is thus still a possibility that we may one day see a live *Nesophontes*.

Some fossil bones dug up in a New South Wales caves in 1896 were found to have belonged to a small opossum-like creature, which lived some 20,000 years ago. The animal was named *Burramys parvus* and put down as a species that had become extinct from natural causes in the far-distant past. In 1966 Dr. Ken Shortman caught a small marsupial that had found its way into the kitchen of a skiing lodge in the Victorian Alps. It looked like a species new to science, but a more thorough examination revealed the startling truth that it was, in actual fact, a live *Burramys*!

Another marsupial, Leadbeater's opossum, *Cymnobelideus leadbeateri*, was known from five specimens, taken between 1867 and 1909. Nothing further was heard of it, and in 1937 its name was added to the list of extinct animals.

In 1961 a population of 15 to 20 of these animals was found in Cumberland Valley, 50 miles north-east of Melbourne, where it now enjoys the strictest protection possible. A naturalist trying to catch live specimens of the tiny honey opossum in January 1967, had the surprise of his life, when he took two marsupial mice or dibblers, *Antechinus apicalis*, out of his trap, members of a species that had not been seen for 83 years and was therefore officially listed as extinct. As the female soon afterwards produced a litter of eight, there is some hope that it will be possible to build up a colony of these creatures, which seem at one time to have been not uncommon in the area of the Swan and King George's Rivers.

Many of Madagascar's lemurs have been sadly reduced in numbers, and some must be regarded as seriously threatened. It is, however, most gratifying to know that the two species which were thought to be extinct are, in fact, still surviving. One of them, the broad-nosed lemur, *Hapalemur simus*, was recorded from the vicinity of Lake Aotra a long time ago

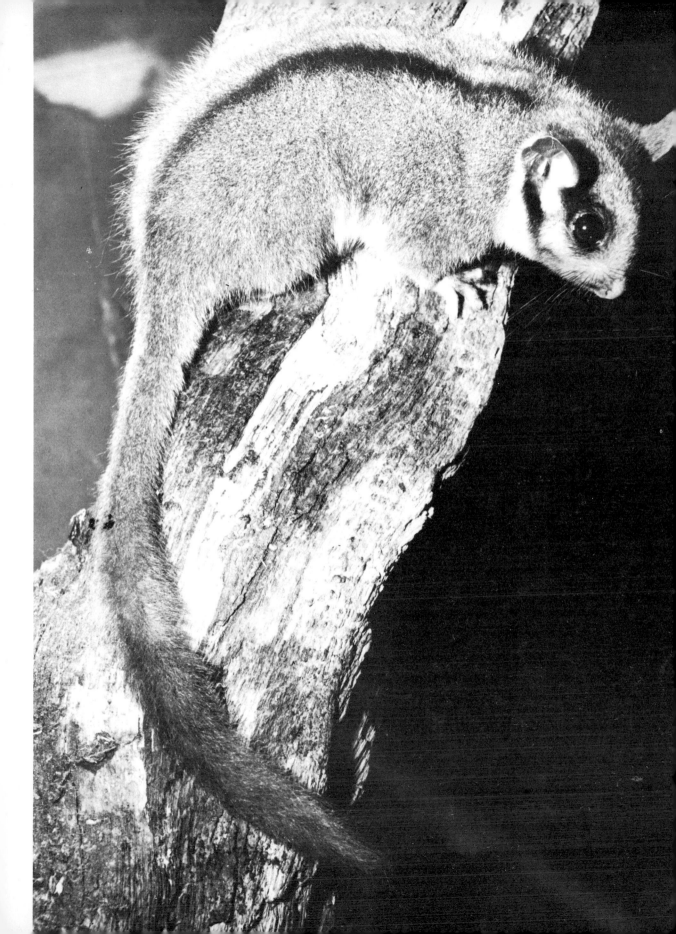

The broad-nosed lemur, Hapalemur simus

Zebra—domestic ass hybrids are sometimes mistaken for the extinct quagga

and then lost sight of, until a few specimens were recently observed in the reed and bamboo thickets surrounding the lake. The description of the other one, the dwarf lemur, *Cheirogaleus trichotis*, published in 1875, was based on a solitary specimen, the exact place of origin of which was unknown. Only two further skins found their way into museum collections, and there was every reason for considering the species as irrevocably lost. It has since been rediscovered near Mananala in 1966.

All of these resuscitated species are, of course, still very much on the danger list. Some may eventually be found to be slightly more numerous than is thought at present, and one or two could even begin to show signs of a recovery. The pink pigeon, *Columba mayeri*, of Mauritius, nowadays quite a common bird, was actually listed as extinct by Lord Rothschild in 1907. Having declined almost to the point of no return, it managed to adapt itself to changed conditions. There are good prospects that the publicity which surrounded some recent rediscoveries will lead to very special care being given to the preservation of the species in question. At the present moment, I should think that the takahé and Leadbeater's opossum have a very much better chance of survival than, let us say, Sclater's monal, the western tragopan, or the anoa of Celebes.

Reports on the survival of a species thought to have been lost long ago, have a tendency to raise hopes that even more sensational rediscoveries might materialize one of these days. Thus Otto Kroesche closes an excellent summary of what is known of New Zealand's moas with the words:

'It is difficult to suppress a secret hope that some moas might still be lurking in the vast mountain forests, to be found by a lucky ornithologist, just as *Notornis* was found a few years ago.'

Some people in South Africa are hopeful that the quagga will be rediscovered in some remote part of the Kalahari or in south west Africa, and from time to time there are rumours of one of these partly-striped zebras having been seen or even shot. Dr. Lutz Heck, the well-known zoologist, following up a number of quagga stories, has come to the conclusion that they are based on occasional hybrids between zebras and domestic asses, perhaps also on zebras of the *burchelli* or *antiquorum* type, characterized by having practically unstriped legs. He is surely right, for south-west Africa, the favourite haunt of the modern 'quagga hunters', lies, after all, far outside the area in which the true quagga was to be found during the first half of the last century.

Chapter 5

Man, the Preserver

In 1806 an expedition under the command of Captains Lewis and Clark was struggling back across the Rocky Mountains, having wintered at the mouth of the Columbia River. In order to cover more ground, the two leaders decided to split their party: Lewis took half of his men over the pass now known as 'Lewis and Clark Pass', while Clark first descended the Jefferson River, then went up the Gallatin and crossed over to the Yellowstone. We can imagine the explorer casting longing glances at the towering mountains he could see upstream, wondering what they might hide, itching to discover the source of the big river. But the resources of the expedition were exhausted, and there was no time left for further exploration. Resolutely, Clark turned his back on the unknown and descended the Yellowstone to rejoin Lewis on the Missouri.

Among the soldiers accompanying Lewis and Clark on their highly successful transcontinental expedition, there was a former hunter and trapper by the name of John Colter. Having again had a taste of wilderness life, Colter decided to return to the adventurous existence of a frontiersman, and when the expedition reached the villages of the friendly Mandan Indians, he asked for his discharge from the army. This was granted, and in 1807 Colter returned to the Rocky Mountains, ascended the Yellowstone and found that it came out of a lake. In the vicinity the trapper came across a variety of strange and wonderful sights, such as bubbling mud pools, hot springs and gigantic fountains which, at fairly regular intervals, threw boiling water high up into the air. The training he had received under Lewis and Clark enabled Colter to draw an amazingly accurate map of the upper Yellowstone and Snake River area, which he afterwards gave to Captain Clark. The explorer incor-

porated it under the heading 'Colter's Route 1807' in his own splendid map of the American West, and he probably accepted Colter's story of what he had seen around Lake Yellowstone. Not so the general public: frontiersmen had a reputation for talking big, and Colter was thought to be no exception. Facetious spirits began to refer to 'Colter's Hell'.

More than 20 years were to pass before 'Colter's Hell' received another visitor. This was James Bridger, also a famous frontiersman, and the tales he brought back were even more colourful than those of his predecessor. But when Warren Angus Ferris, a very sober and matter-of-fact official of the American Fur Company, soon afterwards published an account of a trip to Lake Yellowstone, people stopped laughing. It began to look as if 'Colter's Hell' was fact and not fiction. James Bridger had the satisfaction, in 1851, to act as guide to the first scientific expedition to reach the headwaters of the Yellowstone, and the two leaders, Captain Reynolds and Dr. Hayden, were duly impressed with what he had to show them. In 1870 a much more formidable party, led by General Henry D. Washburn, Surveyor-General of Montana, entered 'Colter's Hell', or the 'Land of Wonders', as it began to be called. Among its members were Lieutenant Gustavus C. Doane, Nathaniel Langford and Judge Cornelius Hedges. The explorers had to brave hostile Indians and were caught by early snow storms, but the canyons, waterfalls and geysers made them forget dangers and hardships. On the evening of September 19th, while sitting at the campfire and listening to his companions discussing the advisability of taking up land claims in the area, Cornelius Hedges began to ponder over a new and strange idea. Now that a road had been opened, there would surely be a considerable influx of people

General William Clark, 1830. In 1806 he co-led the Lewis-Clark Expedition. He was made a General in 1813. His map of the American West included the area of present-day Yellowstone National Park. Painted by George Catlin

into this virgin wilderness. What would happen to it and all its marvels? It was not difficult to foresee that it would be defaced and irrevocably spoiled. Could it not be preserved intact for generations to come, perhaps by being declared the property of the whole nation? Could it be turned into some kind of park, a national park, open to all who wanted to find their recreation in the wilds, but safeguarded against the ravages of human greed? Hedges communicated his thoughts to his companions and managed to enlist the enthusiastic support of most of them. Washburn's official account and a series of articles Langford wrote for 'Scribner's Monthly' caused a great sensation and provided an excellent basis on which Judge Hedges could bring his idea to the notice of Congress.

Many people tend to sneer at the 'materialism' of the last century, preening themselves as fully fledged 'idealists', but how long does it usually take to get a new wildlife reserve properly established, even though a delay of only a few months can, under present-day conditions, be quite sufficient for irreparable damage to be done? Hedges visited the wonderland of

Yellowstone in 1870, and the bill turning it into a national park was signed by President Grant as early as March 12th, 1872. Langford, whose article had contributed so much to the speedy success of the scheme became the park's first superintendent.

Today, with hundreds of national parks in all parts of the world, it is almost impossible to appreciate properly the momentous significance of the concept that took shape on that already far-distant September evening beside a roaring campfire in what is now Yellowstone National Park. We must remember that this was happening at a time when man had only just begun to really assert his mastery over nature as a whole. He was doing it with ruthless efficiency and determination, for the industrial revolution had made him more powerful than ever. Civilization was forging ahead, advancing into the empty spaces of the globe, pushing roads and railways over ground that had been untrodden by white men a few short decades earlier. Age-old forests fell before the onslaught. On the American prairies, the herds of bison were being exterminated. Islands in Arctic and Antarctic waters had their seal populations massacred. The

Yellowstone—Colter's Hell

death of the last quagga in captivity was only a few years off. But what did it matter that there were no quaggas left alive on the veld? Who cared about bisons going the same way? The animal kingdom had anyway been carefully classified into species 'useful' and 'harmful' to man—not only by the general public, but by reputable scientists as well. No one shed a tear for a beautiful landscape disfigured by factory buildings, mining installations or ugly, sprawling hotels. They were, after all, glorious symbols of progress and expansion. There were quite enough unspoiled wildernesses left anyway, the quicker they, too, were made to give up their treasures of timber, minerals and furs, so much the better. That was the general attitude, and it was against such a background that the idea of 'national parks' had been born, the idea of a wilderness that was not to be engulfed by civilization, where there would be no boom towns, no lumber camps, no mining, hunting or trapping. The fact that the response was so immediate and

widespread, can certainly be regarded as one of the most amazing aspects of the whole story.

Conservationists owe a tremendous debt of gratitude to the United States of America, for the creation of Yellowstone National Park started a movement that has, with steadily growing momentum, embraced the whole world, jumping all barriers of nationality, creed, ideology and race. It has paid off handsomely in preserving intact many of the most magnificent scenic displays and in saving numerous species of animals and plants from certain extinction.

Yellowstone National Park, the world's most spectacular thermal region, with over 10,000 geysers, hot springs, steam jets and mud volcanoes, instantly attracted visitors and their rapidly increasing numbers provided full justification for the congressional decision of 1872. The recognition of this fact made congressmen all the more willing to listen to Colonel George W. Steward who, towards the end of the 1880s, started a campaign to save the 'Giant Forest'

Unprecedented drilling and prospecting for minerals in Alaska is robbing much of the countryside of its natural beauty

Waterton Lake—Waterton Lakes National Park, Alberta

of sequoia trees in the High Sierras. In 1890, commercial considerations were frustrated by the establishment of the Sequoia National Park. The same year brought national park status to the stupendous Yosemite Valley, which had already been a reserve for a considerable time.

Meanwhile, the fame of Yellowstone National Park had spread far and wide, and other countries began to show interest in the idea of giving absolute protection to areas not yet desecrated by the march of progress. The first to follow the example of the United States were the Canadians who, in 1886 and 1887, created Glacier National Park in the majestic Selkirk Range and Banff National Park, with lovely Lake Louise as its central attraction. In 1891 it was Australia's turn, with Belair National Park. New Zealand followed suit in 1894 and protected a thermal area with hot springs and geysers, similar to that of Yellowstone, which became the nucleus of Tongariro National Park. Mount Buffalo National Park of Victoria, Australia, was founded in 1898.

New parks were now created in rapid succession: Waterton Lake in Canada (1895), Mount Rainier in the United States (1899), Mount Egmont in New Zealand (1900), Crater Lake in the United States (1902), Wilson's Promontory (1905) and Wyperfeld (1909) in Australia, Mesa Verde in the United States (1906), and Jasper in Canada (1907). During the first decade of the 20th century, conservation efforts in the United States received a tremendous boost through the presidency of Theodore Roosevelt. During his term as President he gave full proof that a true sportsman can also be an ardent conservationist, and the far-sighted policies he instigated have benefited American wildlife long after his death.

In 1909, the idea propagated more than thirty years earlier by Judge Hedges was at last taken up in Europe, and in that year the Government of Sweden declared several areas of great scenic beauty as national parks. At the same time the Swiss naturalists and explorers Paul and Fritz Sarasin, ably supported by Dr. Coaz, Chief Inspector of the Federal Forestry Service, began

propagating a project for the establishment of an alpine nature reserve of a type similar to the North American national parks. Their efforts brought into being the Swiss National Park, situated among the mountain ranges south of the Engadine Valley. The decree establishing this splendid sanctuary was signed on April 3rd, 1914.

The United States and Canada, however, remained in the lead, and one could almost have thought that the two neighbouring countries were running a competition to determine which of them could take better care of what was left of its priceless natural heritage. From 1910 to 1922 the citizens of the United States were presented with Glacier National Park in Montana, adjoining Canada's Waterton Park, Rocky Mountain Park in Colorado, Lassen Peak Volcanic Park in Northern California and magnificent Mount McKinley National Park in Alaska. Canada kept in step with Elk Island, Mount Revelstoke, Kootenay and Wood Buffalo National Park. Australia, too, was enriched by three more parks, Lamington, south of Brisbane, Mount Field and Cradle Mountain—Lake St. Clair, both on the island of Tasmania.

During the early decades of conservation efforts, the choice of a site to be declared a national park was, as a rule, strongly influenced by the scenic beauty it had to offer. Towering mountains, mirroring their snow-capped peaks in glassy lakes, majestic forests, thundering waterfalls, stupendous canyons, volcanic curiosities, those were the attractions an area had to have if it were to be given protection under national park status. Such scenic gems were, of course, mostly to be found in the depth of some remote wilderness still teeming with wildlife, and the animals within the park boundaries, finding themselves free from human persecution, soon began to lose their age-old fear of man. Visitors were able to watch wild beasts which, before, had only been seen by intrepid big game hunters. The bears of Yellowstone National Park rapidly acquired world-wide fame. The big horn sheep, mountain goats and moose of Banff National Park turned out to be as great an attraction as the superlative beauty of the mountain scenery surrounding Lake Louise. Visitors to the Swiss National Park, while enjoying the splendour of a corner of the rugged alpine world, unspoiled by crowded resorts, souvenir shops and cogwheel railways, would have been greatly disappointed if they had not seen chamois, ibex, red deer, marmots and golden eagles. As the surrounding lands were progressively emptied of their game ani-

mals, the national parks acquired a steadily increasing importance as wildlife sanctuaries. The time was fast approaching when the presence of a spectacular concentration of animals or the occurrence of some rare and threatened species would be regarded as sufficient justification for the establishment of a national park!

Game reserves were, of course, nothing really new. It had long been the custom of royalty and nobility to preserve wild animals for sport, and this practice was by no means restricted to Europe. In the old Peruvian empire, for instance, hunting was a privilege of the Inca caste and of the regional tribal rulers, and any ordinary man caught in one of their game reserves was dealt with harshly and without mercy. A genuine game sanctuary, the Kärpf Game Sanctuary, where all animals were to be left in peace, was created in the Swiss Canton of Glarus in 1548, at the instigation of Magistrate Joachim Bäldi, and we can only marvel at the enlightened thinking of the man who decided upon such a step long before game animals were regarded as anything but objects of the chase. Kärpf Game Reserve has remained inviolate ever since and is still in existence, over 400 years after its creation. It contains a wonderful array of alpine wildlife—a noble monument to a remarkable pioneer in conservation!

There were many early attempts to save declining species from complete extermination. Thus the 17th century Archbishops of Salzburg went to a lot of trouble and expense to preserve the ibex of the Tyrolean Alps. They failed in their efforts, and the wild goats of the Zillertal were gradually killed off by poachers. Similar measures taken in the neighbouring Swiss Canton of Graubünden were equally devoid of success, even though the ibex figured in the Canton's coat of arms, making the authorities especially keen to protect it. The species only survived in the Italian Alps, from where it has been reintroduced in Austria and Switzerland.

The Kings of Poland did their utmost to save the very last herd of aurochs near Warsaw but the herd faded away, and in 1627 the last aurochs, a cow, was found dead. Frederick the Great failed in preventing the extermination of the Prussian herds of European bison, but this species fortunately survived in Poland.

Faunal reserves have become especially important in Africa, which has always been something of a 'continent of animals', with wildlife figuring very prominently in the accounts of almost all African explorers and travellers. When Jan van Riebeck

Left: *Swiss National Park*

Banff National Park—Canada

established a Dutch settelement near the Cape of Good Hope, the surroundings of Table Bay were swarming with game, including elephants, rhinos, and lions. Seventeen years after the founding of Cape Town, a Dutch Governor stopped unrestricted hunting and ordered game licences to be issued. However, in accordance with the attitudes of the time, bounties were paid for the destruction of 'harmful' animals, such as lions, leopards and hyenas. As the settlers moved inland, the number of game animals declined sharply, and Governor Simon van der Stel, appointed to his post in 1679, took strict measures to ensure the survival of certain species threatened with local extinction. In 1753 legislation

was passed in Cape Town, which was to give a considerable amount of protection to hippo, rhino, buffalo, and eland. Unfortunately it was easier to proclaim game laws than to enforce their observance, especially in a pioneer country with a wild and sparsely settled frontier!

The British occupation of the Cape led to the Great Trek of 1835. Pushing northwards the trekkers found the areas, where the Orange Free State and Transvaal now are, full of game and made full use of this bountiful supply of meat and hides. The animals soon began to dwindle away and the quagga became extinct, just as the blue-buck of Swellendam had disappeared at the beginning of the century. Game laws were

Plate XII (top) The tiger needs urgent and effective protection for it is on the decline in practically all its vast area of distribution

Plate XIII Elephants in the Amboseli Reserve of Kenya

Plate XIV Bryce Canyon National Park, in Utah, USA, is famous for its spectacular rock formations. It harbours mule deer, cougars and bobcats

issued by the Free State Authorities in 1837, and by the Transvaal Volksraad (Parliament) in 1846. Poachers had to face the threat of having not only their guns and ammunition confiscated, but also their waggons—yet it was the same sad story once more and the authorities found it beyond their powers to keep effective control. Before blaming the South African settlers for massacring the wildlife of their hard-won lands, we must, however, remember that a good many of them did establish private game reserves on their farms, and it is to these men, and only to them, that we owe the survival of such species as the mountain zebra, the bontebok, the blesbok, and the black wildebeest.

The President of the Transvaal Republic, 'Ohm' Paul Kruger, although a mighty hunter in his younger days, was distressed at the speed with which the game was fading away from his beloved veld. He realized that the only way to ensure a measure of government control was through the creation of game reserves and, despite opposition, in 1894 the Pongola Reserve was proclaimed. In 1897 Natal declared the Hluhluwe area of Zululand a reserve. It has remained a very fine game sanctuary to this day, but the Pongola Reserve was unfortunately de-proclaimed in 1921. President Kruger fought tooth and nail for a second and bigger reserve in what was known as the Low-veld, and in 1898 was able to establish the Sabi Game Reserve. Krüger had to leave South Africa during the Anglo-Boer War and died in exile but the Sabi Game Reserve was to achieve success and fame far beyond anything he could have visualized.

The reserve suffered badly during the war, with hunting commandos of both sides killing great numbers of animals to feed the troops, but the British re-proclaimed it immediately after the Peace Treaty of Vereeniging had been signed. In July 1902 a game warden was appointed. The man selected for the job was James Stevenson-Hamilton, a keen sportsman and field naturalist. No better choice could have been made: Colonel Stevenson-Hamilton held office for forty years—with only a short interruption during the first world war—and when he retired in 1946, the Sabi Game Reserve had, thanks to his ceaseless and persuasive efforts, long since become the Krüger National Park. It was also South Africa's top tourist attraction, visited by thousands of people every year.

The Kruger National Park extends about 200 miles in a south-north direction, with an average width of forty miles. The southern parts are covered with the vegetation characteristic of the bushveld, which changes gradually into savannah as one moves

President Kruger

northwards. The park authorities have established a number of comfortable camps, where visitors can either hire a small hut, or pitch their own tents. Rules and regulations are very strict. You are, for instance, not allowed to get out of your car, you must not leave the tracks, and you have to be back in camp by sunset. Despite the fact that it now has about 250,000 visitors a year, the park has remained quite remarkably unaffected by this invasion, mainly thanks to discipline being rigorously enforced. A research station has been established at Skukuza Camp, and for years scientists have now been studying the general ecology of the area, as well as population dynamics, food habits and animal behaviour.

Tourists are, of course, always especially eager to see lions, and today, just over a thousand of these big cats have their hunting grounds within the park; they have become completely indifferent to cars, which they apparently do not associate with humans. They often rest right in the middle of a track, and when they decide to move on, they casually stroll through the ranks of the vehicles surrounding them. Leopards are present too, though much more difficult to see. There are numerous elephants, buffaloes, giraffes and zebras, as well as hippos and many species of antelopes, such as impala, wildebeest, tsesseby, sable, roan, greater kudu and nyala.

The South African white rhinoceros, *Ceratotherium s. simum*, bigger and much more even-tempered than its black cousin, was once common and widely distributed between the Orange River and the Zambesi. Being easy to kill, the animal was rapidly exterminated and disappeared from the lowveld long before the Sabi Game Reserve came into being. At the turn of the century it was thought to be extinct, but a few individuals were later found to have survived in an area situated between the Black and White Umfolosi Rivers in Natal. The Umfolosi Reserve was created to give them adequate protection, and under the devoted guardianship of F. Vaughan-Kirby, another sportsman turned conservationist, the species made a spectacular recovery. White rhino spread from Umfolosi to parts of the neighbouring Hluhluwe Reserve, and there are now enough of them in Natal to allow the restocking of other game sanctuaries. A few years ago the white rhino returned to its former haunts in the Kruger National Park, where a population of over 100 individuals has now been built up. How Stevenson-Hamilton, who died in 1957, would have enjoyed this!

The Kruger National Park, even though existing as an important reserve since the nineties of the last century, just missed being the first African national park. This distinction goes to the southernmost portion of the Albert National Park in the eastern Congo, which encompasses the Virunga Mountains, a range of volcanic cones straddling the Central African Rift Valley just north of Lake Kivu. While climbing Mount Sabino in 1902, Oskar von Beringe, a German officer exploring the border area between German East Africa, the Congo and Uganda, spotted a group of big apes and managed to shoot two of them. He discovered that they were not chimpanzees as he had thought, but gorillas, which had hitherto been known only from far-away West Africa—especially from Cameroon and Gaboon. These gorillas were found to differ somewhat from their West African cousins, and the zoologist Matschie described them as a new species which he named *Gorilla beringei*. It is now generally thought that the so-called mountain gorilla must be regarded as a subspecies of the lowland gorilla, and the name has accordingly been changed to *Gorilla gorilla beringei*.

Museums all over the world were keen to secure specimens and a number of expeditions set out for the Virunga Volcanoes. In 1921, Carl Akeley, the American naturalist and taxidermist, collected the five gorillas which now form the splendid habitat group in the American Museum of Natural History. He also made a preliminary study of the animals and obtained the first movie picture ever taken of gorillas in their native habitat. Akeley felt certain that the continued interest of museum collectors and animal trappers would eventually prove fatal to the mountain gorilla and drew up plans for a gorilla sanctuary on the Virunga Volcanoes. His proposals were passed on to King Albert of Belgium, who had shown a keen interest in conservation ever since he had visited the Yellowstone and Yosemite National Parks. Little persuasion was therefore needed, and in 1925 Mounts Mikeno, Karisimbi and Visoke were made a national park by royal decree.

In 1929 the Albert National Park was considerably enlarged, so as to include not only the still active volcanoes Niragongo and Nyamuragira and the wonderful game fields of the Rwindi Plains swarming with elephants, buffaloes, hippos, topi and kob, but part of the snow-covered Ruwenzori range north of Lake Edward as well. A scientific organization had already been set up, which was to take in hand the detailed exploration of the Albert Park, and of all further national parks that might be established in the Congo and in the mandated territories of Ruanda-Urundi. Three more parks were, in fact, created from 1934 to 1939, the Kagera Park in Ruanda, the

White rhinoceros: Hluhluwe Reserve

Giraffes at waterhole in Kruger National Park

Garamba Park on the Congo–Sudan border, and the Upemba Park in Katanga. The long series of monographs issued by the Institute of Congo National Parks forms a splendid and enduring monument to the very thorough and enlightened efforts of the Belgian conservationists.

For some time it has been very difficult to get a reliable report on the damage which the Congo parks suffered during the various upheavals that have shaken that unhappy country. It was known for certain that the white rhinos of the Garamba Park had been badly decimated by poachers, but what had happened to the Upemba and Albert Parks? In 1967 Kai Curry-Lindahl, the Swedish zoologist, was able to visit these two reserves, and conservationists were eagerly awaiting his reports. It turned out that the southern part of the Upemba Park had been devastated by UN troops who invaded the sanctuary on various occasions between 1960 and 1962 and slaughtered the game with automatic weapons, whereupon Katangese gendarmes and Congo troops quite naturally followed the example set by the blue-

helmets. One must hope that UNESCO immediately lodged a strong protest with UN, and that drastic steps have been taken to prevent further acts of banditry. The northern part of the Upemba Park was found to be teeming with game, even though Baluba tribesmen had plundered the main station, burnt the rangers' quarters and destroyed road bridges.

Very much better news came from the Albert Park, where Curry-Lindahl found the situation as good as ever. Despite the fact that Congo troops were operating against rebels in the northern sector, there were no signs of poaching, and the large numbers of hippo, elephant, kob and waterbuck, which form such a feature of Ishango on the upper Semliki River, appeared entirely undisturbed.

In South Africa, the Kalahari Gemsbok National Park was proclaimed in 1931, a large area of huge red sand dunes, scrub-covered valleys and dry river beds, inhabited by lions, oryx—the gemsbok of the Dutch settlers—wildebeest, red hartebeest, eland and springbok. Within the boundaries of the park, springbok can be seen in herds of many hundreds.

The famous Addo Bush near Port Elizabeth was also made a national park in 1931, mainly to protect the last herd of elephants surviving in the Cape Province. There are, it is true, some left in Knysna Forest, but they are so few in number that there is not much hope of their holding out much longer. The Addo elephants, on the other hand, are doing well.

A few years later, an area near Craddock was proclaimed a national park to give permanent shelter to the last few Cape mountain zebra. These animals can be met with on steep mountain slopes, among huge boulders and sheer rocky bluffs—called 'krantzes' in South Africa—where one would expect to find wild goats or sheep, but never a member of the horse family. For a long time it looked as if protection for this species had come too late, and in 1950 the number of mountain zebra in the Craddock area dropped to 11 individuals. Things then took a turn for the better, and in September 1965, 58 of these animals—25 males and 33 females—were counted. This may still seem a desperately small population but the vividly coloured bontebok, *Damaliscus dorcas dorcas*,

of which only 17 were left in 1931, has made such a good recovery that in 1965 the total population was estimated at about 750. A considerable proportion of these are to be found in the Bontebok National Park, a reserve which was first established near Bredasdorp in 1931. The grazing turned out to be poor, and the animals did so badly that in 1960 they were moved to a new Bontebok National Park on the Breede River near Swellendam.

An antelope closely related to the bontebok, the blesbok, *Damaliscus dorcas albifrons*, was, at one time, also approaching extinction, but thanks to protection in parks, reserves and on farms there are again several thousand individuals. The black wildebeest, *Connochaetes gnou*, has increased from about 300 in 1938 to 2,117 in 1965.

When explorers penetrated eastern Africa during the second half of the last century, they encountered a wealth of game animals quite as spectacular as what had been seen by the early South African hunters and trekkers. After these newly discovered lands had been partitioned into German East Africa, British

Bontebok in Bontebok National Park

Leopard with prey in Serengeti National Park

East Africa (Kenya) and Uganda, the colonial governments acted with commendable promptitude to preserve at least part of this magnificent array of wildlife, and extensive game reserves were proclaimed shortly after the turn of the century. One of the finest of East Africa's game fields, the Serengeti Plains in the northern part of German East Africa, was so remote and inaccessible that it became more widely known only after the first world war when the German colony had been made a League of Nations' Trust Territory under the new name of Tanganyika. With motorcars replacing the porter caravans of prewar days, hunters, both of the sportsman and killer type, began flocking to the Serengeti. During the twenties, it happened that one single party massacred from 60 to 65 lions! Despite an attempt by the Tanganyika administration to stop the slaughter by gazetting part of the plains as a reserve in 1929, it was not until 1937 that hunting was prohibited over the greater part. Thus the full protection for which the gamewarden, Monty Moore, and his wife had

fought and campaigned since 1931, was at last granted to the much-harassed Serengeti lions, and they quickly responded by taking as uninterested an attitude to motor-cars as those in the Kruger National Park. The reserve was given full national park status in 1940.

At one time, the fabulous Ngorongoro Crater formed a part of the Serengeti National Park, but after the second world war a Governor of Tanganyika demonstrated his dislike of game conservation and of conservationists by excising Ngorongoro and the whole Crater Highlands from the national park. The ensuing uproar prevented him from opening the region to general slaughter, and he compromised by turning it into what he was pleased to call a 'conservation area'. The animals were still protected theoretically, but the wonderland of Ngorongoro had been opened to controlled human exploitation, with all the dangers this entails for wildlife, and one cannot help considering the whole episode as a most deplorable blunder. Ngorongoro Crater must surely be regarded as meriting national park status as much as any other place on earth! The Serengeti National Park is, today, as good lion country as it has ever been. Prides numbering from 15 to 20 or even 30 individuals are common. In addition, the vicinity of Seronera Lodge may well be the best place in all Africa to see and study leopards, which are usually so secretive in their ways. C. G. Schillings, the pioneer animal photographer, once said of them that they were literally 'everywhere and nowhere', and many people have spent a lifetime in Africa without ever catching a glimpse of one. Along the Seronera River and its tributaries the spotted cats have taken on at least partly diurnal habits, and they have become as indifferent to motor-cars as the lions. It is by no means unusual to encounter three or four in a single morning's drive.

Between Seronera Lodge and Lake Victoria there is savannah country with permanent water courses. East of Seronera, a vast expanse of open grassland stretches to the foot of the Crater Highlands, wonderfully green during the rains, but yellowish-brown, dusty and waterless in the dry season. This change brings about far-reaching movements of game herds, involving about 200,000 wildebeest, 200,000 gazelles, and 50,000 zebras. If you are lucky enough to be in the right spot at the right time, you will be privileged to witness a spectacle which, in our days, is probably unique on earth. To see the treeless plains covered with wildebeest gives the awed observer some idea of what the American prairies must have been like before the slaughter of the bison began in earnest.

When the Tanganyika authorities decided to establish a reserve on the Serengeti Plains, their decision may have been strongly influenced by the convention worked out at the International Conference for the Protection of African Fauna and Flora which opened in London on November 8th, 1933. All governments of African countries were urged to establish game sanctuaries, preferably with national park status. Lists of animals particularly in need of protection were drawn up, and there was a lengthy discussion of definitions covering the various types of reserves, such as: special reserves—to ensure the survival of just one threatened species; game reserves —where there was to be no shooting, but within the borders of which other human activities were not curtailed; and national parks which were to be kept free of human exploitation of any kind. Over this last point there arose considerable differences of opinion. What did freedom from human exploitation really entail? While some representatives wanted to

see national parks as 'total reserves', open only to accredited scientific investigators, others put considerable stress on their recreational and educational potential. The concept of the 'total reserve' was whole-heartedly adopted by the Belgians who put it into practice in the Congo. Visitors found themselves just barely tolerated in certain restricted areas of the Albert Park, while the rest of the reserve, as well as the Upemba and Garamba Parks, were kept rigorously closed. The South Africans, on the other hand, decided to open up the Kruger Park to tourism, providing sufficient safeguards for the region's wildlife by framing the rules and regulations already alluded to.

The vivid interest shown in African faunal reserves had its effect in other parts of the world. It was suddenly realized that the wildlife of southern Asia, too, had gone into a stage of very rapid decline. Of the Asiatic lion, once widely distributed in northwestern India, there were only a few survivors in the Gir Forest of Kathiawar. The Indian cheetah was declared to be 'very scarce everywhere' by an author who wrote in 1928. The Indian rhinoceros was being systematically exterminated by poachers. The Javan rhinoceros had long ago disappeared from the Ganges Delta, and there were grave doubts about its continued existence in Sumatra, Burma, and Malaya. There was, in fact, only one place where it could definitely be said to occur: the peninsula of Udjung Kulon, at the western tip of Java, which the Dutch authorities had declared a game reserve as early as 1921. The two-horned Sumatran rhinoceros was considered as 'thinly distributed' in Burma, and a naturalist working in Sarawak gave it as his opinion in 1930 that the fate of this animal would soon be sealed so far as the island of Borneo was concerned, large numbers of them being killed every year. Theodore Rathbone Hubback, who made an excellent study of the species in Malaya, found that it was only just holding out in the most inaccessible jungles of the main mountain range and the higher foothills.

Hubback had come to Malaya in 1895, and for many years he was a keen big game hunter, acquiring an unrivalled knowledge of the jungle and its inhabitants. When he saw the environment being devastated by mining operations and giving way almost everywhere to rubber plantations, when he became aware of the horrifying speed at which elephants, gaur and rhinos were being exterminated, he gave up hunting and devoted his time to observing and photographing the animals he had formerly

Sumatran rhinoceros

killed. He secured the first snapshots ever taken of the Sumatran rhinoceros. These pictures are still the best that exist of this rare and elusive animal. Hubback also began campaigning for the protection of what was left of the once rich wildlife of Malaya. Like Stevenson-Hamilton of the Kruger Park, he was very persuasive and through his persistent efforts brought about the setting up of a proper game department, and the creation of the King George V National Park, which was gazetted in 1938. It straddles the border areas of the States of Pahang, Kelantan and Trengganu and miraculously survived the second world war and the communist guerilla activities which followed it. The park still harbours tiger, leopard, Malay bear, sambhar deer, the rare seladang or Malay gaur, Asiatic tapir, and a few Sumatran rhinos.

One of Hubback's closest collaborators was E. O. Shebbeare, who became chief game warden of Malaya. Before the Sumatran rhinos of Malaya were made Shebbeare's responsibility, he played a major part in protecting the Indian rhino. The Jaldapara Reserve of Bengal, where today there are about 50 of these animals, owes its existence almost entirely to his untiring efforts.

India's most famous game reserve, the Kaziranga Wildlife Sanctuary*, which at present harbours about 400 rhinos, was gazetted in 1926. The authorities in charge first adopted the view that the rhinos' interests would be best served by keeping the reserve closed to all visitors, but this unfortunately resulted in the so-called sanctuary becoming a real haven for the poachers who were after rhino horns. When a timely change of policy led to the reserve being opened up in 1938, 40 rhino carcasses and numerous poachers' camps were found. Kaziranga has been efficiently managed and guarded ever since.

The Corbett National Park in northern India is a stronghold for tigers, bears, elephants and various species of deer. Established in 1935, as the Hailey National Park, it was later renamed after Jim Corbett, the splendid field naturalist and slayer of man-eating tigers and leopards. In Ceylon, two national parks were gazetted during the thirties, to give some protection to the rapidly dwindling herds of elephants.

The Japanese have always been noted for their aesthetic appreciation of nature, and it is by no means surprising, therefore, that they accepted the concept of national parks with great enthusiasm. From 1934 onwards a large number of parks came into being,

---

* Kaziranga has just been given National Park status.

119

Tiger in Corbett National Park: India

many of them too small to be of great biological importance, but some of considerable extent and giving shelter to such interesting animals as Asiatic black bears, raccoon dogs, serows and macaques.

The Soviet authorities have declared it their policy to protect substantial samples of all the habitats found within their boundaries, and a number of reserves, equivalent to the national parks of other countries, were established during the twenties and thirties. The Russian wildlife reserves—there are said to be about 90 of them—safeguard the survival of Caucasian and Siberian ibex, argali sheep, Asiatic bighorn sheep, gazelles, bears and snow leopards. The Sikhote Alin and Suzukhe Reserves shelter specimens of the gigantic Amur tiger, *Panthera tigris altaica*, which has become extinct in most of its former haunts. If they were opened to international tourism, the reserves of the Caucasus, of the Central Asiatic mountain ranges, and of Siberia and Kamchatka could easily become centres of pilgrimage for nature lovers from many lands, just like the national parks of North America and Africa.

In South and Central America, the years between the two world wars brought the creation of quite a number of national parks, especially in Chile, Argentina and Mexico. In Guyana, an area around the Kaieteur Falls was given national park status in 1930, while Brazil established a reserve at the spectacular Iguassu Falls.

During the second world war people had little or no time to concern themselves with nature conservation. In Europe and in southern Asia the insane holocaust engulfed many a valuable reserve. The European bison was nearly wiped out, and we shall never know how many of the Asiatic rhinoceroses were slaughtered in eastern jungles. Game departments and national parks authorities the world over had to do their work—if that were still possible—with a sadly depleted staff and drastically cut finances. On the famous Athi Plains outside Nairobi, which had been a game reserve for several decades, military camps sprang up, there were shooting ranges, bombing targets, and the game herds were sprayed with machine gun bullets or scattered by shattering explosions. In northern Kenya thousands of wild animals were massacred in order to feed the prisoners of war brought down from Abyssinia. It must be mentioned, however, that during the forties several important reserves did come into existence in the French African colonies, such as the Bamingui-

Bangoran and the Saint Floris National Parks in Ubangi-Shari and the Mount Nimba Reserve in Guinea.

When the war ended, conservationists not only found much of their work destroyed and nullified, but they could not help feeling that they were facing a very uncertain future. Human populations increased by leaps and bounds, pressing upon the few empty areas still left in the world, clamouring for land and food. In many parts of Africa illicit hunting became big business, and the colonial administrators refused to do anything about it. They preferred to close their eyes and let events take their course, hoping that the poachers would make a clean sweep of it. Once the game had gone, nobody could ask them to make themselves unpopular by protecting it. Jeeps and Land Rovers were able to penetrate the remotest wildernesses, one solitary bulldozer did an amount of work for which an army of men had been needed a few years earlier. Economists and planners threw their weight about as never before. They were getting ready to change the face of the world once and for all, and they were not going to have a few nature-loving cranks get in their way.

There had to be a reaction to these sinister trends, and it came quickly and forcefully. A century ago,

The beautiful Siberian taiga forest

when the deadly threat to nature as a whole was first realized, there were no organizations which could have taken up the fight for conservation. They had to be created gradually, as the necessity arose—national park services, game departments, societies for the protection of nature, bird clubs and similar associations. For many decades their members battled for their ideals, doggedly and courageously, not taken very seriously by those in power and laughed at by the masses. Suddenly, these organizations saw their ranks swelling rapidly. More and more people came to realize that they were on the verge of losing values which could never be replaced. The discordant clangour of progress forced them to turn to nature, to seek their recreation outdoors, away from the enervating bustle of a civilization off course. Mountaineering, camping, bird-watching, botanizing and similar activities became amazingly popular. There was a rapidly growing interest in national parks, in wildlife sanctuaries of any kind. Many humans, feeling themselves threatened by the juggernaut of technocracy, began to understand the plight animals were in. The tremendous upsurge of support for conservation could no longer be shrugged off, and, despite the contemptuously negative attitude of many politicians, economists and planners—or perhaps because of it—a great number of reserves and national parks came into being during the post war years. By far the most significant event was, however, the forming of the World Wildlife Fund, which took place on September 11th 1961 in Zurich, Switzerland. The occasion has been aptly characterized as 'The Launching of a New Ark', and, ever since, conservationists in all parts of the world have been cheered on by the knowledge that, if necessity arises, they can turn to a powerful international organization and that a helping hand will reach out and assist them.

This was not yet the case in 1946, when nature lovers in Kenya, ably led by Colonel Mervyn Cowie, forced a reluctant administration into gazetting a part of the Athi Plains as Nairobi National Park. A few years later, when large portions of the rather unmanageable 'Southern Game Reserve' were given up, the Government had to compensate for this by establishing the Tsavo National Park. In 1952, the Government of Uganda proclaimed the Queen Elizabeth and Murchison Falls National Parks. Similar reserves sprang up in Rhodesia, Gaboon, Cameroon, Senegal and other parts of Africa. Many politicians and administrators took a highly cynical view of these proceedings.

'All right,' they said, 'have your useless national parks if you must. They will be abolished quickly enough when all these African countries get their independence. The game animals you make such a fuss about will then be slaughtered and eaten—and that is just about the only thing they are good for!'

One cannot expect everybody to have an appreciation of the ethical and aesthetical points of conservation, but it does seem strange that so many of those who should have known better utterly failed to visualize the tremendous economic potential of African national parks and game reserves. In a book which was published in Nairobi in 1949, I wrote: 'Year after year sportsmen, camera hunters and tourists are coming in ever greater numbers to the game haunts of eastern Africa, where fortunately a unique and wonderful array of wildlife can still be found and where, with a small amount of goodwill and an intelligent realization of its enormous value as one of East Africa's best assets, this array of wildlife can easily be preserved for generations to come.'

As these words came from a mere zoologist, and not from an august politician or an omniscient financial wizard, little attention was paid to them, and for years afterwards economic experts never lost an opportunity to point out that tourism could not possibly make a material contribution to the revenue of the East African countries. To expect national parks and wildlife to become paying propositions, they argued, was nothing but a pipe-dream.

Economists can be wrong; one cannot help having a horrid suspicion that they very often are. By the time the East African countries attained independence, tourism had become such an important source of revenue that the national parks and game reserves were not abolished, nor was there a general massacre of wild animals. On the contrary, the independent governments created new reserves, and punishment for poaching became more severe. Wildlife had, in fact, become an extremely valuable asset!

Other African countries, whose national parks had not yet been properly developed, looked to Kenya, Uganda and Tanzania with a certain amount of envy and began to draw up plans which were to secure a slice of this lucrative tourist industry.

At present, no year goes by without a few wildlife sanctuaries being proclaimed in one part of the world or another. It must be considered as highly significant, that the number of reserves is biggest in the most intensely industrialized countries where, one

Right: *The spectacular Murchison Falls*

122

The Hoge Veluwe; Holland's biggest reserve

would have thought, land could least be spared for 'unproductive' exercises of this kind. Thus, the United States National Park Service administers 181 units, amounting to 24 million acres or 3·21% of the nation's total area, while the Nature Conservancy of the United Kingdom is in charge of 95 national reserves, of which the smallest cover 4, and the largest 40,000 acres. Their total surface equals 5·28% of the British Isles. Holland has 200 reserves, West Germany 750, Poland over 500—among them the famous forest of Bjalowiesa, where the European bison is on the increase again. The Swedes have created 16 national parks and over 750 other reserves, and there are 469 reserves, including one national park, in Switzerland. The Japanese parks have already been mentioned; their area equals 6·45% of the national territory.

Taking into consideration what highly industrialized and densely populated countries have been able to achieve, one cannot but help thinking that there must be room for more wildlife sanctuaries in Africa, Asia, South and Central America. In many of the Latin American countries conservation has, unfortunately, sadly lagged behind, but there are definite and gratifying signs of a change. In Venezuela, six national parks came into existence between 1952 and 1962. Brazil has established seven parks and similar reserves from 1959 to 1962, and several more are in the planning stage. The Xingu National Park in the Brazilian State of Matto Grosso, which is to have an area of 84,920 square miles, may well become one of the world's most famous nature reserves. The Government of Ecuador earned itself the gratitude of all biologists when in 1963 and 1964 it agreed to give effective protection to the Galapagos National Park, thus preserving part of the evolutionary laboratory which inspired Darwin.

It is, of course, not sufficient to declare a certain

area a national park or a national reserve, mark it as such on a map, and then sit back feeling satisfied to have done something for conservation. As long as money can be made through the sale of game meat, horns, tusks, skins, furs and feathers, a faunal reserve will always be a temptation to poachers and to the crooks who direct their activities. To be a sanctuary, not only in name, but in practice, a reserve has to be patrolled and guarded by a strong corps of reliable and incorruptible game wardens and game guards. It is useless to enlist a few poor and uneducated native hunters, give them rangers' badges and very little pay, and to expect them to protect rhinos, elephants and other valuable animals. They will promptly go into partnership with the poachers, or turn poachers themselves. It is certainly advisable to choose one's rangers from among people with a deeply rooted hunting tradition, for they will be well versed in practical nature lore, but they must also be thoroughly trained and instructed and, most important of all, they must be adequately paid in accordance with the arduous and dangerous duties they have to perform while protecting one of the nation's treasure houses. They must be made to feel proud of their job and genuinely interested in conservation. Several African countries already have a considerable number of devoted game guards who are ready to risk their lives in fighting off poachers. This is the kind of staff one has to build up in a wildlife sanctuary, if it is to be of any value at all.

As to the much debated question of whether a national park should be open to the public or not, it must be realized that very few countries can afford the luxury of having total reserves, tracts of country set aside for purely scientific purposes only. Well-guarded national parks cost money, and this money, or part of it, will mostly have to come from tourism. There is also the example of Kaziranga—and many other reserves—to show that poachers can operate with much greater ease in a hermetically closed area than in a reserve that is continuously traversed by visitors. This does not mean, however, that tourism in national parks can be regarded as an unmixed blessing; far from it! In some countries visitors are even becoming a real threat, the danger paradoxically arising out of the enormous popularity national parks are at present enjoying. In 1925 the national parks of the United States were visited by two million people; by 1966, this figure had risen to near 80 million! This puts a terrible strain not only on the park staff, but on all the facilities serving tourists, such as hotels, camps, lodges, roads, tracks and airstrips. The authorities are easily tempted to over-develop the parks in an effort to cope with this rapidly swelling

Game-wardens of Wankie National Park rounding up giraffes for transportation into another reserve

flood of visitors, to build too many hotels and air-strips, too dense a network of roads, to install shopping centres, ski-lifts, golf courses and other amenities which have absolutely no place in a wildlife sanctuary. The powers that be may feel forced to give in to all kinds of smart alecs, who want to get a foothold inside the parks in order to cash in on the tourist bonanza. National parks undoubtedly have a very important recreational function, but they must not be allowed to become human playgrounds.

Much as tourism is appreciated and must be catered for, conservation has to take first place, and the interests of fauna and flora are to be considered as of paramount importance. There are definite limits to the tourist facilities a park can carry, and installations should never become obtrusive. Visitors must be made fully aware that they have entered a nature sanctuary, where they are welcome guests as long as they behave themselves and keep to the rules, and the park authorities should not hesitate to enforce strict discipline. It may be the wisest course to develop certain regions of a park reasonably well without, however, indulging in unnecessary luxuries, to keep other parts so difficult of access that they are only visited by the real enthusiasts, and to have some closed areas, tucked away here and there, more or less 'sanctuaries within the sanctuary'.

The United States have led the world in making full use of the educational possibilities, for which, in national parks, there is almost unlimited scope. The visitor has access to reference collections, he can study diagrams and reliefs, attend lectures and instructional film shows and join conducted tours; it is most certainly not the fault of the park authorities if he does not come away with a better understanding of nature.

Educational aspects sometimes tend to over-shadow the purely scientific work that is done in national parks, but the importance of research cannot be stressed enough. The continued existence of many reserves may eventually depend on policies formulated on the basis of a vast amount of data accumulated through the work of biologists and ecologists. The total reserve, free of even the slightest amount of human interference, has turned out to be something of a chimera. Nature, even if left severely alone, is by no means static. Things are, in fact, in a constant state of flux, and the gradual changes may well prove harmful to the animals one is trying to protect. In addition, it must never be forgotten that even the most extensive reserves are islands in a world that is being changed and re-changed by human activity, and they cannot remain entirely unaffected by what is going on outside their bound-

Savannah forest destroyed by elephants in Tsavo National Park

Hippopotamus in Queen Elizabeth National Park

aries. Intelligent and adaptable animals, such as elephants, do not take long to discover where they are safe from persecution, and whole herds will leave an area open to hunting in order to take refuge in a neighbouring game sanctuary. As they respond extremely well to protection, their numbers begin to increase rapidly. Elephants are great destroyers of trees, and, wherever they become too numerous, bushy savannahs may be turned into grasslands. I have seen this happen in parts of the Tsavo National Park. In places where 15 years ago there was a visibility of 100 to 150 yards, you now overlook miles of open plain with widely scattered trees. The change has brought an influx of grazing animals, such as wildebeest, hartebeest, Thomson's gazelles and zebra, but it is detrimental to black rhinos, lesser kudu, gerenuk and other browsers.

There is a distinct tendency to lose sight of the fact that man and man-like creatures have been an ecological factor for an enormously long span of time, and primitive hunters played their part as predators, exerting a certain amount of control over the numbers of animals which are fairly safe from big cats, wild dogs and hyenas. They were not able to exterminate or even seriously reduce a species like the hippopotamus, but their activities must have put a check on too rapid a growth of hippo populations.

Enjoying complete protection, the hippos of the Queen Elizabeth National Park of Uganda became so numerous a few years ago, that they destroyed their own grazing—and, of course, the grazing of buffaloes, kobs, and other species as well. In former times a large proportion would simply have spread to adjoining areas, but under present conditions, this is not possible, any animals wandering across the park borders being either killed or wounded. The hippos remained where they felt safe, and there was no other way out of the dilemma than to make a study of their population dynamics and to reduce their numbers according to a carefully worked out plan. By restricting the shooting to certain limited sectors of the park, disturbance was kept to a minimum, and hippos living in areas unaffected by control measures did not become frightened and shy. The action was highly successful, and grazing has vastly improved. In the Murchison Falls National Park it has been found necessary to control elephants, and something will most probably have to be done about the more than 25,000 elephants of the Tsavo National Park.

It must be stressed that any kind of control within a national park has to be based on data provided by a responsible team of research workers and not on the unsupported recommendations of certain individuals keen on doing a little easy shooting or swayed by unscientific emotionalism. Many well-meaning conservationists have, for instance, made a point in advocating predator control in order to give the ungulates a better chance. Wolves have therefore been hunted almost to extinction in American and Russian reserves, while game wardens in Africa often show an implacable and wholly unreasonable hatred for the hunting dog. Unscientific control measures of this type certainly will bring about an increase in the numbers of herbivores, but they also lead to unnatural herding, to overgrazing and over-browsing, to habitat deterioration, and finally to a physical decline in the ungulates. Before the last stage is reached, the park authorities usually step in, and game wardens have to turn hunters in order to reduce the ungulate populations, thus doing something that the predators could all along have done much more efficiently.

The Hluhluwe Reserve in Natal was established after lions, cheetahs and hunting dogs had long been eradicated from the area. As soon as the complete cessation of hunting pressure made itself felt, the reserve began to deteriorate disastrously due to overgrazing. The game wardens had to shoot thousands of animals in an attempt to bring about a recovery. They have now released a number of cheetahs within the reserve to provide natural predators.

The northernmost sector of the Kruger National Park, cut off from the rest of the reserve by a range of hills, underwent severe habitat deterioration after its lion population had moved across the boundary into Portuguese territory, where they were shot. Conditions only improved when, after a good number of years, some lions came across the hills from the south, took over the empty hunting grounds and re-established the balance of nature.

In Yellowstone National Park the wapiti—or elk, as they are rather confusingly called in America— have become a serious problem. There are about 13,000 of them, and, if left to themselves, they would soon eat the moose, mule deer, beaver, bighorn sheep and themselves out of existence. The popu-

lation has therefore to be thinned out periodically by park rangers, and in neighbouring Grand Teton National Park public hunting of elk is permitted under licence. One cannot help thinking that all this might not be necessary if there were more lynxes, pumas and especially wolves to provide natural control.

These examples should give sufficient proof that predators—be they lions, leopards, tigers, pumas, wolves, hunting dogs, coyotes or eagles—have a vitally important part to play, and that control of predators in national parks demonstrates a sad lack of ecological understanding. Under the fairly natural conditions usually encountered in a spacious national park or equivalent reserve, large carnivores hardly ever become too numerous for their prey. Things are, however, entirely different where successful and highly adaptable species of omnivorous habits, like crows, magpies and certain gulls, are concerned, and in a bird sanctuary of limited extent it may be necessary to apply very strict control measures if any nests are to escape their predatory attentions. One might even be tempted to call them vermin, though, as a whole, I should prefer to reserve this term for predators introduced into foreign areas, for foxes in Australia, stoats in New Zealand, mongooses in Hawaii and mink in Great Britain.

Despite the tremendous popular support conservation has gained in recent years, and more especially since the establishment of the World Wildlife Fund under the leadership of such well-known personalities as Prince Bernhard of the Netherlands, the Duke of Edinburgh, Peter Scott, David Attenborough, Professor Grzimek, Roger Tory Peterson and Sir Landsborough Thomson, the battle is by no means over. The national parks are always in danger and, if we are not constantly on guard, we may suffer serious losses. The threat mainly comes from that section of the public, whose ruthless exploitation of nature has made the creation of national parks a necessity in the first place, from the people who cannot bear to look at a strip of land that is not exploited and made to fill somebody's— preferably their own—pockets. The presence of nature reserves worries their progressive minds, so they amuse themselves by drawing up plans for hydro-electric schemes which may require the flooding of bird sanctuaries, game reserves or national parks. Apparently they are unaware of the fact that humanity has entered the age of atomic power, in which hydro-electric power stations will sooner or later become obsolete. They are desperately eager to get their

Plate XV A rhino has been drugged so that it can be transported to the safety of a game reserve

Plate XVI Sparrowhawks have been persecuted mercilessly by gamekeepers and are now fairly rare in many parts of Europe. This is another example of the sad lack of ecological understanding that has always characterised man's attitude to predators

African hunting dogs—much hated as predators but very necessary for maintaining ecological balance

hands on any minerals or other resources that might be present in a national park, using the most amazing arguments in order to achieve their ends. In Canada, for instance, there have been ugly murmurs that the parks should be made to pay their way through the exploitation of their timber stands! One might think that a country as rich and highly developed as Canada, which has always been in the forefront of conservation, would not find it necessary for parks to pay their way.

Of the animals now listed as threatened, very many are not represented in any national park or other major wildlife refuge. Such species need the most effective legal protection that can be given to them, if they are to survive. It may sometimes be possible to assure their safety by creating special reserves of limited extent. Thus the breeding areas of rare birds are frequently put under protection, if not for the whole year then at least during the breeding season, and single nests or small groups of nests have, on occasion, been carefully guarded day and night until the young have flown. Each endangered species confronts conservationists with a problem differing from all the others. Circumstances sometimes help to facilitate the task, as in the case of the New Zealand tuatara, *Sphenodon punctatus*, a reptile that has come to us almost unchanged from Mesozoic times. It once occurred both on North and South Island, but was quickly wiped out by cats, dogs, weasels and pigs, surviving only on about twenty small islets off the North Auckland coast, in the Bay of Plenty and in Cook's Strait, of which Stephen Island contains the biggest population. It has been shown that insular faunas are very vulnerable and easily become sadly depleted owing to habitat destruction or to the depredations of introduced predators, but a small area can, on the other hand, be extremely well guarded against destructive outside influences. While such a place has often proved to be a death-trap for its animal inhabitants, it may, if man wills it, be turned into an ideal sanctuary. This has happened in the case of the tuatara, and with the strict and effective protection it now enjoys, the future of this fascinating living fossil can be viewed with considerable optimism.

An interesting experiment in conservation is at present being carried out in Madagascar, where on the two square mile island of Mangabey in the Bay of Antongil, a reserve for the fast disappearing aye-aye has been established. At the time of writing, four males and five females which were caught on the mainland have already been released on Mangabey, and it is hoped thus to build up a population of this interesting lemur in a locality where it can easily be protected and kept under control.

In certain instances specimens of a species which, for some reason or other, could not be adequately protected within its original area of distribution have been moved to a nearby national park. This has been done with white rhinoceroses of the northern race, *Ceratotherium simum cottoni,* which are facing extinction in the West Nile District of Uganda. A number of these animals were brought to the east bank of the Nile and released in the Murchison Falls National Park. They established themselves very quickly and are now doing well, which is all the more gratifying, as the outlook for the northern white rhinos in the southern Sudan and in the northeastern Congo seems at present quite as bad, if not worse, than in western Uganda.

Hunter's hartebeest, *Damaliscus hunteri,* need not be regarded as being in immediate danger, but as it is very localized, existing only in a narrow strip of bush country extending from the Tana River of Kenya to southern Somalia, it has been thought wise to transfer a small herd to the northern sector of the Tsavo National Park, into a habitat very similar to that north of the Tana.

Birds, being so much more mobile than reptiles and mammals, can pose exceedingly difficult problems. Large species in particular do not easily confine themselves to small areas, and the battle for their survival may become a nationwide affair. Not so long ago the California condor, *Gymnogyps californianus,* was quite abundant, ranging from the Columbia River to northern Baja California, but in 1936 it was already restricted to the coast range of southern

California, and ornithologists estimated that there were not more than about 20 birds left alive. This may have been somewhat too pessimistic an assessment, for in 1960 between 60 and 65 were known to survive. In 1964, however, only about 40 were left, of which one-third had not yet reached breeding age. The species has long ago been put under strict protection, and a reserve, the Sespe Condor Sanctuary, was established in an area which was assumed to contain most of the nesting sites. Worried by the continued decline, the United States Fish and Wildlife Service has now instigated an intensive study of the California condor, for effective conservation is only possible on the basis of an intimate knowledge of the species to be protected. A field station has recently been established, and exploring trips were made into all parts of the condor's present range. It was soon realized that there is a considerable amount of nesting outside the Sespe Sanctuary. This fact will necessitate a thorough review of the conservation measures already taken, but it also reduces the possibility of some single hazard wiping out the whole population. Observations made in 1966 showed that at least 51 condors were still living, 14 of them young birds. This seems to point to a very good rate of reproduction, and there is perhaps some hope that the California condor can be saved from extinction.

It is important never to despair, even though one may be expecting the worst. There was, after all, at one time very little hope for the trumpeter swan, *Cygnus buccinator.* Strict protection and the establishment of breeding colonies in national wildlife refuges, especially in the Red Rock Lakes Migratory Waterfowl Refuge, near the town of Yellowstone, brought about a most gratifying increase, and at present the total population of these fine birds is estimated at 2,100.

The magnificent whooping crane, *Grus americana,* 5 ft. tall, and with a wing spread of up to 9 ft. can never have been very common. Audubon only saw it in flocks of 20 to 30 or of two or three times that number. Robert E. Allen who made a detailed study of the species estimates that there may have been no more than 1,500 individuals around the middle of the last century. The whooping crane was thought, by an author of the 1930s, to be doomed to early extinction but it still survives, even though in desperately small numbers.

Its winter range is restricted to the Aransas National Wildlife Refuge, on the Texas coast, and at times less than 20 birds arrived. In 1963/4, 33 were seen, among them 7 in juvenile plumage. A year later 42 birds came back from their nesting grounds. The migration route of the cranes is well known, and everything possible is being done to protect the birds while they are on their way. The people of Texas, Oklahoma, Kansas, Nebraska, South and North Dakota are implored through Press and radio to allow them safe passage.

Six nests, each with two eggs, were located in Wood Buffalo National Park in 1967 and Canadian and American biologists decided to take one egg from each nest to the Patuxent Wildlife Research Centre in Maryland, where five chicks were successfully hatched. It is now hoped that they will form the nucleus of a flock of cranes breeding in captivity. The species would then be sure to survive, even if it should prove impossible to preserve the last remnants of the wild population. The descendants of the captive flock could possibly be induced to breed in Louisiana, as some whooping cranes did in the past, thus sparing the birds the long and very dangerous journey to Wood Buffalo National Park.

Wildlife Research Centres and Zoological Gardens may have an increasingly important part to play in safeguarding the existence of species which are becoming extinct in their native habitat. The classic example of an animal that has only survived thanks to its being kept in captivity is, of course the mi-lu, or Père David's deer. This strange ungulate was discovered in 1865 by Father Armand David, the famous French naturalist, not in remote Mongolia or in the wilds of Muping, but in the Imperial Hunting Park of Peking: no wild specimen had been known for many years. In 1869 the British Ambassador in China was able to ship a pair of live mi-lu to the London Zoo, and during the following years a few more went to various European countries. When the flood waters of the Huang-ho breeched the walls of the hunting park in 1894, most of the deer escaped and were massacred by hungry Chinese farmers. The small herd that remained, was wiped out during the Boxer Rising, except for two individuals, of which the last one died around 1921. This could well have been a tragedy similar to the extermination of the quagga or the passenger pigeon, but in 1898 the Duke of Bedford had bought all the Père David's deer available in Europe, using them to build up a breeding herd in his private zoo at Woburn Abbey. Through this timely move the species was preserved, and, at the time of writing, over 400 mi-lu are being kept in a number of zoos. A few have been sent back to China.

This success story has inspired several enterprises of a similar kind. When the population of the ne-ne or Hawaiian goose, *Branta sandvicensis,* thought to have numbered 25,000 when the islands were discovered, dropped to a mere 33, an increase was brought about by breeding in captivity, especially in the grounds of Peter Scott's Severn Wildfowl Trust. The species was then re-established in its habitat. In 1962 there were 150 geese in their native haunts, and

There was little hope at one time for the beautiful trumpeter swans—now thriving near Yellowstone

The mi-lu or David's Deer at Woburn Abbey—it only survives in captivity

the population has since increased to about 285. Two sanctuaries, totalling 18,000 acres, have been proclaimed, and the United States Congress has voted a yearly grant of U.S. $15,000 to finance ecological studies and the continuation of the propagation programme. With over 200 ne-ne in captivity, it will be possible to strengthen the Hawaiian colonies of free-living birds whenever this should be thought necessary. While the ne-ne is again doing very well in its Hawaiian homeland, from which it so nearly disappeared, the Arabian oryx, *Oryx leucoryx*, may be destined to survive only in captivity.

This antelope, once ranging over most of the Arabian peninsula, has always been under considerable hunting pressure, and its decline set in a long time ago. It was speeded up enormously, however, when oil sheikhs started hunting oryx in Jeeps and Land Rovers, equipped with machine guns. The *Red Data Book* estimates the number of survivors at a few hundred. Other sources speak of only about 100 individuals. In Muscat and Oman the species is now protected by decree of the Sultan— but can this protection be made really effective, and what will happen should there be a political upheaval in the area? It was decided, therefore, to establish a breeding herd in a safe place, and several expeditions have entered the southern Arabian deserts in order to catch a number of oryx antelopes.

The animals were subsequently transferred to the Phoenix Zoo in Arizona, where no less than five calves have meanwhile been born. In September 1965 the herd numbered nine males and four females, and there is no reason why the Arabian oryx should not have as good a chance of survival as the mi-lu, even if it should get wiped out in its natural desert environment.

Until quite recently zoological gardens were essentially places of entertainment and popular instruction, where many kinds of strange and beautiful creatures could be admired by the curious. If a zoo director managed to breed certain species, that was regarded as an interesting experiment and not much else. Nowadays the propagation of rare animals has become one of the main functions of any reputable zoo, and spectacular successes have been obtained with such species as okapi, Indian rhino, gorilla and orang-utan. The pygmy hippo and the Asiatic tapir are doing well in captivity and it is to be hoped that great stress will be put on breeding the various beautiful pheasants, many of which seem to be vanishing rapidly from the troubled and war-torn countries which form their homelands. One day we may have huge animal farms in areas with favourable climates—both political and weather-wise —which make it their business to breed dozens or even hundreds of endangered species for distribution to zoos and eventually for re-introduction into their former homes, once conditions become suitable for such an enterprise.

It cannot be denied that unscrupulous animal dealers have done their share in reducing certain species to danger level. That delightful South American monkey, Goeldi's tamarin, *Callimico goeldii*, is threatened because too many of them are exported and sold on the pet market. The decline of three other monkeys, the bald uakari, *Cacajao calvus*, the red uakari, *C. rubicundus*, and the black-headed uakari, *C. melanocephala*, is partly due to their being hunted for food by the natives of the Amazonian forests, but it has been accelerated by the rapidly increasing export of live specimens. Trapping and transport are unfortunately causing very heavy losses, and it is said that of every four red uakaris caught three die before they reach the dealer's establishment. The orang-utan, badly hit by hunting and habitat destruction, is now being brought to the verge of extinction by a large-scale illegal trade in juveniles. The capture of a young orang-utan almost invariably brings about the death of its mother, and the youngster itself may be so badly hurt or suffer such ill-treatment from its captors that it succumbs before it can even be smuggled to one of the centres where the poor apes are assembled for export. A considerable number of orangs are thus killed for every one that is seen in a zoo. It would, however, be unjust to blame the zoological gardens for this sad state of affairs, and it must be stressed that the International Union of Directors of Zoological Gardens is in the forefront of the fight against the nefarious trade. The zoo directors have introduced very strict regulations prohibiting the purchase of orangs offered on what might be called the 'black market'.

It is estimated that not more than 5,000 orangs are now left in Sumatra and Borneo, but there is some hope that the species may be saved in some of the forest reserves of northern Borneo, and especially in

Four Arabian oryx ready to be shipped to the Phoenix Zoo in Arizona where a breeding centre has been established to conserve this rare species

the Mount Kinabalu National Park, where they occur among the durian trees of the lower slopes. Young apes confiscated from smugglers and illicit dealers are released in reserves, after having been rehabilitated to life in the forest. The Yerkes Laboratory in the United States has established a breeding colony of captive orangs.

The example of the Pribilov Island fur seals has shown that conservation can act under the guise of exploitation. Much as the animal lover deplores the slaughter of a certain number of seals that takes place each year, the existence of the species can most certainly be regarded as fully safeguarded. Game preservation for hunting purposes has kept most of Europe's game animals from extermination, and out of old-fashioned preservation has now emerged the science of game management, which has achieved truly spectacular successes in both Europe and North America.

Owing to the political convulsions which passed over Europe early in the last century, red deer were exterminated in Switzerland, roe deer nearly so, and chamois became very rare. Reasonable game laws brought about a recovery of the last two species, while red deer re-entered Switzerland from adjoining countries. Under steadily improving methods of game management, the situation reached a point where, in 1934, no less than 270 red deer, 13,647 roe deer and 3,908 chamois could be shot without endangering the breeding stocks. In 1964, the hunters of Switzerland were able to kill 2,429 red deer, 25,616 roe deer, and 9,759 chamois. If such miracles of game management are possible in a small and over-crowded country in the heart of Europe, what could be done in the still existing wide open spaces of Africa!

The popular idea of the tropics as an uninterrupted belt of fabulously fertile lands is far from true, and the so-called 'marginal areas' of Africa are, in reality, vast regions with poor soils where the ecological balance is very precariously maintained. Intense agriculture is quite out of the question, but they are commonly used as grazing lands for domestic stock. The results are painfully evident in the clouds of dust that trail for miles behind the herds of emaciated scrub cattle, making it quite obvious that the country is gradually being turned into a desert. Yet these same soils, poor as they are, have for thousands of years supported large concentrations of game without undergoing any deterioration. Under natural conditions, wild animals are in an ecological balance with their habitat. The use they make of it does not

Browsing gerunuk

lead to destruction. Some are browsers, feeding almost entirely on the leaves and twigs of bushes and trees; among the grazers, there are many specialists that eat only certain grasses and leave others strictly alone. Thus one species may prefer its grazing short and soft, another one will go for the high, hard grasses. Where domestic cattle grow so thin that you could almost hang up your hat on their protruding hip bones, zebras and antelopes remain sleek and fat. Leading ecologists have suggested that it would be wiser to leave the marginal lands of Africa under game instead of dooming them to become deserts as a result of overgrazing by domestic stock. Under proper management the game herds could provide protein-hungry populations with meat of better quality and in greater quantity than can be obtained from starving scrub cattle. The idea of wholesale extermination of game, as it is still from time to time advocated by self-styled apostles of progress, woefully ignorant of the ecological facts of life, but with an eye for gaining a quick penny, should have been dispelled as a completely out-of-date concept several decades ago. If a really intelligent and progressive use is to be made of the marginal lands outside the game reserves and national parks, the answer lies in the establishment of well-organized and scientifically run game management schemes.

Anyone who questions the practicability of such schemes would do well to take a look at what the Russians have done with the saiga antelope of their steppes and semi-deserts.

The saiga, *Saiga tartarica*, stands about 75 cm. at the shoulder, weighs up to 69 kg. and has a strangely inflated, proboscis-like nose. During the 18th century it could be found in the Kalmuk Steppes of southern Russia, in Kazakhstan, in the Ala-Kul Basin, in Dzungaria, and on the western edge of the Gobi Desert. Travellers often encountered it in enormous herds. As was the case with so many other animals, the second half of the 19th century brought a rapid decline. The saiga disappeared from many areas where it had been common, and its numbers diminished alarmingly. When the authorities became aware of what was happening, hunting was prohibited, first in Russia in 1919, and then in Kazakhstan in 1923. Protection may not have been very well enforced at first, for in the thirties the species was found to be in a really precarious position. There were just over 1,000 saigas left, a few hundred on the Astrakhan Steppe, west of the Volga, a few hundred in Kazakhstan and a couple of dozen in Dzungaria. A tightening up of conservation measures brought about a rapid increase, and, in due course, the saiga became the object of a large-scale game management scheme. By 1960 there were again nearly 2 million saiga—400,000 west of the Volga, and 1·5 million in Russian Asia—and this despite the fact that a considerable number of animals had already been shot under licence. When hunting was opened on the Astrakhan Steppe in 1951, 10,000 saiga were killed in the first year. In Kazakhstan exploitation began in 1954, with a total annual bag of 50,000 antelopes. In 1956 a State centre for saiga management, the 'Astrakhan Promchos', was established, the task of which it has become to ensure the preservation of the species, to control the population density and to arrange for the yearly harvesting of surplus animals. Considerable revenue is obtained from the sale of meat, which resembles mutton, from skins and from

Strict protection saved the Saiga antelope of Russia and Russian Central Asia from extinction. It is now exploited under a State Game Management Scheme, the sale of meat and skins from the surplus animals providing considerable revenue

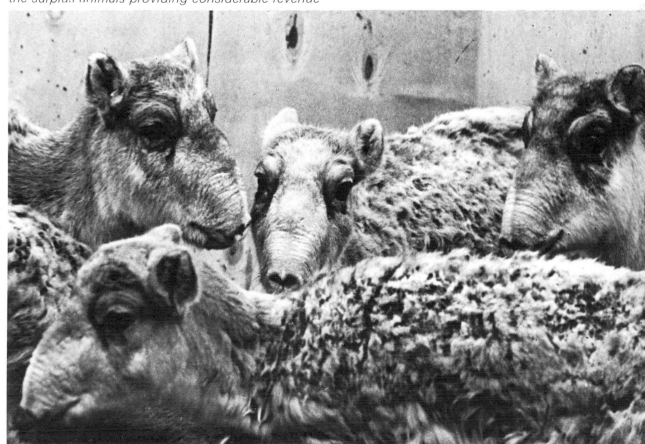

the fat of the animals, which not only serves as food, but is used for industrial purposes as well. The saiga management scheme can thus be rated as a splendid success, and there is ample scope for similar enterprises in countries like Botswana, Zambia, Tanganyika—the mainland part of Tanzania—Kenya, Uganda, Somalia, Sudan and Chad, in all of which game can still be found in considerable quantities outside reserves and national parks. It would certainly be much more remunerative to manage the herds of addax and white oryx of the Sahara Desert in the way shown by the Russian Saiga scheme, instead of allowing them to be massacred and exterminated through unrestricted hunting on the part of roving tribesmen!

While no one could possibly question the wisdom of exploiting animal resources on the basis of sound game management, or deny that national parks and game refuges have become valuable assets, controversial questions still remain: what does it really matter if there are no more rhinoceroses, orang-utans or whooping cranes? why should a piece of land remain untouched for the sake of a few animals, even if these animals attract a prodigious stream of tourists, when its minerals, its timber stands and the hydro-electric power of its rivers might bring in as great or even greater material returns? With equal justification we can ask: of what use are the performances of plays and operas given in expensive and often state-subsidized theatres and opera houses? Why do we build costly museums to house paintings and sculptures? why should the Mona Lisa and the Venus of Milo be preserved so carefully? Why was £275,000 paid for the 'Adoration of the Magi' by Rubens? Why are medieval castles and Greek temples kept from falling into ruins? Why were enormous sums of money spent on saving the rock temple of Abu Simbel from being engulfed by the waters of the Aswan Dam?

All of these things appeal to many people by their beauty; they captivate the interest, they fascinate and impress by their magnificence. It is felt that their disappearance would leave the world a poorer place. Exactly the same applies to nature—to animals, to trees and flowers. There are some who may shake their heads and snigger in disbelief—but what about the unprecedented popularity of zoological gardens and nature films? Why is there an unending and still rising flood of animal books and magazines? Why do so many countries reproduce their most characteristic and beautiful animals on postage stamps? And why do so many people from Europe and America under-

take expensive trips to Africa, just to see elephants, rhinos, lions, giraffes, zebras, and antelopes in their natural habitats? All this provides conclusive evidence that animals do mean something to a considerable number of people, that there are those among us who feel moved by the honking of wild geese, who experience an unforgettable thrill at the sight of a grizzly bear, who are awed by the majesty of a lion walking over the veld, gilded by the rays of the setting sun; that there are those who take a deep aesthetic pleasure in watching the graceful leap of an impala, the flight of a flock of white egrets, the aerial mastery of a soaring eagle.

Need we wonder at this? Man has been a hunter, wholly dependent on wild animals, for the major part of his existence on earth, and it is only natural that an interest in wildlife should have become deeply rooted in our system. In every one of us, there is at least a vestige of the hunting instinct that was predominant throughout palaeolithic and mesolithic times. It is this vestige that has maintained a hunting tradition in even the highest civilizations, but it is also responsible for all other interests in wildlife which have become so varied and so important in our time. I am fully aware that in his meditations on hunting, Ortega y Gasset claims the true hunting instinct exclusively for the man with the gun, stating positively that the real hunter can only be satisfied with the physical possession of the animal he pursues, and that photography will never be a substitute for the chase. This may, of course, be perfectly true so far as the eminent Spanish philosopher himself is concerned, but in its generalized application it is as wrong as such generalizations, philosophical or otherwise, invariably are. Great is the number of sportsmen who have, in fact, put aside their rifles and found greater and more enduring pleasure in game photography and even in mere game watching, and many of them have, in due course, become ardent conservationists. Moreover, there are people who, for one reason or another, have never gone through what we may perhaps call the destructive phase, but who probably get a deeper and more intense pleasure from their contacts with wildlife than Ortega y Gasset's mere killer ever will.

I grew up in an environment which, although extremely pleasant in every way, was pretty sterile with regard to natural history, and especially to

Right: *On McNeil River, Alaska brown bears romping undisturbed make a wonderful spectacle*

zoology, but somehow I showed a keen interest in creeping and crawling things at a very early age, and as I grew up, it was always clear to me that any profession not entirely devoted to animals was not worth choosing. My reading consisted mainly of books on hunting, and I pictured myself shooting all kinds of wild animals, especially lions and elephants. The career of a museum collector appeared to me as just about the highest ideal that could possibly be attained. I repeat that there was absolutely nothing in my surroundings to steer me in that direction, and it was only after I had been a professional zoologist for a good many years that, to my great amazement, I heard of a great-grandfather who had been a forester and game warden on a princely estate. I then knew from where the spark had come!

As things turned out, I did not become a hunter or a museum collector. Instead of a rifle, I bought a camera and forthwith took up animal photography. To get good pictures, I had to watch and study my subjects and I learned that live animals are so much more interesting than dead ones. In all my time in Europe and in Africa, I have never shot a game animal; observation and photography have proved sufficient outlets for my hunting instincts. But I admit that had I lived in the last century, before suitable cameras for fieldwork were available, I might quite probably have taken to the rifle. I am sure that, like so many well-known sportsmen, I would often have felt genuine regrets for my victims, but the irresistible urge to hunt would nevertheless have driven me from one killing to the next. I have fortunately been spared all this, and, after many years of hunting with a camera and of studying animals intimately in their wild habitats, I would now feel quite incapable of shooting a lion, an elephant or any other game beast for pleasure, and I do not think I could do it for scientific reasons either. The fun of hunting, I am sure, is not so much in the possession of the quarry, but in the pursuit.

I have seen a similar development in many friends and colleagues, and I am therefore convinced that it is the old hunting urge, inherited from our Palaeolithic and Mesolithic ancestors, which makes people become naturalists, field zoologists, animal photographers, butterfly collectors and ornithologists, be they humble bird watchers totting up annual tallies or scientists producing erudite papers. I have no hesitation in also including all those who simply take pleasure in catching just a glimpse of a deer, a hare or a fox on their Sunday walks, who cast an occasional friendly glance at the birds coming to their window in winter time, who now and then visit a zoo or read a book about animals. In them the spark may be hardly visible, but it is there, and it sometimes does not take much to let the almost dying ember take on new life. People have suddenly discovered a keen interest in wildlife which they had never suspected as forming part of their mental make-up.

Thus many of us get considerable enjoyment of one kind or another out of wildlife, and we must make it quite clear that we have a right to this, that we intend to see wildlife protected and safeguarded. Rhinoceroses, orang-utans and whooping cranes are as worthy of preservation as the Mona Lisa, the Venus of Milo, the Parthenon and the Temple of Abu Simbel; national parks and sanctuaries are as important and educationally valuable as theatres, art galleries and historical museums. Animals have, after all, been man's longest and most fundamental preoccupation, they were closely connected with his first tentative excursions into the spiritual world, and they formed the first, and, for a very lengthy period, practically the only subjects of his most ancient artistic endeavours. After having progressed beyond the stage of the primitive hunter, humanity has, for a long time, derived enjoyment and relaxation from the animal world, even though the combination of man's increasing mastery of nature with his inherent predatory instincts made it inevitable for this enjoyment to be mainly of the destructive kind. The time has now come for man to turn away from destruction and to play the part of the preserver, not casually or accidentally, but wholeheartedly and on a world-wide basis.

What has been shaped by the hands of man can, if necessary, be shaped again: what has been created by nature will never be replaced, once it has been wantonly destroyed. An animal that has become extinct is lost for ever. No one can bring back the dodo, the quagga, the great auk and the passenger pigeon. If we fail to guard our nature reserves against over-development and harmful intrusion, if we do not insist that uncontrolled slaughter be replaced by wise and sensible exploitation of animal resources, many more spectacular and wonderful creatures will soon be lost to us.

World Survey

A continent by continent guide to national parks and wildlife sanctuaries, their principal flora and fauna incorporating a detailed list of extinct and endangered species of the world.

Europe

In the ancient centres of civilization of the Mediterranean area, wildlife came under heavy pressure at a very early date, and much of it has gone long ago and for ever. In western, central, northern and eastern Europe, the sporting instincts of a powerful nobility led not only to centuries of game preservation, but also to the conservation of a considerable amount of forest habitat. If game was to be preserved, forests had to be preserved, as well, and had their rulers not developed this overriding passion for the chase, European countries would have been stripped of a lot more of their covering than was actually the case. In course of time, man and wildlife reached something like a state of commensalism or of co-existence, and despite the steady growth of Europe's populations, despite a very intensive utilization of the land and of natural resources, irretrievable losses have been amazingly few.

The industrial revolution and the population explosion of the last few decades, not to mention political extravaganzas such as revolutions and wars, have greatly endangered this co-existence, but it cannot be denied that many European countries are making tremendous efforts to save as much of their wildlife as they possibly can, and the overall picture is, perhaps, not quite as dismal as might have been. There is growing collaboration between sportsmen and conservationists—the hunters recognizing the urgent need for national parks, game reserves, wildfowl refuges and strict legalisation—the protectors appreciating the necessity and the advantage of a reasonable amount of hunting based upon the principle of sound game management. The way the Wildfowlers' Association of Great Britain and Ireland decided to join forces with the conservationists within the framework of the Wild Fowl Trust, is a good and highly encouraging example of this trend.

European species and subspecies lost:
Aurochs, *Bos primigenius;*
European wild horse, *Equus caballus gmelini* (or *Equus ferus silvestris);*
Portuguese ibex, *Capra pyrenaica lusitanica;*
Caucasian bison, *Bos bonasus caucasicus;*
The bald ibis or waldrapp, *Gèronticus eremita,* disappeared from localized outposts in Switzerland, Austria and Hungary early 17th century. It still occurs in Morocco, Algeria and the Middle East.

European mammals and birds in danger:
Spanish lynx, *Felis lynx pardina;*
Novaya Zemlya reindeer, *Rangifer tarandus pearsoni;*
Pyrenean ibex, *Capra p. pyrenaica;*
Corsican red deer, *Cervus elaphus corsicanus;*
Spanish imperial eagle, *Aquila heliaca adalberti;*
Audouin's gull, *Larus audouini* (Mediterranean and North Africa).
European bison, *Bos. b. bonasus.* Figures on the official list of threatened species after facing near extinction in both world wars, but now increasing very satisfactorily.

Spanish imperial eagle—endangered

139

European brown bear, common lynx, wild cat, wolf and wolverine, are not included in the official list as their overall numbers have not dropped to danger level. However, due to the popular prejudices against predators this may soon be the case.

European lynx

European wolf

European National Parks and Wildlife Reserves:

Great Britain:

The IUCN lists ten national parks in Britain. They cannot, however, be regarded as 'national parks' in the same sense as it is understood in the more spacious parts of the world. Unlike the great parks of South Africa and North America these parks are inhabited, contain many works of man and there is considerable exploitation of natural resources. It is hoped, however, that 'national park' status will protect them from the ravages of urbanization, industrialization and exploitation. They are:

Lake District, 866 sq. m.
Snowdonia, 845 sq. m.
Yorkshire Dales, 680 sq. m.
North York Moors, 553 sq. m.
Peak District, 542 sq. m.
Brecon Beacons, 515 sq. m.
Northumberland, 398 sq. m.
Dartmoor, 365 sq. m.
Exmoor, 265 sq. m.
Pembrokeshire Coast, 255 sq. m.

National Nature Reserves:

There are 108 of which 22 surpass 1,240 acres, while 34 have an area between 247 and 1,240 acres. Many are of great faunal interest, but only a few can be included in this enumeration.

Cairngorms, Inverness-shire, 91·9 sq. m. Dotterel, ptarmigan and snow bunting on mountain tops, capercaillie in forests. Golden eagle. Osprey have nested there in recent years. Deer, roedeer, blue hare.
Inverpolly, Ross-shire, 41·4 sq. m.
Rhum, Inverness-shire 41·2 sq. m: Deer, grey seal.
Caerlaverock, Dumfries and Kirkudbright, 21·1 sq. m. Famous winter refuge for whooper swans, barnacle geese from Spitsbergen, pinkfeet and greylag geese from Iceland.
Beinn Eighe, Ross-shire, 16·4 sq. m. Deer, blue hare, wild cat, marten, golden eagle, ptarmigan.
Hermaness, Shetland, 3·7 sq. m: Bird sanctuary.
St. Kilda, 3·2 sq. m. One of Britain's finest bird sanctuaries. Big colonies of fulmars and puffins, gannets, St. Kilda wren.
Scolt Head, Norfolk, 2·8 sq. m. Of great ornithological interest.

Of the smaller reserves, between 250 and 1,250 acres, the following are of great interest:
Hickling Broad,   Loch Lomond,
North Rona,   Sula Sgeir.

Besides the national nature reserves, there are many excellent bird sanctuaries administered by the National Trust, the Royal Society for the Protection of Birds, and various local bodies:
Ramsay Island,   Skomer Island,
Skokholm Island,   Grassholm Island,
—all within the Pembrokeshire Coast National Park.
Havergate—avocet breeding.
Blakeney Point,   Dungeness,
Minsmere,
Farne Islands, a sanctuary for seals as well as sea birds. Britain has many wildfowl refuges giving protection to migrating geese, ducks and waders.

Ireland

As yet no national parks but quite a few important reserves:

Bourn Vincent Memorial Park, 16·4 sq. m. near the Killarney Lakes. Deer.

Ross Island Nature Reserve.
North Bull Island, 5·3 sq. m. Bird sanctuary.
Mayo Bird Sanctuary, 14·8 acres. Breeding place of red-necked phalarope.
The Skelligs. About 10,000 pairs of gannets.
Cambay Island, 610 acres. Grey seal, sea-birds.

Map 1: Great Britain and Ireland

1. Lake District
2. Snowdonia
3. Yorkshire Dales
4. North York Moors
5. Peak District
6. Brecon Beacons
7. Northumberland
8. Dartmoor
9. Exmoor
10. Pembrokeshire Coast
11. Cairngorms
12. Inverpolly
13. Rhum
14. Caerlaverock
15. Beinn Eighe
16. Hermaness
17. St. Kilda
18. Scolt Head
19. Hickling Broad
20. Loch Lomond
21. North Rona
22. Sula Sgeir
23. Havergate
24. Blakeney Point
25. Dungeness
26. Minsmere
27. Farne Islands
28. Bourn Vincent Memorial Park
29. Ross Island Nature Reserve
30. North Bull Island
31. Mayo Bird Sanctuary
32. The Skelligs
33. Cambay Island

GREAT BRITAIN AND IRELAND

Puffins on St. Kilda

Spain:

Montaña de Covadongo National Park, 65·3 sq. m.
Rocky mountain area west of the Picos de Europa.
Cantabrian chamois, roedeer, wild boar, bear, wolf.
Valle de Ordesa National Park, 7·8 sq. m. Pyrenees.
Pyrenean chamois (isard), Pyrenean ibex, lammergeyer.
Coto Doñana Reserve, 27 sq. m. Famous reserve in the
delta of the Guadalquivir. Deer, wild boar, Spanish lynx.
Of great ornithological interest. Flamingoes. Breeding area
of purple heron, little egret, night heron, bittern, spoonbill,
imperial eagle, booted eagle, pratincole, pin-tailed
sandgrouse.
Sierra de Gredos Game Reserve. West Spanish ibex.
Serrania de Ronda Game Reserve. South Spanish ibex.

Portugal:

Gerês National Park, on the northern border. Decreed
1954, but not yet properly established.
Arrabida National Park, being planned on Setubal
Peninsula.

France

Vanoise National Park, Murienne and Tarantaise,
235·4 sq. m. In the Vanoise Mountains. Chamois, Alpine
ibex.
Eastern Pyrenees National Park, Basses and Hautes
Pyrenees, 193 sq. m. Along Spanish border, adjoining
Ordesa National Park. Bear (about 60 said to occur
mainly in Basses Pyrenees), Spanish lynx, Pyrenean
chamois, capercaillie, lammergeyer, Egyptian vulture, black
vulture, eagle owl.
Port Cros National Park, 2·4 sq. m. An island of the Hyères
Archipelago. Entomologically very interesting. Refuge for
migrating birds.

France has 14 national game reserves and three
Game Reserves of National Interest, of which the
following are worthy of special mention:
Chambord, Loire-et-Cher, 21 sq. m. Deer, roedeer, wild
boar. Also of ornithological interest.
Burrus, Ariège, 16·9 sq. m. Pyrenean chamois, ptarmigan,
capercaillie.
Bauges, Savoie and Haute Savoie, 15·7 sq. m. Chamois,
roedeer, mouflon (introduced), marmot.
Bavella-Sambucco, Corsica, 15 sq. m. Mouflon.
Cauterets, Hautes Pyrenees, 12·6 sq. m. Pyrenean chamois,
variable hare, ptarmigan, blackcock.
Chizé, Deux-Sèvres, 7·9 sq. m. Roedeer, wild boar.
Casabianda, Corsica, 6·8 sq. m. A few Corsican red deer.
Belval, Ardennes, 3·5 sq. m. Deer, roedeer, mouflon
(introduced), wild boar.
Sept Iles, 202 acres. Two islands off the coast of Brittany.
Gannets, guillemots, auk, cormorant, kittiwake, peregrine
falcon, raven.
Mercantour, 107·5 sq. m. Alpes Maritimes. Chamois and
other mountain game.
The Société National de Protection de la Nature
administers what is probably the best-known French
wildlife reserve the *Zoological and Botanical Reserve of
the Camargue,* Bouches-du-Rhone, 36 sq. m. It is of great
ornithological interest. Breeding colony of greater flamingo.
Whiskered tern, black-winged stilt, avocet, purple heron,
night heron, squacco heron, little egret, pratincole, Kentish
plover. Near the mouth of the Rhone there is also the
Beaver Reserve of La Sèze.

Vanoise National Park—France

Pyrenean ibex

142

Italy

Stelvio National Park, 369 sq. m. Alpine area with deer, chamois, roedeer, marmot.
Gran Paradiso National Park, 216 sq. m. Alpine reserve in the Val d'Aosta region. Ibex, chamois, marmot, golden eagle, eagle owl, ptarmigan, rock partridge.
Abbruzzi National Park, 112·5 sq. m. Situated in the Abbruzzi Mountains. Abbruzzi chamois, bear, wolf, wild cat.
Circeo National Park, 28·7 sq. m. Oak forest. Wild boar.
Cossogno Total Reserve, about 4 sq. m. of alpine forest with chamois and golden eagle.
Sasso Fratino Total Reserve, 111 acres. Apennine forest.
Poggio tre Cancelli Total Reserve, 123 acres. Mediterranean bush (maquis).

Map 2: Spain, Portugal, France and Italy

1. Montaña de Covadongo National Park
2. Valle de Ordesa National Park
3. Coto Doñana Reserve
4. Sierra de Gredos Game Reserve
5. Serrania de Ronda Game Reserve
6. Gerês National Park
7. Vanoise National Park
8. Eastern Pyrenees National Park
9. Port Cros National Park
10. Chambord Reserve
11. Burrus Reserve
12. Bauges Reserve
13. Bavella-Sambucco Reserve
14. Cauterets Reserve
15. Chizé Reserve
16. Casabianda Reserve
17. Belval Reserve
18. Sept Iles Reserve
19. Mercantour Reserve
20. Zoological and Botanical Reserve of the Camargue
21. Stelvio National Park
22. Gran Paradiso National Park
23. Abbruzzi National Park
24. Circeo National Park
25. Cossogno Total Reserve
26. Sasso Fratino Total Reserve
27. Poggio tre Cancelli Total Reserve

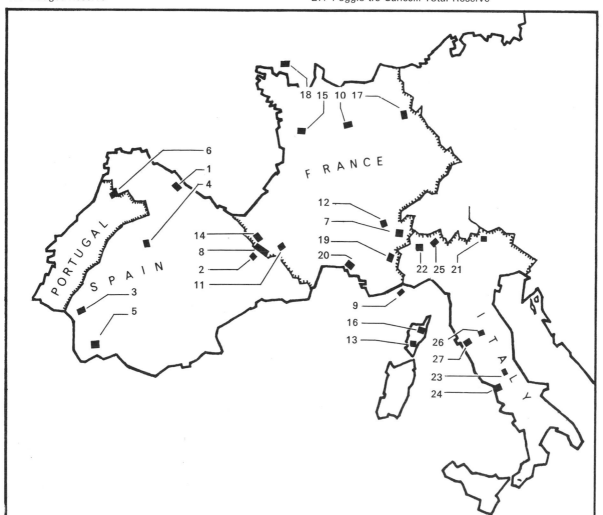

Belgium

Hautes Fagnes Nature Reserve, 7·7 sq. m. Peat bogs. Mostly of botanical and entomological interest.
Westhoek Nature Reserve, 1·3 sq. m. Coastal area with dunes. Of botanical and ornithological importance.
Lesse et Lomme, 3·7 sq. m. At the confluence of the rivers Lesse and Lomme. Limestone area of scenic interest, with deciduous forest.
Vague des Gomhets, 116 acres. Swampy area surrounded by forest. Deer, roedeer, wild boar, wildcat.

Belgium has many bird sanctuaries administered by the Society Les Réserves Naturelles et Ornithologiques de Belgique, such as:

Kalmthout, 2·8 sq. m. Heathland, marshes, dunes. Blackheaded gull, black tern, shelduck, curlew, godwit, blacknecked grebe.
Genk, 543 acres. Marshland in the Stiembeck valley. Black tern, marsh harrier, nightjar.
Zwin, 308 acres. Saltmarshes at the old mouth of the river Zwin. Avocet, shelduck, little tern, hoopoe.

Holland

Hoge Veluwe National Park, 22 sq. m. Forest and heathland. Deer, roedeer, mouflon (introduced), wild boar, blackcock.
Veluwezoom National Park, 17·3 sq. m. Mixed forest and heathland. Deer, wild boar, fox, blackcock.
De Wieden National Park, 9·6 sq. m. Ponds and marshes. Bird sanctuary. Breeding colonies of cormorants and purple herons.
Kennemeerduinen National Park, 4·7 sq. m. Dunes along coast. Sea birds and migrants.
Veluwe Randmeeren and Zwarte Meer, 21·2 sq. m. Artificial lake. Bird sanctuary. Bearded tit.
Boschplaat, 16·9 sq. m. Terschelling Island. Bird sanctuary. Small breeding colony of spoonbills.

Schorren Achter de Polder Eendracht op Texel, 11·5 sq. m. Texel Island. Important bird sanctuary. Avocet, tern, gulls. Famous refuge for migrating waders.
Geul and Westerduinen, 6·4 sq. m. Texel Island. Freshwater pond. Gulls, spoonbills.
Dwingelosche and Kraloër Heide, 4·6 sq. m. Heathlands, Blackheaded gull, curlew, blackcock.
Oostvornse Duinen, 4 sq. m. Old dunes with small lakes and marshes. Blackheaded gull, blackcock, red-crested pochard, shelduck.
Biesbosch, 3·1 sq. m. Ponds and reed beds of great ornithological interest. Some night herons.
Naardermeer, 2·8 sq. m. A very important bird sanctuary with spoonbill, purple heron, cormorant, black tern. Despite the fact that it is one of the most densely populated countries in the world—or, perhaps, because of it—Holland has 112 reserves of over 250 acres!

Map 3: Belgium and Holland

1. Hautes Fagnes Reserve
2. Westhoek Nature Reserve
3. Lesse et Lomme
4. Vague des Gomhets
5. Kalmthout
6. Genk
7. Zwin
8. Hoge Veluwe National Park
9. Veluwezoom National Park
10. De Wieden National Park
11. Kennemerduinen National Park
12. Veluwe Randmeeren and Zwarte Meer
13. Boschplaat
14. Schorren Achter de Polder Eendracht op Texel
15. Geul and Westerduinen
16. Dwingelosche and Kraloer Heide
17. Oostvornse Duinen
18. Biesbosch
19. Naardermeer

Spotted deer in Hoge Veluwe National Park—Holland

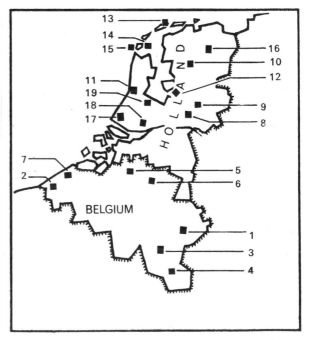

Denmark

Hansted, 11·5 sq. m. Dunes, heathland, marshes, lakes. Interesting bird sanctuary. Breeding place of golden plover.
Hirsholmene, Archipelago of ten islands, 1·1 acre of sea. A refuge for waders and sea birds, only Danish breeding colony of kittiwakes.
Vorsø, 1·1 sq. m. Islands in Horsenfjord. Colonies of cormorants and herons.
There are many game reserves, partial game reserves and bird sanctuaries, such as **Graesholmen** with auks, guillemots and eiders, and **Jordsand,** in Northern Friesia, a famous refuge for sea birds and migrants.

Norway

Börgefjell National Park, 386 sq. m. Mountain area of great scenic beauty, with lakes and rivers. Elk, wolverine. Wolf as sporadic visitor. Willow grouse, ptarmigan and many other interesting birds.
Rondane National Park, 222 sq. m. Mountain area with elk, reindeer, otter, fox and 124 species of birds.
Fokstumyra National Reserve, 3·47 sq. m. Situated on Dovrefjell; of great ornithological interest.
There are several other reserves, such as the **Nordmarka Faunal Reserve** of 10·8 sq. m. and the **Nordkapp-Hornvika Reserve,** famous for its sea birds.

Sweden
Lappland:
Padjelanta National Park, 787 sq. m. Wild mountain area with large lakes.
Sarek National Park, 753 sq. m. Mountains and narrow valleys.
Stora Sjöfallet National Park, 580 sq. m. Adjoining the lakes from which the Stora Lule Alv springs.
These three adjoining parks form a continuous wilderness area of 2,120 sq. m., and we are told that 'map and compass are indispensable when hiking.' There are reindeer, elk, bear, wolverine, wolf, arctic fox, lemming, ptarmigan, dotterel, snowy owl, snow bunting, golden eagle, bluethroat, brambling. Sarek National Park has 22 species of mammals and 102 species of birds.
Muddus National Park, 190 sq. m. In the coniferous belt of northern Norrland. Forests and bogs around Lake Muddusjaure. Reindeer, elk, bear, pine marten, otter, capercaillie, golden eagle, hawk owl, crane, whooper swan.
Peljekaise National Park, 564 sq. m. Grazing area for Lapp reindeer herds.
Abisko National Park, 29 sq. m. On Lake Torne Träsk, Mountain birch forest, barren rock. Elk, reindeer, marten, wolf, otter. Of ornithological interest.
Vaddetjakko National Park, 9·4 sq. m. North-west of Lake Torne Träsk, on Norwegian border. Lakes, willow thickets, marshes. Elk, reindeer, arctic fox, blue hare, lemming, rough-legged buzzard, ptarmigan.

Central Sweden:
Sonfjället National Park, 10·4 sq. m. Isolated mountain. Coniferous forest, peaks above timber line. Bear.
Töfsingdalen National Park, 5·25 sq. m. Virgin coniferous forest. Bear, wolverine, golden eagle.

Southern Sweden:
Gotska Sandön, 14 sq. m. Island north of Gotland. Of botanical and entomological interest. Herring gull, great black-backed gull, tern, eider.

Golden plover

Abisko National Park—Sweden

S. C. Porter/Bruce Coleman Ltd

Gosta Hakansson/Bruce Coleman Ltd

There are six national parks of under 300 acres, mainly of botanical importance. In addition, Sweden has numerous County Council National Parks. Many of the State Forests are game reserves with elk, reindeer and other animals.

Finland

Pallas-Ounastunturi National Park, 193 sq. m. Fjell-landscape with reindeer and many interesting birds.
Lemmenjoki National Park, 148·6 sq. m. On Lemmenjoki River. Reindeer, bear, wolf, whooper swan.
Oulanka National Park, 41·3 sq. m. A very wild area along Oulankajoki River. Reindeer, whooper swan, smew, golden eagle.
Phyätunturi National Park, 11·5 sq. m. Fjell-landscape. Elk, reindeer.
Phyähäkki National Park, 3·9 sq. m. Natural coniferous forest. Elk, blue hare.
Linnansaari National Park, 3·1 sq. m. A group of islands in Lake Saimau. Elk, common seal. Of ornithological interest. Osprey.
Petkeljärvi National Park, 2·5 sq. m. Karelian coniferous forest, lakes.
Rokua National Park, 1·6 sq. m. On Lake Leisjärvi. Elk.

There are also 15 'nature parks', for instance.
Kevo Nature Park, 132 sq. m. Great canyon of Kevoioki River. Reindeer, arctic fox, gyr falcon.
Jussarö Nature Park, 98 acres of islands in the Finnish Gulf. Of ornithological interest. Auks, eider, Caspian tern, arctic skua, geylag.

Finnish Travel Information Centre

Pyhätunturi National Park—Finland

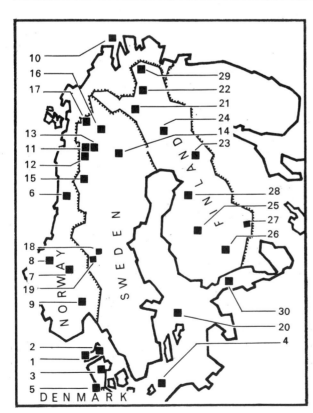

Map 4: Denmark, Norway, Sweden and Finland

1. Hansted
2. Hirsholmene
3. Vorsø
4. Graesholmen
5. Jordsand
6. Björgefjell National Park
7. Rondane National Park
8. Foksumyra National Reserve
9. Nordmarka Faunal Reserve
10. Nordkapp—Hornvika Reserve
11. Padjelanta National Park
12. Sarek National Park
13. Stora Sjöfallet National Park
14. Muddus National Park
15. Peljekaise National Park
16. Abisko National Park
17. Vaddetjakko National Park
18. Sonfjället National Park
19. Töfsingdalen National Park
20. Gotska Sandön
21. Pallas-Ounastunturi National Park
22. Lemmenjoki National Park
23. Oulanka National Park
24. Pyhätunturi National Park
25. Pyhähäkki National Park
26. Linnansaari National Park
27. Petkeljärvi National Park
28. Rokua National Park
29. Kevo Nature Park
30. Jussarö Nature Park

Germany (West)

At present there are 33 nature parks (Naturschützparke), areas of great scenic beauty, not too densely inhabited and little industralized. Two of them can be regarded as coming very close to the criteria demanded of a real national park. They are:

Lüneburgerheide Nature Park, Lower Saxony: 77 sq. m. of heathland with 40 species of mammals and 380 species of birds.

Siebengebirge Nature Park, Rhineland-Northern Westphalia, 16·2 sq. m. Mountain area of special botanical interest.

There are about 900 nature reserves, of which only a few can be mentioned:

Ammergebirge, Bavaria, 104·2 sq. m. Natural forest and alpine pastures. Chamois, deer, marmots.

Königssee, Bavaria, 79·4 sq. m. Mountain area near Berchtesgaden. Ibex (introduced), chamois, deer, golden eagle, ptarmigan.

Karwendel, Bavaria, 73·3 sq. m. Mountain area around Garmisch-Partenkirchen. Very rich alpine flora and fauna. Chamois, deer, marmot.

Holzmaden, Baden Württemberg, 30·8 sq. m. Of mainly palaeontological interest.

Mellum, Lower Saxony, 13·5 sq. m. Grassland area between rivers Jade and Weser. Important bird sanctuary. Common tern, Sandwich tern, oyster catcher, common gull, herring gull.

Lister Dunes, 7·8 sq. m. On the Island of Sylt, Schleswig-Holstein. Important bird sanctuary.

Dümmer, Lower Saxony, 5·8 sq. m. Of great ornithological importance. Breeding area for eight species of duck. Tern, curlew, ruff, golden plover, bittern.

Federsee, Baden-Württemberg, 5·4 sq. m. Of ornithological interest.

Wollmatingerried, Baden-Württemberg, 1·67 sq. m. Marshy area on Lake of Constance. Important bird sanctuary. Breeding area, refuge for migrants.

There are many other bird sanctuaries, as well as excellent game reserves.

Lüneburgerheide Nature Park—West Germany

Eberhard Jüttner

Germany (East)

East Germany has no national parks or nature parks, but there are numerous game reserves and bird sanctuaries, of which the following may be mentioned:

Darss Reserve, Pomerania. Breeding area of crane.
Rügen, of great ornithological interest.
Mulde, Gordsdorf and **Pinnowsee Reserves** serve to protect the beaver.
Müritzsee, 26·3 sq. m. Mecklenburg. An important bird sanctuary. Main breeding area of crane in Germany.
Kyffhäuserbergland, 21·6 sq. m. A mountain area of considerable botanical interest and rich in game.
Sächsische Schweiz, 540·4 sq. m. Spectacular scenery, good game area.

Austria

Rothwald Total Reserve, 2·3 sq. m. Largest vestige of primeval forest in Central Europe.
Tauern Nature Park, 19·3 sq. m. Adjoining two reserves of 35 and 77 sq. m. Important high Alpine area.
Neusiedlersee and Seewinkel Reserves, 66 sq. m. Lake surrounded by steppe. A very important bird sanctuary with spoonbill, purple heron, great white heron.
Karwendel Partial Reserve, 278 sq. m. Alpine area north of Innsbruck.

Grossglockner and Pasterze Partial Reserve, 14·2 sq. m. Alpine area of great scenic beauty, with interesting flora and fauna. Chamois.
Reserve Steinernes Meer and Hagengebirge, 135 sq. m. South of Salzburg. Ibex (introduced).
Lainzer Tiergarten, 8·8 sq. m. Part of the famous Vienna Woods.

Switzerland

Swiss National Park, 65 sq. m. An excellent and very strictly guarded Alpine reserve among the mountains of the Engadin. Magnificent scenery. Ibex (introduced), chamois, deer, roedeer, marmot, golden eagle, black woodpecker, ptarmigan, blackcock, capercaillie, wall creeper.
Aletschwald Reserve, approx. 1 sq. m. A forest of cembra pines near the Aletsch glacier. Of mainly botanical and scenic interest.
Virgin Forest of Derborence, 126 acres. Only vestige of a primitive forest to be found in Switzerland. Situated in the Canton of Valais; of mainly botanical interest.
In addition, there are 466 other total or partial reserves, covering an area of about 210 sq. m. Of these 92 are administered by the Swiss League for the Protection of Nature. A number of very interesting bird sanctuaries have been established by the Swiss Society of the Study and Protection of Birds.

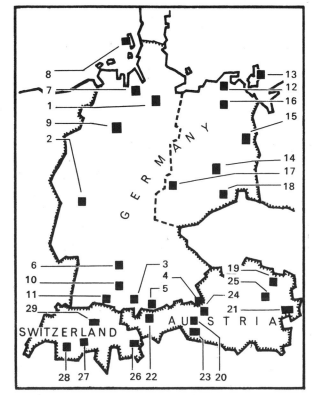

Map 5: Germany, Austria and Switzerland

1. Lüneburgerheide Nature Park
2. Siebengebirge Nature Park
3. Ammergebirge Nature Reserve
4. Königssee Nature Reserve
5. Karwendel Nature Reserve
6. Holzmaden Nature Reserve
7. Mellum Nature Reserve
8. Lister Dunes Nature Reserve
9. Dümmer Nature Reserve
10. Federsee Nature Reserve
11. Wollmatingerried Nature Reserve
12. Darss Reserve
13. Rügen Reserve
14. Gordsdorf Reserve
15. Pinnowsee Reserve
16. Müritzsee Reserve
17. Kyffhäuserbergland Reserve
18. Sächsische Schweiz
19. Rothwald Total Reserve
20. Tauern Nature Park
21. Neusiedlersee and Seewinkel Reserves
22. Karwendel Partial Reserve
23. Grossglockner and Pasterze Partial Reserve
24. Reserve Steinernes Meer and Hagengebirge
25. Lainzer Tiergarten
26. Swiss National Park
27. Aletschwald Reserve
28. Virgin Forest of Derborence
29. Kärpf Game Reserve

Austrian State Tourist Dept.

Karwendel Partial Reserve—Austria

Marmot in Swiss National Park

C. A. W. Guggisberg/Bruce Coleman Ltd.

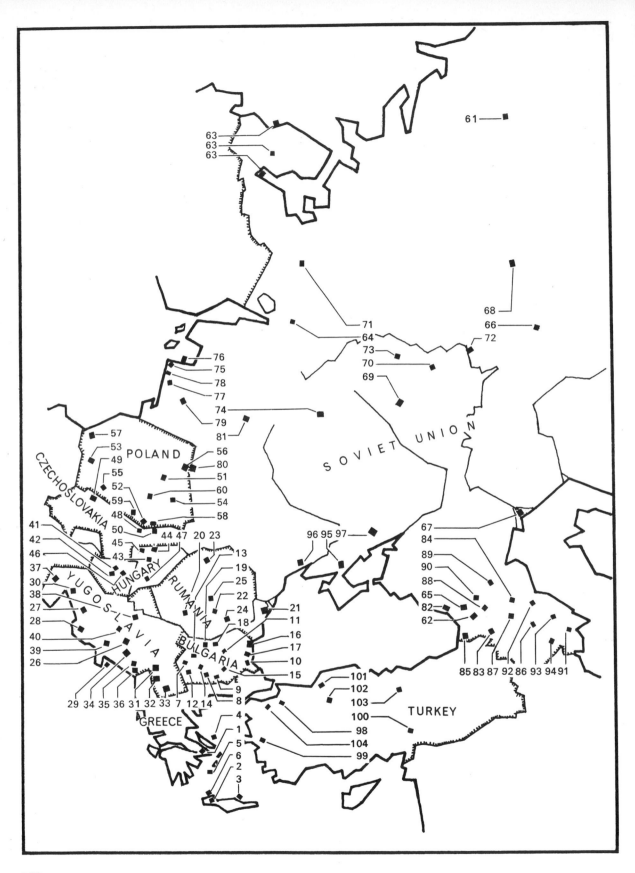

61

63
63
63

71
64
73
70
69

68
66
72

76
75
78
77
74
79
81

57
53
49
55
52
59
48
50

POLAND

56
80
51
60
54
58

CZECHOSLOVAKIA

SOVIET UNION

41
42
46
37
30
38
27
28
40
39
26

YUGOSLAVIA

HUNGARY

45
43
44 47 20 23

13
19
25
22
24
18

RUMANIA

BULGARIA

96 95 97

67
84
89
90
88
65
82
62

21
11
16
17
10
15

101
102
103
100

85 83 87 92 86 93 94 91

29 34 35 36 31 32 33 7 12 14

9
8

TURKEY

GREECE

4
1
5
6
2
3

98
104
99

150

Map 6: Greece, Bulgaria, Rumania, Yugoslavia, Hungary, Czechoslovakia, Poland, Soviet Union (European part) and Turkey

1. Mount Parnis National Park
2. Samarias National Park
3. Dias Island Reserve
4. Guioura Island Reserve
5. Antimylos Island Reserve
6. Theodora
7. Vitocha Park
8. Vikhren Park
9. Steneto Park
10. Ropotamo Park
11. Djendema Reserve
12. Parangalitza Reserve
13. Maritza Lakes
14. Baevi Doupki
15. Vassil Kolarov
16. Kaliakra
17. Kamtchia
18. Milka
19. Switov
20. Retezat National Park
21. Danube Delta Reserve
22. Bucegi Reserve
23. Pietrosul Reserve
24. Snagov Reserve
25. Piatra Craiului Mare
26. Sutjeska National Park
27. Plitvice Lakes National Park
28. Paklenica National Park
29. Mljet National Park
30. Risnjak National Park
31. Mavrovo National Park
32. Galicica National Park
33. Pelister National Park
34. Durmitor National Park
35. Biogradska Gora National Park
36. Lovcen National Park
37. Triglav National Park
38. Fruska Gora National Park
39. Hutovo Blato Reserve
40. Obedska Bara Reserve
41. Tihany National Park
42. Little Balaton Reserve
43. Baradla Cave Reserve
44. Peace Cave Reserve
45. Szalajka Valley Reserve
46. Velence Lake Reserve
47. Féhér Nature Reserve
48. Tatra National Park
49. Krkonose National Park
50. Pieniny National Park
51. Kampinos National Park
52. Tatra National Park
53. Wielkopolski National Park
54. Holy Cross Mountain National Park
55. Karkonosze Mountain National Park
56. Bialowieza National Park
57. Wolin National Park
58. Pieniny Mountain National Park
59. Babiagora National Park
60. Ojcow National Park
61. Pechora-Ilych
62. Caucasus
63. Kandalakcha-Lappland
64. Darwin
65. Tberda
66. Bashkirie
67. Astrakhan
68. Ilmen
69. Voronesh
70. Oka
71. Kivatch
72. Volga-Kama
73. Pri500-Terrasny
74. Centralno-Chernoziemnyi
75. Slitere
76. Engure
77. Moritsala
78. Grini
79. Juvintas
80. Bielovieja
81. Berezina
82. Ritza
83. Borjom
84. Lagodekhi
85. Kintrich
86. Wachlowan
87. Saguram
88. Adjamet
89. Botsara
90. Satapli
91. Kyzil Agatch
92. Zakataly
93. Turiantchai
94. Gokgol
95. Askania Nova
96. Chernomorskii
97. Ukrainski Stepnoi
98. Uludag National Park
99. Kusadasi National Park
100. Karatepe National Park
101. Yedigöller National Park
102. Kizilçahaman National Park
103. Yosgat National Park
104. Lake Manyas National Park

Greece

Mount Parnis National Park, 14·3 sq. m. Game park with deer and roedeer.

Samarias National Park, 11·5 sq. m. In the White Mountains of Crete. Wild goat.

Dias Island Reserve, 4·6 sq. m. Small island off Crete. Wild goat (introduced).

Guioura Island Reserve, 3·8 sq. m. Island of the Northern Sporades group. Wild goat.

Antimylos Island Reserve, 3·1 sq. m. Island of the Cyclades group. Wild goat.

Erimomilos Island Reserve, 2·9 sq. m. Wild and feral domestic goats; hybrids.

Theodora. Small island off Crete. Reserve for introduced wild goats.

There are eight game reserves, mainly for the protection of deer. **Nestos Marsh,** on the Greco-Bulgarian border, has been set aside as a bird sanctuary in 1966.

Bulgaria

Vitocha Park, 88 sq. m. Forest area in the Rila Mountains.
Vikhren Park, 26 sq. m. Mountain area with chamois and bear.
Steneto Park, 6·4 sq. m. Steneto Gorge of the Tcherni Ossame River. Ancient forests. Deer, roedeer, chamois, bear, eagle.
Ropotamo Park, 3·2 sq. m. Black Sea, south of Ropotamo River. Dunes. Deer, roedeer, wild boar, of ornithological interest.

Of the many Bulgarian reserves, **Djendema, Parangalitza, Maritza Lakes, Baevi Doupki** and **Vassil Kolarov** are situated in mountain areas and give protection to bear and other game, such as deer, roedeer and chamois. **Kaliakra,** on the Black Sea, is a bird sanctuary and also serves as a refuge for the rare monk seal.

Kamtchia, near the Black Sea, protects part of an ancient forest with deer, roedeer, wild boar and black stork. **Milka** and **Switov** are important bird sanctuaries on the Danube.

Rumania

Retezat National Park, 43 sq. m. Forested mountain area.
Danube Delta Reserve, 154·4 sq. m. A very important bird sanctuary, containing Europe's biggest breeding colony of pelicans. Little egret, great white heron, night heron, squacco heron, spoonbill, glossy ibis, cormorant, pygmy cormorant, sea eagle.
Bucegi Reserve, 18·4 sq. m. Bucegi Mountain. Chamois.
Pietrosul Reserve, 10·4 sq. m. Mountain area, into which chamois have been re-introduced.
Snagov Reserve, 6·8 sq. m. Forest and lake on the Danubian plain.
Piatra Craiului Mare, 1·76 sq. m. Mountain area. Chamois. There are a considerable number of other reserves.

Yugoslavia

Sutjeska National Park, Bosnia, 66·6 sq. m. Forest area. Deer, roedeer, chamois, bear (very rare), capercaillie.
Plitvice Lakes National Park, Croatia. 74 sq. m. Karst area. Bear (very rare), wild cat, otter, marten.
Paklenica National Park, Croatia, 14 sq. m. Bear, wild cat, marten, griffon vulture, golden eagle.
Mljet National Park, Croatia. 12 sq. m. Mljet Island, near Dubrovnic. Refuge for the rare monk seal.
Risnjak National Park, Croatia, 12 sq. m. Karst area in the Dinaric Alps. Deer, chamois, bear, wild cat, marten, wolf, capercaillie.
Mavrovo National Park, Macedonia, 305·2 sq. m. Coniferous forest. Roedeer, chamois, bear, lynx.
Galicica National Park, Macedonia, 89 sq. m. Bear, lynx.
Pelister National Park, Macedonia, 40·1 sq. m. Chamois, roedeer, bear.
Durmitor National Park, Montenegro, 124 sq. m. of which 4·6 sq. m. are under total protection. Wild mountain area. Chamois, bear (very rare), capercaillie.
Biogradska Gora National Park, Montenegro, 13·9 sq. m. Roedeer, bear, capercaillie.
Lovcen National Park, Montenegro, 7·7 sq. m. Mountain area between Cetenje and Kotor. Of archaeological and historical interest. Rock partridge.
Triglav National Park, Slovenia, 7·7 sq. m. Julian Alps. Chamois, blue hare, blackcock, eagle owl.
Fruska Gora National Park, Serbia, 85 sq. m. Mixed forest.

While some of the Yugoslav National Parks can be regarded as total reserves, others are divided into zones of total protection and areas where hunting—under 'strict control'—is tolerated. As the sale' of bears to wealthy sportsmen from western countries has become quite a lucrative source of state revenue, one cannot help feeling that this much-persecuted species is the main object of the 'controlled hunting' within national parks.

In addition to national parks, Yugoslavia has a number of very interesting reserves, such as:

Hutovo Blato, Bosnia, 13 sq. m. Marshy area. Important bird sanctuary. Great white heron, egret, pygmy cormorant, sea eagle.
Obedska Bara, Serbia, 2·9 sq. m. Forest, meadows, marshland. Important bird sanctuary.

Hungary

Tihany National Park, 4·2 sq. m. Geologically interesting peninsula in Lake Balaton.
Little Balaton Reserve, 5·4 sq. m. Marshy area. Ornithologically very important. Great white heron, little egret, purple heron, squacco heron, spoonbill, glossy ibis, cormorant.
Baradla Cave Reserve, 3 sq. m. Karst area with caves.
Peace Cave Reserve, 2·5 sq. m. Karst area with caves.
Szalajka Valley Reserve, 2·1 sq. m. Mountain area. Palaeolithic site.
Velence Lake Reserve, 1·6 sq. m. Lake surrounded by reed beds. Interesting bird sanctuary. Great white heron.
Fehér Nature Reserve, 4·6 sq. m. Bird sanctuary. Avocet, spoonbill.

Plitvice Lakes National Park—Yugoslavia

Yugoslav National Tourist Office

Plate XVII (opposite page 152) Until very
recently the life of the Barren Ground
Eskimo was regulated by the migratory
movements of the caribou. The wandering
herds provided them with food, clothing,
tents, tools and weapons

Plate XVIII (left) Gannets—adult and
young—on Bass Rock

Plate XIX (above) Nikko National Park on
Honshu Island, Japan. An area of great
scenic beauty which harbours sika deer,
serow, black bear and macaques

Plate XX African nature reserves are famous for their array of game animals, but they also have much to offer to the ornithologist. Our photograph shows the weaver bird at its half-finished nest

Czechoslovakia

Tatra National Park, 193 sq. m. Part of the Slovak Carpathians. Chamois, bear, wolf, wild cat, lynx, marmot.
Krkonosc National Park, 146·7 sq. m. Situated in the Riesengebirge' of Bohemia. Ringousel, nutcracker, Alpine shrew.
Pieniny National Park, 8·3 sq. m. Gorge of River Dunajec.

Czechoslovakia has many national reserves, such as:

Maly Velky Tisy, 2·3 sq. m. Two ponds forming a bird sanctuary.
Lednicke rybniky, 2·1 sq. m. Ponds in an old river bed. Refuge for migrating birds.
Novozamecky rybnik, 1·3 sq. m. Sanctuary for water birds.

Poland

Kampinos National Park, 86·3 sq. m. An old arm of the Vistula, surrounded by forest. Elk, crane, heronries.
Tatra National Park, 85·2 sq. m. Mountain area adjoining the Slovak Tatra National Park. Chamois, bear, lynx, marmot, golden eagle, eagle owl.
Wielkopolski National Park, 20·7 sq. m. Situated in Pomerania. Mixed forest with deer, roedeer, black stork, eagle owl.
Holy Cross Mountain National Park, 23·3 sq. m. Densely forested mountain range. Roedeer, wild boar, blackcock.
Karkonosze Mountain National Park, 21·4 sq. m. Adjoining the Krkonose National Park of Bohemia. Deer, roedeer, wild boar.
Bialowieza National Park, 19·6 sq. m. Poland's most famous nature reserve Virgin forest with European bison, elk, wild horse, lynx, beaver, black stork, capercaille, eagle owl.
Wolin National Park, 17·8 sq. m. On the Baltic coast. Sea eagle, osprey, cormorant, Arctic tern.
Pieniny Mountain National Park, 10·4 sq. m. On both sides of the Dunajec River. Deer, wild cat, lynx, eagle owl, wall creeper (an otherwise Alpine species), Parnassius butterfly.
Babiagora National Park, 6·6· sq. m. Mountain area with vestiges of virgin Carpathian forest. Deer, lynx, wild cat, eagle owl.
Ojcow National Park, 6·4 sq. m. Karst area with many caves. Interesting cave fauna.

Poland has 520 nature reserves, of which only a few can be mentioned here:

Czerwone Bagno, 8·4 sq. m. Forest marshland, with elk, blackcock.
Jezioro Karas, 2·6 sq. m. Marshy lakes, of ornithological importance.
Jezioro Lukniany, 2·4 sq. m. Lake of ornithological importance. Mute swan.
Nart Czerkies, 1·8 sq. m. Forest area. Black stork.
Borki, 573 acres. Mixed forest. Deer. European Bison, Beaver Reserves of **Kdypy** and **Marycha.**

Soviet Union (Europe)

Pechora-Ilych, 2,757 sq. m. Mountain area north of Ural. Taiga forest with reindeer, elk, sable, bear, beaver (introduced), capercaillie.
Caucasus, 1,027 sq. m. Chamois, West-Caucasian ibex, European bison (introduced), deer, bear, leopard.
Kandalakcha-Lappland, 696 and 85 sq. m. Islands in Kandalakcha Bay; seven islands in Barents Sea; Ainos Island, Barents Sea; part of Kola Peninsula, with Lake Imandra. Reindeer, elk, bear, otter; on the islands seal and

European bison

Kola Peninsula in winter—USSR

Novosti Press Agency

153

sea birds: guillemots, auk, cormorant, kittiwakes, eider.

Darwin, Vologda, 435 sq. m. Elk, bear, lynx, wolf. Important bird sanctuary: capercaillie, blackcock, hazelhen.

Tberda, Caucasus, 348·5 sq. m. Caucasian ibex, chamois, bear.

Bashkirie, Ural, 278 sq. m. Forest area with elk, deer, roedeer, burunduck, flying squirrel, bear, capercaillie, blackcock.

Astrakhan, 169·8 sq. m. Very important bird sanctuary. Egret, cormorant, pelican, flamingo, geese, duck.

Ilmen, Ural, 124 sq. m. Forest area. Elk, roedeer, lynx, beaver.

Voronesh, 119·6 sq. m. Deciduous forest. Elk, deer, wild boar, beaver, Russian desman.

Oka, Ryazen, 84·9 sq. m. Mixed forest. European bison, elk, deer, Russian desman.

Kivatch, Karelia, 39·8 sq. m. Karelian taiga forest. Elk, bear, otter. Refuge for migrating birds.

Volga-Kama, 29·3 sq. m. Taiga forest at junction of rivers Volga and Kama. Elk, fur-bearing animals.

Prioksko-Terrasny, Moscow, 18·5 sq. m. On River Oka. European bison, roedeer, wild boar, beaver.

Centralno-Chernoziemnyi, Kursk, 16·2 sq. m. Steppe, oak forests. Bustard.

Slitere, Latvia, 31·17 sq. m. Roedeer, wild boar.

Engure, Latvia, 5·1 sq. m. Bird sanctuary on an island in Riga Bay.

Moritsala, Latvia, 3·4 sq. m. Moritz Island in Lake Ousman. Roedeer. Of ornithological interest.

Grini, Latvia, 3 sq. m. On Baltic coast. Deer, roedeer, wild boar.

Juvintas, Lithuania, 19·6 sq. m. Lake Juvintas. Of ornithological interest. Large colony of mute swans.

Bielovieja, White Russia, 285·6 sq. m. Forest with European bison, wild boar, deer, capercaillie.

Berezina, White Russia, 284 sq. m. Forests and marshes. Elk, roedeer, wild boar, bear, otter, beaver, capercaillie.

Ritza, Georgia, 61·5 sq. m. Eastern Caucasian forest and coastal area of Black Sea. Deer, roedeer, bear.

Borjom, Georgia, 69·8 sq. m. Mountains of eastern Georgia. Oak forests with deer, wild boar and bear.

Lagodekhi, Georgia, 51·3 sq. m. Southern Caucasus. Ibex, chamois deer, roedeer.

Kintrich, Georgia, 23·1 sq. m. Forested mountains, Deer, wild boar, pheasants.

Wachlowan, Georgia, 22·9 sq. m. Forests with bear, wild boar.

Saguram, Georgia, 19·6 sq. m. Near Tiflis. Deer, roedeer.

Adjamet, Georgia, 17·8 sq. m. Oak forests.

Botsara, Georgia, 13·4 sq. m. Of mainly botanical interest.

Satapli, Georgia, 1·33 sq. m. Cave with remains of cretaceous dinosaurs. Cave fauna.

Kyzil Agatch, Azerbeidjan, 339·6 sq. m. Bird sanctuary on the Caspian Sea.

Zakataly, Azerbeidjan, 97·6 sq. m. Eastern Caucasus. Chamois, roedeer, deer, wild boar, bear, wolf, lynx, wild cat.

Turiantchai, Azerbeidjan, 49 sq. m. Situated at foot of Caucasus. Wild boar, wolf, jackal.

Gokgol, Azerbeidjan, 28·9 sq. m. Mountain forests, subalpine meadows, lakes. Roedeer, bear, marten.

Askania Nova, Ukraine, 38·6 sq. m. Vestiges of Ukrainian steppe. Marmot, souslik, eagles, bustard. Introduced: Mongolian wild horse, onager and many other ungulates.

Chernomorskii, Ukraine, 37·4 sq. m. Steppe along Black Sea. Of ornithological interest.

Ukrainski Stepnoi, Ukraine, 8·5 sq. m. Steppe area with marmots.

Tberda: Caucasian chamois

Astrakhan: Grey herons and spoonbills

North America (excluding Mexico)

In North America, and more especially in the part we know as the United States, the impact of civilization has been highly dramatic. A vigorous and energetic race invaded a pristine wilderness, in which hunters and primitive agriculturists had, for thousands of years, lived in a state of balance with nature. Encountering a congenial climate and fertile soil, the intruders multiplied rapidly and spread westwards across the continent. Having freed themselves from their ties with Europe and having discarded the laws and traditions which in their old homelands prevented the country people from cutting forests and slaughtering game, they proceeded to lay waste the newly won countries. In the youthful exuberance characteristic of all pioneers. They effected tremendous changes and caused an enormous amount of habitat destruction. A new and aggressive civilization arose in what had a short while ago been a continent of vast forests and of immeasurable prairies swarming with game. Wildlife received a frightful battering, and the losses were heavy.

Reaction set in early, and no nation has done, and is still doing more for conservation than the United States. In Canada, the clash between civilized man and nature was somewhat tempered by a harsher climate and more hostile wilderness. Even today, there still are areas which have remained almost as untouched as they were when Champlain sailed up the St. Lawrence River. But the Canadians, too, awoke to an early realization of what the march of progress was doing to the continent, and their conservation efforts have ever since rivalled those of their southern neighbours.

North American species and subspecies of mammals lost:

Gull island mouse, *Microtus pennsylvanicus nesophilus;*
Eastern bison, *Bison bison pennsylvanicus;*
Oregon bison, *Bison bison oregonus;*
Eastern wapiti, *Cervus c. canadensis;*
Arizona wapiti, *Cervus c. merriami;*
Badlands bighorn, *Ovis canadensis auduboni;*
Long-eared kit fox, *Vulpes m. macrotis;*
Sea mink, *Mustela macrodon;*
Newfoundland wolf, *Canis lupus beothucus;*
Florida red wolf, *Canis n. niger.*

Some authors give a considerably longer list of extinct mammals, adding to the above mentioned forms no less than 16 species and subspecies of grizzly bears. In 1918 a museum zoologist, C. H. Merriam, did in fact subdivide the brown and grizzly bears of America into two genera, 14 super-species 71 species and 15 subspecies, all of which he neatly labelled and named, even though many of his descriptions were based on nothing more than a skull or two. Bears are notorious for showing an enormous range of individual variation, and this quite obviously explains Merriam's over-enthusiasm. His taxonomic Eiffel-tower was later reduced to 14 species and four subspecies by H. E. Anthony, and other zoologists have since come to the conclusion that the grizzlies and brownies cannot be considered as specifically different from the Old World brown bear, *Ursus arctos.* For the moment, it is probably best to distinguish between the gigantic brown bear of Alaska, *Ursus arctos middendorffi,* and the grizzly bear, *Ursus arctos*

Alaska brown bear catching salmon

horribilis, and to forget about the 16 species and subspecies. It is, however, a sad fact that gtizzly bears have disappeared from many areas where they formerly occurred. In the United States they can be found in a couple of National Parks and are very rare elsewhere. In the Canadian Rockies they have fared somewhat better, but the so-called 'barren ground grizzly' of the far north must also be considered as threatened, and there are not more than 1,000 left, with 500 probably being a much nearer estimate.

North American birds now extinct:

Labrador duck, *Camptorhychus labradorius;*
Passenger pigeon, *Ectopistes migratorius;*
Carolina parakeet, *Conuropsis carolinensis;*
Heath hen, *Tympanuchus c. cupido.*

North American mammals and birds in danger:

Kaibab squirrel, *Sciurus kaibabensis;*
Delmarva Peninsula fox squirrel, *Sciurus niger cinereus;*
Eastern fox squirrel, *Sciurus niger vulpinus;*
Utah prairie dog, *Cynomys parvidens;*
Salt-marsh harvest mouse, *Recthrodontomys raviventris;*
Block Island meadow mouse, *Microtus pennsylvanicus provectus;*
Black meadow mouse, *Microtus breweri;*
The two surviving subspecies of the red wolf, *Canis niger gregoryi* and *Canis niger rufus;*

Black-footed ferret, *Mustela nigripes;*
Florida cougar, *Felis concolor coryi;*
Eastern cougar, *Felis concolor cougar;*
Tule wapiti, *Cervus canadensis nannodes;*
Key deer, *Odocoileus virginianus clavium;*
Columbia whitetailed deer, *Odocoileus virginianus leucurus;*
Sonoran pronghorn antelope, *Antilocapra americana sonoriensis;*
Wood bison, *Bison bison athabascensis* (subspecies threatened through interbreeding with introduced plains bison):
California condor, *Gymnogyps californianus;*
Everglades kite, *Rostrhamus sociabilis plumbeus;*
Southern bald eagle, *Haliaeetus l. leucocephalus;*
Attwater's prairie chicken, *Tympanuchus cupido attwateri;*
Greater prairie chicken, *Tympanuchus cupido pinnatus;*
Whooping crane, *Grus americana;*
Yuma clapper rail, *Rallus longirostris yumaensis;*
Eskimo curlew, *Numenius borealis;*
Ivory-billed woodpecker, *Campephilus p. principalis;*
Cape sable sparrow, *Ammospiza mirabilis;*
Dusky sparrow, *Ammospiza nigrescens;*
Ipswich sparrow, *Passerculus princeps.*

American conservationists are fully aware of the dangers threatening the above-mentioned species and subspecies, and everything possible is being done to save them from extinction.

Southern bald eagle *Haliaeetus l. leucocephalus*—endangered

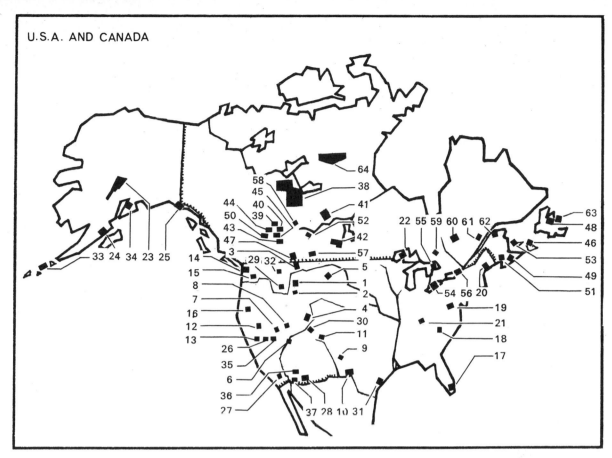

Map 7: U.S.A. and Canada

1. Yellowstone National Park
2. Grand Teton National Park
3. Glacier National Park
4. Rocky Mountain National Park
5. Théodore Roosevelt National Memorial Park
6. Grand Canyon National Park
7. Zion National Park
8. Bryce Canyon National Park
9. Carlsbad Caverns National Park
10. Big Bend National Park
11. Mesa Verde National Park
12. Yosemite National Park
13. Sequoia-Kings Canyon National Park
14. Olympic National Park
15. Mount Rainier National Park
16. Lassen Volcanic National Park
17. Everglades National Park
18. Great Smoky Mountains National Park
19. Shenandoah National Park
20. Acadia National Park
21. Mammoth Cave National Park
22. Isle Royal National Park
23. Mount McKinley National Park
24. Katmai National Monument
25. Glacier Bay National Monument
26. Death Valley National Monument
27. Joshua Tree National Monument
28. Organ Pipe Cactus National Monument
29. Craters of the Moon National Monument
30. Natural Bridges National Monument
31. Aransas National Wildlife Refuge
32. National Bison Range
33. Aleutian Island National Wildlife Refuge
34. Kenai National Moose Range
35. Desert Game Range
36. Kofa Game Range
37. Cabeza Prieta Game Range
38. Wood Buffalo National Park
39. Jasper National Park
40. Banff National Park
41. Prince Albert National Park
42. Riding Mountain National Park
43. Kootenay National Park
44. Glacier National Park
45. Yoho National Park
46. Cape Breton Highland National Park
47. Waterton Lakes National Park
48. Terra Nova National Park
49. Kejimkujik National Park
50. Mount Revelstoke National Park
51. Fundy National Park
52. Elk Island National Park
53. Prince Edward Island National Park
54. Point Pelee National Park
55. Georgian Bay Island National Park
56. St. Lawrence Island National Park
57. Cypress Hills Provincial Park
58. Dinosaur Provincial Park
59. Algonquin Provincial Park
60. Vérandrye Provincial Park
61. Laurentides Provincial Park
62. Gaspesian Provincial Park
63. Pitts Pond Provincial Park
64. Thelon Game Reserve

North American National Parks and Wildlife Reserves

United States

Yellowstone National Park, Wyoming. 3,472 sq. m. Mountains, forests, lakes, thermal areas. Moose, wapiti, mule deer, pronghorn antelope, bighorn, bison, grizzly, black bear, coyote, beaver, white pelican, trumpeter swan. One of the world's most famous national parks.

Grand Teton National Park, Wyoming, 484 sq. m. Magnificent views of the spectacular Teton Range. Moose, wapiti, mule deer, bighorn, grizzly, black bear, coyote, beaver, Barrow's golden-eye duck, ruffed grouse, Clark's crow, water ouzel.

Glacier National Park, Montana, 1,583 sq. m. Mountain area with 60 glaciers and 200 lakes. Moose, wapiti, mule deer, whitetailed deer, bighorn, mountain goat, grizzly, black bear, coyote, beaver.

Rocky Mountain National Park, Colorado, 405 sq. m. Mountain area with 65 peaks of 10,000 ft. and over. Many lakes. Wapiti, mule deer, bighorn (numerous), bobcat, black bear, coyote, beaver, golden eagle, broadtailed hummingbird, ptarmigan.

Theodore Roosevelt National Memorial Park, North Dakota. 110 sq. m. Theodore Roosevelt's Elkhorn Ranch. Pronghorn antelope, deer, bison.

Grand Canyon National Park, Arizona, 1,052 sq. m. The world's mightiest gorge. Mule deer, pronghorn antelope, coyote, ringtail, bobcat, a few cougar, Kaibab squirrel, calliope humming bird, canyon wren.

Zion National Park, Utah, 223 sq. m. Zion Canyon, eroded rocks. Mule deer, bighorn, cougar.

Bryce Canyon National Park, Utah, 56 sq. m. Spectacular rock formations. Mule deer, cougar, bobcat, coyote, grey fox.

Carlsbad Caverns National Park, New Mexico, 77 sq. m. Limestone caverns with bat colonies. Mule deer, ringtail, coyote, grey fox.

Big Bend National Park, Texas, 1,106 sq. m. On the Rio Grande. Mountains, canyon, desert country. Pronghorn antelope, mule deer, Arizona whitetailed deer, peccary, cougar, black bear, kit fox, roadrunner, lucifer hummingbird.

Mesa Verde National Park, Colorado, 80 sq. m. Of great archaeological interest. Mule deer, black bear, bobcat, coyote, prairie dog. Bighorn and wild turkey re-introduced.

Yosemite National Park, California, 1,189 sq. m. Glacier-eroded valleys, waterfalls, canyons, giant sequoias. Mule deer, black bear, coyote, yellow-bellied marmot, Steller's jay, water ouzel.

Sequoia and Kings Canyon National Park, California, 1,314 sq. m. High Sierra. Sequoia groves. Mule deer, bighorn, black bear, coyote, grey fox, mountain beaver.

Olympic National Park, Washington, 1,400 sq. m. From Pacific Ocean beach to snow peaks. Rain forest. Roosevelt wapiti, blacktailed deer, snowshoe rabbit, black bear, cougar, beaver, mountain beaver.

Mount Rainier National Park, Washington, 377 sq. m. Cascade mountains, with Mount Rainier, 14,408 ft. extinct volcano. Mountain goat, wapiti, blacktailed deer, black bear, marmot, snowshoe rabbit, mountain beaver, sooty

Lake Macdonald in Glacier National Park—Montana

United States Information Service

grouse, whitetailed ptarmigan, golden eagle, bald eagle.

Lassen Volcanic National Park, California, 163 sq. m.
Lassen Peak, active volcano, which had many eruptions
between 1914 and 1921. Sulphur and steam fumaroles.
Blacktailed deer, mule deer.

Everglades National Park, Florida, 2,188 sq. m. Subtropical
wilderness. Whitetailed deer, manatee, cougar, alligator,
American crocodile. Bird-life enormously rich: roseate
spoonbill, wood ibis, seven species of herons, three species
of egrets, anhinga, limpkin.

Great Smoky Mountains National Park, Tennessee-North
Carolina, 798 sq. m. Last remnant of southern primeval
hardwood forest. Whitetailed deer, black bear, fox,
raccoon, bobcat, ruffed grouse, turkey.

Shenandoah National Park, Virginia, 302 sq. m. Blue Ridge
Mountains. Whitetailed deer, opppossum, flying squirrel,
woodchuck, chipmunk.

Acadia National Park, on Mount Desert Island, off Coast of
Maine, 64·3 sq. m. Coniferous forest. Deer, beaver, osprey,
bald eagle, ruffed grouse.

Mammoth Cave National Park, Kentucky, 78 sq. m.
Enormous system of caverns with interesting fauna, such
as cave crickets, eyeless fish, eyeless crayfish.

Isle Royal National Park, Michigan, 210 sq. m. Island in
Lake Superior. Moose, coyote, beaver, osprey, Canada jay,
bald eagle.

Mount McKinley National Park, Alaska, 3,030 sq. m.
Wilderness area dominated by 20,300 ft. Mt. McKinley—
Denali of the Indians. North America's most magnificent
park. Caribou, Dall sheep, moose, 'Tocklat' grizzly, timber
wolf, wolverine, red fox, lynx, coyote, parka squirrel,
porcupine, marmot, golden eagle, willow ptarmigan.

There are a number of small parks of lesser wildlife
importance. Altogether, the National Park Service is
responsible for 32 parks in the United States and
the Hawaiian Islands. It also administers 42
National Monuments. Seven of these are of purely
archaeological importance, the others are faunal
reserves or serve to protect botanical or geological
features. We can mention only a few of them:

Katmai National Monument, Alaska, 4,214 sq. m. Within
this reserve is the Katmai Volcano, which erupted violently
in 1912, and the Valley of Ten Thousand Smokes, formed
during the eruption. Volcanic activity has now largely died
down. The area is rich in wildlife: caribou, moose, brown
bear, wolverine, lynx, beaver.

Glacier Bay National Monument, Alaska, 3,590 sq. m.
Untouched wilderness around Muir Glacier. Brown and
black bear. Canada geese.

Death Valley National Monument, California, 2,981 sq. m.
A desert area with interesting small mammals and
reptiles.

Joshua Tree National Monument, California, 1,344 sq. m.
Part of the Mojave and Colorado Deserts. Of great
botanical interest. Protects a stand of Joshua trees, a large
species of yucca. Desert bighorn, mule deer, coyote,
bobcat.

Mountain scenery in Olympic National Park

Organ Pipe Cactus National Monument, Arizona, 516 sq. m. Sonoran desert area with interesting flora. Desert bighorn, pronghorn antelope, Arizona whitetailed deer, desert mule deer, peccary, coati, Gambel's quail, canyon wren, cactus wren, vermilion flycatcher, roadrunner.

Craters of the Moon National Monument, Idaho, 74 sq. m. Studded with craters and other volcanic features. Of mainly geological importance.

Natural Bridges National Monument, Utah, 4 sq. m. Three natural sandstone bridges. Caves, Indian cliff dwellings.

No less important than the areas under the National Park Service are the many National Wildlife Refuges, administered by the Fish and Wildlife Service, such as:

Aransas National Wildlife Refuge, Texas, 74 sq. m. Bird sanctuary. Winter refuge of the few surviving whooping cranes.

National Bison Range, Montana, 29 sq. m. 3—400 bison, wapiti, whitetailed deer, pronghorn antelope, bighorn.

Aleutian Island National Wildlife Refuge, 4,250 sq. m. Fifty islands, extending from Unimak to Atto. Brown bear, wolverine, harbour seal, bearded seal, sea otter. Tremendous amount of waterfowl.

Kenai National Moose Range, Alaska, 3,214 sq. m. West side of Kenai Peninsula. Moose, Dall sheep, mountain goat, brown bear, black bear, coyote.

Pribilov Islands Reserve, Bering Sea. Fur seal.

Desert Game Range, Nevada, 3,745 sq. m. Nelson's bighorn, pronghorn antelope, mule deer. A total of 60 species of mammals.

Kofa Game Range, Arizona, 1,031 sq. m. of desert.

Cabeza Prieta Game Range. 1,034 sq. m. On the Mexican border. Only remaining herd of Sonoran pronghorn antelope.

There are 89 State Parks and numerous other reserves, particularly bird sanctuaries, administered by the Audubon Society such as **Corkscrew Swamp,** in Florida, and the **Rainey Wildlife Sanctuary,** in Louisiana.

Canada

Wood Buffalo National Park, Alberta, 17,300 sq. m. Situated between Lake Athabasca and Great Slave Lake. Forests and prairies. Established to safeguard the northern subspecies of the bison. Plains bison were, however, introduced into one area and there has been considerable interbreeding. Whooping cranes breed in the reserve.

Jasper National Park, Alberta, 4,200 sq. m. Mountain area around Mt. Edith Cavell. Moose, wapiti, mule deer, caribou, mountain goat, bighorn, grizzly, black bear.

Banff National Park, Alberta, 2,564 sq. m. Rocky Mountains. Magnificent scenery. Moose, wapiti, mule deer, mountain goat, bighorn, grizzly, black bear, cougar.

Prince Albert National Park, Saskatchewan, 1,496 sq. m. Forest, lakes and river. Wapiti, black bear, wolf, coyote, lynx, beaver.

Riding Mountain National Park, Manitoba, 1,148 sq. m. Wooded plateau. Moose, wapiti, black bear, coyote, wolf, beaver, pelican, swan.

Kootenay National Park, British Columbia, 543 sq. m. Mountain goat, mule deer, wapiti, black bear.

Glacier National Park, British Columbia, 521 sq. m. Selkirk Range. Forest, tundra. Mountain goat, caribou, moose, wapiti, mule deer, grizzly, black bear.

Yoho National Park, British Columbia, 507 sq. m. Western slope of Rockies, on both sides of Kicking Horse River. Of great scenic beauty.

Cape Breton Highland National Park, Nova Scotia, 367 sq. m. Hills and mountains. Whitetailed deer, moose, lynx, beaver, sea birds.

Waterton Lakes National Park, Alberta, 203 sq. m. Adjoining Glacier National Park of Montana, U.S.A. Very wild, densely forested. Black and whitetailed deer, mule deer, moose, wapiti mountain goat, bighorn, a few bison, grizzly bear, black bear.

Terra Nova National Park, Newfoundland, 153 sq. m. Moose (introduced) caribou, black bear, lynx, beaver.

Kejimkujik National Park, Nova Scotia, 140 sq. m.

Mount Revelstoke National Park, British Columbia, 100 sq. m. Mountain area noted for grizzly bear. Also black bear, caribou, mule deer.

Fundy National Park, New Brunswick, 79·5 sq. m. Hilly plateau. Moose, whitetailed deer, black bear, fur-bearing animals. Of great ornithological interest.

Elk Island National Park, Alberta, 75 sq. m. Mostly wooded area surrounding Island Lake. Bison, mule deer, wapiti, moose.

Prince Edward Island National Park, Nova Scotia, 77 sq. m. On north coast of Prince Edward Island Of ornithological interest.

Point Pelee National Park, Ontario, 6 sq. m. Peninsula in Lake Erie. Refuge for migrating birds. Deer, raccoon, coyote.

Georgian Bay Island National Park, Ontario, 5·4 sq. m. 42 islands in Lake Huron.

St. Lawrence Island National Park, Ontario. Twelve of the 'Thousand Islands' in Lake Ontario, made famous by J. F. Cooper's novel *The Pathfinder.*

Besides the Federal Parks mentioned above, there are numerous Provincial Parks such as:

Cypress Hills Provincial Park, Alberta, 75·2 sq. m. On Elkwater Lake. Moose, wapiti, whitetailed deer. Of considerable ornithological interest.

Dinosaur Provincial Park, Alberta, 34 sq. m. 'Badlands' with deer, pronghorn antelope, coyote. Important palaeontological site.

Algonquin Provincial Park, Ontario, 2,909 sq. m. Moose, black bear, wolf.

Vérandrye Provincial Park, Quebec, 4,408 sq. m. Hilly area with lakes and rivers. Moose, black bear, wolf.

Laurentides Provincial Park, Quebec, 3,581 sq. m. Numerous lakes and rivers. Moose, black bear, wolf.

Gaspesian Provincial Park, Quebec, 492 sq. m. Chic-choc Mountains. Coniferous forest. Caribou, moose, black bear.

Pitts Pond Provincial Park, Newfoundland, 15·8 sq. m. Caribou, moose (introduced), black bear, beaver.

Canada has a number of game reserves, bird sanctuaries and wilderness areas. Of special interest are the **Thelon** and **Twin Island Game Reserves** in the North West Territory, the first created as a refuge for musk ox and caribou, the second for the protection of polar bears.

Canada Geese

Yoho National Park

South and Central America (including Mexico)

In South America, the impact of civilization has, on the whole, been less forceful than in North America. Penetration was more gradual, less immediately destructive, and in many countries it was very seriously hampered by tropical conditions. Within the last few decades destruction has, however, been enormously speeded up, and today the situation is very grave indeed. The urgency of conservation has hardly been realised, and there are large areas without proper national parks. Where such reserves have been established, they are often very inadequately guarded. There exists little or no legislation to curb uncontrolled hunting and exploitation of animal resources is therefore still in its crudest and most devastating form. The pet trade, for instance, is rapidly developing into a major menace for many South American monkeys and birds.

Argentina, where the ravages of civilization have made themselves felt considerably earlier than in the tropical areas farther north, has so far taken the lead in conservation, but even in that country, there is still room for many improvements. However, the battle for effective conservation is now on in most parts of South America, and we can only hope that it will bring definite results before it is too late. Actual losses have, so far, been negligible, but a large number of mammals and birds must be regarded as endangered.

South and Central American species lost:
Slender billed grackle, *Cassidix palustris* (Mexico)

South and Central American mammals and birds in danger:
White-nosed saki, *Chiropotes albinasus;*
Woolly spider monkey, *Brachyteles arachnoides;*
Bald uakari, *Cacajao calvus;*
Red uakari, *Cacajao rubicundus;*
Black-headed uakari, *Cacajao melanocephala;*
Goeldi's tamarin, *Callimico goeldii;*
Giant armadillo, *Priodontes giganteus;*
Lesser pichiciego, *Chlamyphorus truncatus;*
Volcano rabbit, *Romerolagus diazi;*
Chinchilla, *Chinchilla laniger;*
Maned wolf, *Chrysocyon brachyurus;*
Bush dog, *Speothos venaticus;*
Spectacled bear, *Tremarctos ornatus;*
Giant otter, *Pteronura brasiliensis;*
Mountain tapir, *Tapirus pinchaque;*
Central American tapir, *Tapirus bairdii;*
Pampas deer, *Ozotoceros bezoarticus;*
Chilean pudu, *Pudu pudu;*
Amazonian manatee, *Trichechus inunguis;*
Andean grebe, *Podiceps andinus;*
Junin's grebe, *Podiceps taczanowskii;*
Atitlan grebe, *Podilymbus gigas;*
Titicaca grebe, *Rollandia micropterus;*
Mexican duck, *Anas diazi;*
Cozumal curassow, *Crax rubra griscomi;*
Whiteheaded curassow, *Pipile pipile;*

Horned guan, *Oreophasis derbianus;*
Horned coot, *Fulica cornuta;*
Thickbilled parrot, *Rhynchopsitta pachyrhyncha;*
Imperial woodpecker, *Campephilus imperialis;*
Nicaraguan grackle, *Cassidix nicaraguensis;*
Columbia red-eyed cowbird, *Tangavius armenti.*

If the deplorable craze of wearing the skins of various spotted cats persists, we may soon have to add the jaguar and the ocelot to this list.

Maned wolf, *Chrysocyon brachyurus*—endangered

Russ Kinne/Bruce Coleman Ltd.

Chinchilla, *Chinchilla laniger*—endangered

Russ Kinne/Bruce Coleman Ltd.

Map 8: South America

1. Nahuel Huapi National Park
2. Los Glaciares National Park
3. Lanin National Park
4. Rio Pilcomayo National Park
5. Los Alerces National Park
6. Perito Francisco P. Moreno National Park
7. Tierra del Fuego National Park
8. Iguazu National Park
9. El Rey National Park
10. Chaco National Park
11. Laguna Blanca National Park
12. Petrified Forest National Monument
13. Cape Horn National Park
14. Nahuelbuta National Park
15. Fray Jorge National Park
16. Tolhuaca National Park
17. Mount Sajama National Park
18. Paso del Puerto National Park
19. Cabo Polonia National Park
20. Iguaçu National Park
21. Monte Pascoal National Park
22. Brastlia National Park
23. Aparados da Serra National Park
24. Itatiaia National Park
25. Soòretama Biological Reserve
26. Serra dos Orgãos National Park
27. Caparão National Park
28. Scto Cidades National Park
29. Tijuca National Park
30. Jacarepagua Biological Reserve
31. Kaieteur National Park
32. Kaysergebergte Nature Reserve
33. Coppename River Nature Reserve
34. Tafelberg Nature Reserve
35. Wia-Wia Nature Reserve
36. Nature Reserve at mouth of Coppename River
37. Brinckheuvel Nature Reserve
38. Canaima National Park
39. Guatopo National Park
40. Henri Pittier (Rancho Grande) National Park
41. El Avila National Park
42. Yacambu National Park
43. Yurubi National Park

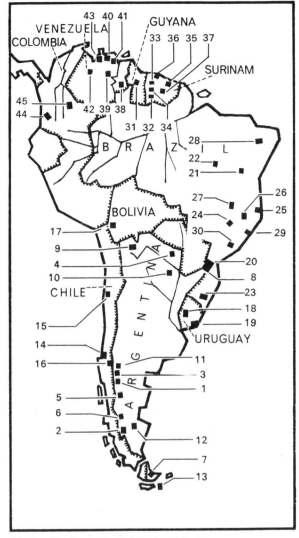

44. Las Farallones de Cali National Park
45. Macarena Reserve

South and Central American National Parks and Wildlife Reserves

Argentine

Nahuel Huapi National Park, 3,030 sq. m. Andean area of great scenic beauty. Pudu, huemul, puma (cougar), condor. Many species of European and Asiatic game animals have been introduced, and some of them should certainly be regarded as vermin within the park boundaries. It would be better to reduce their numbers than to shoot puma, as is still being done.
Los Glaciares National Park, 2,316 sq. m. In the area of Mount Fitz Roy. Nothofagus forests. Pudu, huemul, guanaco, chinchilla, Darwin's rhea, condor.
Lanin National Park, 1,525 sq. m. In the area of Lanin Volcano. Forests. Puma, condor.
Rio Pilcomayo National Park, 1,100 sq. m. At the confluence of Rivers Paraguay and Pilcomayo. Chaco vegetation. Tapir, puma, caiman. Of great ornithological interest.

Los Alerces National Park, 1,015 sq. m. Mountain area in the southern Andes. Lakes, forests. Pudu, huemul, puma.
Perito Francisco P. Moreno National Park, 444 sq. m. Southern Andes. Guanaco, huemul, Patagonian fox, Darwin's rhea, condor. Of considerable ornithological interest.
Tierra del Fuego National Park, 243 sq. m. Forest area. Guanaco; penguins and other sea birds.
Iguazu National Park, 212 sq. m. Subtropical forest area on Brazilian border. Jaguar, ocelot, coati, caiman. Of great ornithological interest.
El Rey National Park, 170 sq. m. Subtropical vegetation. Tapir, jaguar, ocelot, coati, Azara's fox, great ant-eater. Bird life very rich.
Chaco National Park, 58 sq. m. Humid forests of eastern Chaco. Tapir, otter.
Laguna Blanca National Park, 43·4 sq. m. Bird sanctuary. Flamingo, black-necked swan.
Petrified Forest National Monument, 38·6 sq. m. Patagonian steppe with petrified araucaria trees. Guanaco, rhea.

163

Chile

Cape Horn National Park, 243 sq. m. Nothofagus forest. Seal, penguins.
Nahuelbuta National Park, 20·9 sq. m. Araucaria and nothofagus forest.
Fray Jorge National Park, 20 sq. m. Mountain area with vestiges of subtropical forest. Pampas cat. Andean cat, South American skunk, chinchilla.
Tolhuaca National Park, 13·5 sq. m. Araucaria and nothofagus forest.

Several other national parks must be regarded as being of more importance to tourism and recreation than to wildlife and habitat conservation.

Bolivia

Mount Sajama National Park. Contains Keñua Forest, the highest forest in the world, consisting mainly of *Polylepsis tarapacana.* The forest has been sadly depleted, and there are reports of heavy poaching. Efforts are now being made to improve things. Vicuña, chinchilla.
Miriquiri National Park. This reserve was gazetted in 1945, but it does not yet seem to be adequately guarded.

The game reserves of *Huayana-Potosi, Chacaltaya* and *Milluni* are locally considered as 'national parks'. A sportsmen's organization is responsible for their protection.

Three parks that could be important are in the planning stage:

Yapacani-Ichilo, 3,226 sq. m.
Rio Negro-San Martin, 2,841 sq. m.
Guanay Norte, 1,558 sq. m.

Peru

San Andres de Cutervo National Park, 9·6 sq. m. A very interesting area with spectacled bear, puma, deer and caves inhabited by oil birds, but not yet effectively guarded.
Tinga Maria National Park, 5·8 sq. m. In this park, too, there is a cave inhabited by oil birds. The area is not yet effectively guarded.
Vicuña Reserve, 193 sq. m. On a puna (high plateau), south-west of Lima. About 1,000 vicuña, the biggest concentration in existence.

There is a breeding centre for vicuña on Hazienda Callecalle, Lake Titicaca.
Many of the guano islands off the Peruvian coast are protected and thus serve as bird sanctuaries. Pelicans, cormorants, boobies.

Uruguay

Paso del Puerto National Park, 2·3 sq. m. On the confluence of Rio Negro and Aroyo Grande. Said to have been created for the protection of the tinamou, almost exterminated elsewhere in the country.
Cabo Polonia National Park, 17 miles of coastline, to give protection to seals.

Brazil

Iguaçu National Park, 695 sq. m. Subtropical forest near the spectacular Iguassu Falls. Black howling monkey, puma, jaguar, ocelot, capybara, caiman. Bird life very rich.
Monte Pascoal National Park, 143 sq. m. Forest area with howling monkey, tapir, jaguar, otter; enormously rich bird life.

Peruvian guano island

Brastlia National Park, 77·2 sq. m. Wooded savannah of Central Plateau. Black howling monkey, zorra fox, six-banded armadillo, Spix's kerodon, swamp rabbit.

Aparados da Serra National Park, 50·2 sq. m. Coastal mountain ranges, border area of Rio Grande do Sul and Santa Catarina. Pampas cat, seven-banded armadillo, golden opossum. Bird life very rich.

Itatiaia National Park, 46·3 sq. m. Tropical forest of coastal area. Jaguar, ocelot, crab-eating fox, crab-eating raccoon, coati, tamandua. Bird life very rich.

Soòretama Biological Reserve, 46·3 sq. m. Situated in a mountainous area where the coastal vegetation merges into that of the Amazon basin. Howling monkey, tapir, red brocket, peccary, water opossum, harpy eagle, solitary tinamou. The region is especially rich in humming birds, 90% of the species occurring in Brazil being encountered there.

Serra dos Orgãos National Park, 40·5 sq. m. Organ Mountains. Luxuriant vegetation. Titi monkey, brown woolly spider monkey, woolly opossum, paca, agouti. Bird life extremely rich and varied.

Caparão National Park, 40 sq. m. Mountain area of Espirito Santo. Woolly spider monkey, capucin monkey, black-pencilled marmoset, red brocket, nine-banded armadillo, Margay cat.

Sete Cidades National Park, 30 sq. m. Savannah woodland with gallery forests. Brown wood brocket, yaguarundi, rock kerodon, Rabudo rabbit, tamandua, murine opossum, rhea.

Tijuca National Park, 12·3 sq. m. Forest east of Rio de Janeiro. Capucin monkey, black-pencilled marmoset, tavra, grison, Ingram's squirrel, three-toed sloth. Bird life rich and varied.

Jacarepagua Biological Reserve, 10·8 sq. m. Lagoons west of Barra da Tijuca. Of great ornithological interest.

Several important parks are still in course of organisation:

Araguaia National Park, about 7,720 sq. m. On the Island of Bananal, Amazon, which has a very rich fauna and is of particular ornithological interest. Gazetted 1960.

Tocantins National Park, 2,412 sq. m. On the Tocantins River and within the Amazonian Forest area. Gazetted 1961.

Xingu National Park, 8,492 sq. m. On the River Xingu in the Mato Grosso. Gazetted 1961.

In addition, Brazil has 35 state forests and seven state parks.

Guyana

Kaieteur National Park, 43·4 sq. m. Forest area near Kaieteur Falls. Tapir, deer, jaguar, ocelot, sloth, opossum, otter. Bird life very rich: toucan, trumpeter bird, hocco, tinamou.

Surinam

Kaysergebergte Nature Reserve, 617 sq. m.

Coppename River Nature Reserve, 216 sq. m. River with numerous falls and rapids. Savannah country.

Tafelberg Nature Reserve, 154 sq. m. Of mainly botanical interest.

Wia-Wia Nature Reserve, 138 sq. m. Coastal area with lagoons and flooded forests. Especially important as nesting site of green turtle, leathery turtle and loggerhead turtle. Also of ornithological interest: colonies of scarlet ibis and flamingoes.

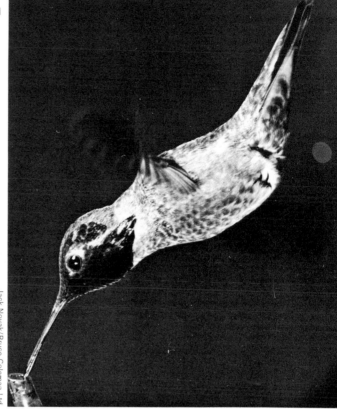

Jack Novak/Bruce Coleman Ltd

Humming bird—*Calypte anna*
Ocelot

Leonard Lee Rue III/Bruce Coleman Ltd

Nature Reserve at mouth of Coppename River, 38·6 sq. m. On sea coast. Manatee, flamingo, scarlet ibis, brown pelican.
Brinckheuvel Nature Reserve, 23·1 sq. m. Savannah. Of mainly geological interest.

Venezuela

Canaima National Park, 3,860 sq. m. Mountain area around Angel Falls, the world's highest waterfall. Forest, savannah. Tapir, peccary, jaguar, paca, caiman.
Guatopo National Park, 357 sq. m. Mountain area. Tapir, peccary, jaguar, paca.
Henri Pittier (Rancho Grande) National Park, 347 sq. m. Cordillera de la Costa. Forest. Peccary, brocket. Bird life very rich and varied, 530 species. Parrots, cock of the rock.
El Avila National Park, 255 sq. m. Mountain area. Brocket, paca, sloth, agouti, crab-eating fox.
Yacambu National Park, 34·7 sq. m. Densely forested mountain area.
Yurubi National Park, 15·4 sq. m. Savannah.

Colombia

Las Farallones de Cali National Park, 1,158 sq. m. Luxurious vegetation. Deer, mountain tapir, spectacled bear.
Purace National Park, 386 sq. m. Extinct volcano, mountain tapir, pudu, spectacled bear.
Macarena Reserve, 4,246 sq. m. An area where Guyanean and Andean vegetation merge into each other. Tapir, three species of deer, spectacled bear; bird life very rich.

Panama Canal Zone

Barro Colorado Reserve, 5·6 sq. m. Administered by the Smithsonian Institution, Washington. Jungle covered island in Gatun Lake. Black howling monkey, marmoset, capucin monkey, squirrel monkey, night monkey, tapir, collared peccary, white-lipped peccary, puma, ocelot, coati, agouti, paca, opossum, water opossum. Of great ornithological interest.

Guatemala

Rio Dulce National Park, approx. 77 sq. m. Rio Dulce and Lake Izabel. Luxuriant vegetation. Geoffroy's spider monkey, whitetailed deer, Baird's tapir, puma, raccoon. Of ornithological interest.
Santa Rosalia National Park, 15·6 sq. m. Hilly country with coniferous forest. Whitetailed deer, raccoon, opossum.
Atitlan National Park, Lake Atitlan. Only habitat of Atitlan grebe.

British Honduras

Chiquibul Forest Reserve, 318 sq. m. Forest area with tapir, puma, jaguar.

There are several other forest reserves, all of which also serve as game reserves.

Mexico

La Malinche, 152 sq. m. Coniferous forests on volcano La Malinche.
Iztaccihuatl-Popocateptl, 99 sq. m. Coniferous forests on the two famous volcanoes:
Pico de Orizaba, 76·2 sq. m. Volcano with coniferous forests.
Bosencheve, 58 sq. m. Laguna del Carmen. Bird sanctuary.
Lagunas de Chacahua, 54·7 sq. m. On Pacific Coast. Lagoons surrounded by mangrove swamps and forests. Deer, pelicans; many other sea birds.
Zoquiapan, 38·6 sq. m. Coniferous forests.
Cofre de Perote, 38·3 sq. m. Volcano. Lower slopes covered with coniferous trees and oaks.
Lagunas de Zempoala, 18 sq. m. Crater lakes surrounded by forest.
Desierto de los Leones, 7·3 sq. m. Forest area.
Insurgente Miguel Hidalgo y Costilla, 7 sq. m. Forest area surrounding artificial lake.
El Chico, 6·1 sq. m. Mountain forest.
Desierto del Carmen, 2 sq. m. Dense forest.

Many of Mexico's parks are not adequately guarded.

Young South American tapir

Raccoon

Caribbean Islands

The Caribbean Islands provide us with a classic illustration of the vulnerability of insular faunas. After some species had already been exterminated, or brought very near to extinction by the indigenous Caribs, the impact of civilization had a truly catastrophic effect. Habitat destruction and the introduction of predators wiped out a considerable part of the fauna and reduced many more species to danger level. Little has yet been done to halt the devastation, and the island area will probably suffer further losses.

Caribbean mammals lost:

Four species of **ground sloths**, which disappeared some time before the arrival of the Europeans.
Five species of **shrews**: *Nesophontes edithae*, Puerto Rico; *Nesophontes micrus*, Cuba, Isle of Pines; *Nesophontes zamicrus*, Hispaniola; *Nesophontes paramicrus*, Hispaniola; *Nesophontes hypomicrus*, Hispaniola;
Lesser falcate-winged bat, *Phyllops vetus*, Cuba;
Puerto Rico long-nosed bat, *Monophyllus frater*;
Jamaican long-nosed bat, *Phyllonicteris aphylla*;
Puerto Rico long-tongued bat, *Phyllonicteris major*;
Hispaniola long-tongued bat, *Phyllonicteris obtusa*;
Cuban yellow bat, *Natalus major primus*;
Barbadan giant rice rat, *Megalomys audreyae*;
Santa Lucia giant rice rat, *Megalomys luciae*;
Martinique giant rice rat, *Megalomys desmarestii*;
Jamaican rice rat, *Oryzomys antillarum*;
St. Vincent rice rat, *Oryzomys victus*;
Cuban short-tailed hutia, *Geocapromys columbianus*;
Bahamian hutia, *Geocapromys brownii ingrahami*;
Least Hispaniola hutia, *Plagiodontia spelaeum*;
Hispaniola hexolobodon, *Hexolobodon phenax*;
Puerto Rico isolobodon, *Isolobodon portoricensis*;
Hispaniola isolobodon, *Isolobodon levir*;
Narrow-toothed hutia, *Aphaetreus montanus*, Hispaniola and San Gabriel;
Six species of **spiny rats**: *Brotomys voratus* and *Brotomys contractus* from Hispaniola, *Boromys offella* and *Boromys torrei* from Cuba, *Heteropsomys insulans* and *Homopsomys antillensis* from Puerto Rico;
Quemi, *Quemisia gravis*, Hispaniola;
Puerto Rico heptaxodon, *Heptaxodon bidens*;
Puerto Rico elasmodontomys, *Elasmodontomys obliquus*.

Caribbean birds lost:

Guadeloupe parrot, *Amazona violacea*, extinct early 18th century;
Martinique parrot, *Amazona martinica*, extinct early 18th century;
Guadeloupe conure, *Aratinga labati*;
Cuban red macaw, *Ara tricolor*, extinct approx. 1885;
Jamaican red macaw, *Ara gossei*, extinct 18th century;
Jamaican green and yellow macaw, *Ara erythrocephala*, extinct early 19th century;
Guadeloupe red macaw, *Ara guadeloupensis*, extinct early 18th century;
Dominican green and yellow macaw, *Ara atwoodi*, extinct late 18th century;
Mysterious macaw, *Ara erythrura*, origin unknown, never seen after 1658;
Martinique macaw, *Ara martinica*, not seen after 1640;
Caribbean storm petrel, *Pterodroma hasitata caribbea*;
Jamaican rail, *Amaurolimnas c. concolor*;
Culebra parrot, *Amazona vittata gracilipes*, Culebra Island, Puerto Rico;
Puerto Rico conure, *Aratinga chloroptera maugei*;
Antiguan burrowing owl, *Speotyto cunicularia amaura*;
Guadeloupe burrowing owl, *Speotyto cunicularia guadeloupensis*;
Jamaican least parauque, *Siphonorhis a americanus*, Hispaniola subspecies surviving but endangered.
Martinique wren, *Troylodytes aëdon martinicensis*;
Guadeloupe wren, *Troglodytes aëdon guadeloupensis*;
St. Christopher finch, *Loxigilla portoricensis grandis*.

Caribbean mammals and birds in danger:

Cuban solenodon, *Atopogale cubana*;
Hispaniola solenodon, *Solenodon paradoxus*;
Cuvier's hutia, *Plagiodontia aedium*, Hispaniola;
Dominican hutia, *Plagiodontia hylaeum*;
Jamaican hutia, *Geocapromys b. brownii*;
Bushy-tailed hutia, *Capromys melanurus*, Cuba;
Dwarf hutia, *Capromys nana*, Cuba;
Cuban tree duck, *Dendrocygnus arborea*;
Gundlach's hawk, *Accipiter gundlachi*, Cuba;
Grenada hook-billed kite, *Chondrohierax uncinatus mirus*;
Cuban hook-billed kite, *Chondrohierax wilsonii*;
Cuban sandhill crane, *Grus canadensis nesiotes*;
Cuban blue rail, *Cyanolimnas cerverai*;
Puerto Rico plain pigeon, *Columba inornata wetmori*;
Grenada dove, *Leptotila wellsi*;
St. Vincent parrot, *Amazona guildingii*;
Imperial parrot, *Amazona imperialis*, Dominica;
Bahama parrot, *Amazona leucocephala bahamensis*, Inagua;
St. Lucia parrot, *Amazona versicolor*,
Puerto Rico parrot, *Amazona vittata*;
Puerto Rico short-eared owl, *Asio flammeus portoricensis*;
Virgin Island screech owl, *Otus nudipes newtoni*;
Puerto Rico whippoorwill, *Caprimulgus noctitherus*;
Hispaniola least parauque, *Siphonorhis americanus brewsteri*;
Cuban ivory-billed woodpecker, *Campephilus principalis bairdii*;

St. Vincent parrot, *Amazona guildingii*—endangered

Jane Burton/Bruce Coleman Ltd.

167

West Indian red-bellied woodpecker, *Melanerpes superciliaris,* Bahamas;
Fernandina's flicker, *Nesoceleus fernandinae,* Cuba;
Euler's flycatcher, *Empidonax euleri johnstonei,* Grenada;
Zapata wren, *Ferminia cerverai,* Cuba;
St. Lucia wren, *Troglodytes aëdon mesoleucus;*
St. Vincent wren, *Troglodytes aëdon musicus;*
Martinique brown trembler, *Cinclocerthia ruficauda gutturalis;*

Martinique white-breasted thrasher, *Ramphocinclus b. brachyurus;*
St. Lucia white-breasted thrasher, *Ramphocinclus b. sanctae-lucinae;*
Isle of Pines solitaire, *Myadestes elisabeth retrusus;*
St. Vincent thrush, *Myadestes genibarbis sibilans;*
Grand Cayman thrush, *Turdus ravidus;*
Barbados yellow warbler, *Dendroica p. petechia;*
Semper's warbler, *Leucopeza semperi,* St. Lucia;
Zapata sparrow, *Torreornis inexpectata.*

Map 9: Central America, Mexico and Caribbean Islands

1. Barro Colorado Reserve
2. Rio Dulce National Park
3. Santa Rosalia National Park
4. Atitlan National Park
5. La Malinche
6. Iztaccihuatl-Popocatepetl
7. Pico de Orizaba
8. Lagunas de Chacahua
9. Zoquiapan
10. Cofre de Perote
11. Lagunas de Zempoala
12. Desierto de los Leones
13. Insurgente Miguel Hidalgo y Costilla
14. El Chico
15. Desierto del Carmen
16. El Vedado Haina-Duey National Park
17. Armando Bermudez and José del Carmen Ramirez National Parks
18. Cupeyal Nature Reserve
19. El Cabo Nature Reserve
20. Jaguani Nature Reserve
21. Cabo Corrientes National Reserve
22. Ciénaga de Zapata National Park
23. Flamencos Reserve
24. Bosque Nacional de Luquillo
25. Derby Island Reserve
26. Virgin Islands National Park
27. Buck Island Reef National Monument
28. Bonaire Flamingo Reserve

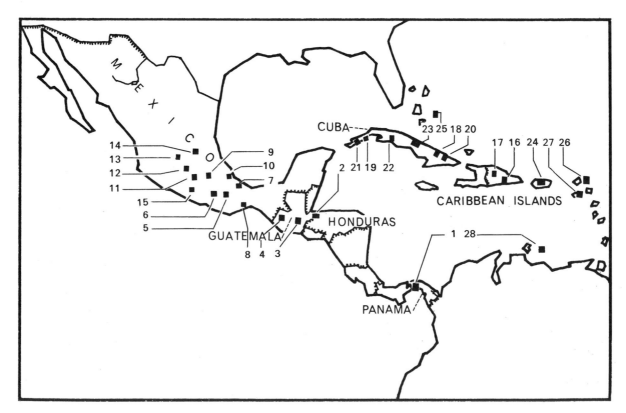

Caribbean National Parks and Reserves

Jamaica

Forest reserves, which also serve as game reserves.

Dominican Republic

El Vedado Haina-Duey National Park, 19·4 sq. m. Forest area.
Armando Bermudez National Park, 301 sq. m. and José del Carmen Ramirez National Park, 297 sq. m. are both situated in the central mountain range, around Pico Duarte.

Cuba

Cupeyal National Reserve, 40 sq. m. Forested mountain area. Gundlach's hawk, solitaire thrush, ivory-billed woodpecker, hutia.
El Cabo Nature Reserve, 29 sq. m. Whitetailed deer, hutia; of ornithological interest.
Jaguani Nature Reserve, 19 sq. m. Ivory-billed woodpecker.
Cabo Corrientes Nature Reserve, 6·1 sq. m. Whitetailed deer, hutia; of ornithological interest.
Ciénaga de Zapata National Park, 193 sq. m.
Flamencos Reserve, Bird Sanctuary. Flamingoes.

Puerto Rico

Bosque Nacional de Luquillo. Bird sanctuary.

Bahamas

Derby Island Reserve. Bird sanctuary. Herons, spoonbill, flamingo.

St. Vincent

Four forest reserves and four bird sanctuaries.

Windward Islands

Three forest reserves.

Virgin Islands

Virgin Islands National Park, 15 sq. m. On St. John Island.
Buck Island Reef National Monument. Administered by the U.S. National Park Service. Buck Island, off St. Croix, with bird colonies and surrounding coral reefs.

Trinidad

Mora Forest Nature Reserve, 580 acres.
Tumana Hill Nature Reserve, 323·7 acres.
Mt. Harris Nature Reserve, 42 acres.
Caroni Swamps Game Reserve, Herons, flamingo, scarlet ibis, spoonbill.

Bonaire

Flamingo reserve

Scarlet ibis

Atlantic Islands

The islands of the Atlantic Ocean have lost the following species:

Falkland Island fox, *Dusicyon australis,* extinct about 1876;
Rothschild's olive ibis, *Lampribis olivacea rothschildi,* Principe Island;
Great auk, *Pinguinus impennis,* Funk Island, islands off Iceland;
St. Helena blue dove, unnamed, seen 1775, but never recorded again;
Ascension Island flightless rail, unnamed, seen in 1656, never recorded again;
Tristan da Cunha flightless rail, *Porphyriornis n. nesiotis;*
Grosbeak weaver, *Neospiza concolor,* São Tomé Island.

Atlantic Island species in danger:

Cahow, *Pterodroma cahow,* Bermuda;
Azores wood pigeon, *Columba palumbus azorica;*
Raza Island lark, *Alauda raza,* Raza Island, Cape Verde;
Tristan bunting, *Nesospiza acunhae;*
Wilkins' bunting, *Nesospiza wilkinsi,* Nightingale and Inaccessible Island;
São Miguel bullfinch, *Pyrrhula p. murina,* São Miguel, Azores;
Fernando Po speirops, *Speirops brunnea.*

National Parks and Reserves on Atlantic Islands

Iceland

Thingvellir National Park, 15·4 sq. m. Volcanic landscape and area of historic interest.
Eldey Nature Reserve, 3·7 acres. This reserve was established in 1940, 96 years too late to save the great auk! But Eldey still has plenty of sea birds and is especially famous for its gannetry.
Skaftafell National Park, of 386 sq. m. and several other reserves are in the planning stage.
There are five partial reserves.

Bermuda
There are several reserves on small islands to give protection to the cahow.

Canary Islands
Two 'national parks'
Teide and **Caldera de Caburiente** exist in name only and are absolutely unguarded.

Falkland Islands
Kidney Island Nature Reserve,
Couchon Island Nature Reserve,
Low Island Nature Reserve,
Beauchene Island Nature Reserve,
Middle Island Nature Reserve.
These sanctuaries mainly serve for the protection of fur seals, penguins and albatrosses. Kidney Island has two species of seals and 27 breeding species of birds.

British Museum (Natural History)

Great auk, *Pinguinus impennis*—extinct

Map 10: Iceland

1. Thingvellir National Park   2. Eldey Nature Reserve

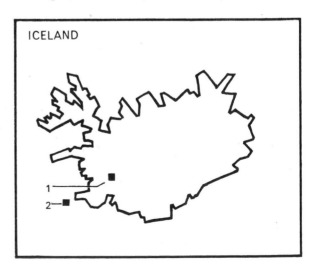

ICELAND

Africa

North African wildlife began to decline in Roman times and has been mercilessly exploited ever since. Hunting pressure has increased enormously during the last few decades, and it is a miracle that anything survives at all.

The history of Africa south of the Zambesi has been very similar to that of North America, with the impact of civilization having the same devastating effect and causing tragic losses which we shall never cease to deplore. The turn of the tide set in during the second half of the last century, and magnificent efforts have since been made to preserve as much as possible of South Africa's fabulous wildlife heritage. Numerous reserves have been established, and they are as well guarded and as efficiently run as any in the world. There are several Government-run game farms, for many land-owners are keen to re-introduce game to the farms which their fathers and grandfathers shot empty.

Between the Zambesi and the southern fringes of the Sahara, the march of civilization was long delayed by tropical conditions. Diseases of many kinds were widespread, and vast areas were kept free of domestic stock through the presence of tsetse flies. While the great waterways of North and South America facilitated European penetration, African rivers were too obstructed with cataracts and rapids to be of any use as easy roads into the interior. In large parts of the continent the fauna thus remained practically undisturbed, and it was only from the middle of the last century onwards that the wildlife of tropical Africa began to feel the impact of civilization. The last three or four decades have, however, been disastrous, and in many regions of West and Equatorial Africa, the fauna has been depleted in a truly horrifying manner. Eastern Africa has suffered too, but things have been somewhat better than elsewhere, and with

African wildlife now a prime target of international tourism, the outlook is certainly better than it was a few years ago. Tanzania, Kenya and Uganda, for instance, have many excellent and well-run reserves, and great efforts are being made to curb illicit hunting. Other African countries are rapidly moving in the same direction.

African species and subspecies of mammals lost:

Blue-buck, *Hippotragus leucophaeus;*
Quagga, *Equus quagga;*
Algerian wild ass, *Equus asinus atlanticus;*
Burchell's zebra, nominate form, *Equus burchelli burchelli* (other subspecies are still numerous);
Bubal hartebeest, *Alcelaphus b. buselaphus;*
Red gazelle, *Gazella rufifrons rufina;*
Cape lion, *Panthera leo melanochaitus;*
Barbary lion, *Panthera leo leo;*
Atlas bear, *Ursus arctos crowtheri.*

As far as we know, no continental African bird has yet become extinct in modern times. The only losses of 'African' birds concern the islands of São Tomé and Principe, and they have been mentioned under the heading of 'Atlantic Islands'.

African mammals and birds in danger:

Tana River mangabey, *Cercocebus g. galeritus;*
Zanzibar colobus, *Colobus badius kirkii;*
Uzangwe colobus, *Colobus badius gordonorum;*
Green colobus, *Colobus verus;*
Pygmy chimpanzee, *Pan paniscus;*
Mountain gorilla, *Gorilla gorilla beringei;*
Brown hyaena, *Hyaena brunnea;*
Simien fox, *Canis simensis;*
Barbary hyaena, *Hyaena hyaena barbara;*
Barbary leopard, *Panthera pardus panthera;*
Nubian wild ass, *Equus asinus africanus;*
Somali wild ass, *Equus asinus somalicus;*
Mountain zebra, *Equus z. zebra;*

Pygmy hippopotamus, *Choeropsis liberiensis*—endangered

Hartmann's mountain zebra, *Equus z. hartmannae;*
Northern white rhinoceros, *Ceratotherium simum cottoni;*
Pygmy hippopotamus, *Choeropsis liberiensis;*
Barbary stag, *Cervus elaphus barbarus;*
Mountain nyala, *Tragelaphus buxtoni;*
Western giant eland, *Taurotragus d. derbianus;*
Jentink's duiker, *Cephalophus jentinki;*
Banded duiker, *Cephalophus zebra;*
Giant sable antelope, *Hippotragus niger variani;*
Scimitar horned oryx, *Oryx tao;*
Addax, *Addax nasomaculatus;*
Bontebok, *Damaliscus d. dorcas;*
Hunter's hartebeest, *Damaliscus hunteri;*
Swayne's hartebeest, *Alcelaphus buselaphus swaynei;*
Beira, *Dorcotragus megalotis;*

Black-faced impala, *Aepyceros melampus petersi;*
Cuvier's gazelle, *Gazella gazella cuvieri;*
Slender-horned gazelle, *Gazella l. leptoceras;*
Pelzeln's gazelle, *Gazella pelzelni;*
Mhorr gazelle, *Gazella dama mhorr;*
Walia ibex, *Capra ibex walia;*
Nubian ibex, *Capra ibex nubiana;*
West African manatee, *Trichechus senegalensis;*
Tadjoura francolin, *Francolinus ochropectus;*
Swierstra's francolin, *Francolinus swierstrai;*
White-headed rock fowl, *Picacarthes gymnocephalus;*
Grey-headed rock fowl, *Picacarthes oreas* (it is highly regrettable that demands for specimens by museums and zoos have put these two most interesting West African birds on the danger list!)

Map 11: Africa (southern part)

1. Kruger National Park
2. Kalahari Gemsbok National Park
3. Addo Elephant National Park
4. Mountain Zebra National Park
5. Golden Gate Highlands National Park
6. Bontebok National Park
7. Tsitsikama Forest Coastal National Park
8. Aughrabies Falls National Park
9. Cape of Good Hope Nature Reserve
10. Goukama Nature Reserve
11. Umfolozi Game Reserve
12. Hluhluwe Game Reserve
13. St. Lucia Game Reserve
14. Mkuzi Game Reserve
15. Giant's Castle Game Reserve
16. St. Lucia Park
17. Ndumu Game Reserve
18. Royal Natal National Park
19. False Bay Park
20. Kamberg Nature Reserve
21. Loteni Nature Reserve
22. Oribi Gorge Nature Reserve
23. Coleford Nature Reserve
24. Umlalazi Nature Reserve
25. Willem Pretorius Game Reserve
26. Loskop Dam Nature Reserve
27. Hans Merensky Nature Reserve
28. Barberspan Nature Reserve
29. Percy Fyfe Nature Reserve
30. Etosha Game Park
31. Milwane Game Sanctuary
32. Wankie National Park
33. Victoria Falls National Park
34. Rhodes Matopos National Park
35. Rhodes Inyanga National Park
36. Mushandike National Park
37. Chimanimani National Park
38. Ngesi National Park
39. Robert McIlwaine National Park
40. Sebakwe National Park
41. Zimbabwe National Park
42. Chewore Game Reserve
43. Matusadona Game Reserve
44. Chizarira Game Reserve
45. Mana Pools Game Reserve
46. Quiçama National Park
47. Iôna National Park
48. Cangandala Nature Reserve
49. Luando Nature Reserve
50. Gorongoza National Park
51. Kafue National Park
52. Luangwa Valley Game Reserve
53. Mweru Marsh Game Reserve
54. Sumbu Game Reserve
55. Lunga Game Reserve
56. Lusenga Game Reserve
57. Kasanka Game Reserve
58. Malawi National Park
59. Serengeti National Park
60. Ruaha National Park
61. Mikumi National Park
62. Lake Manyara National Park
63. Ngurdoto Crater and Momella Lakes National Park
64. Ngorongoro Crater Conservation Area
65. Tarangire Game Reserve
66. Gombe Stream Game Reserve
67. Biharamulo Game Reserve
68. Kilimanjaro Game Reserve
69. Mkomazi Game Reserve
70. Tsavo National Park
71. Meru National Park
72. Aberdare National Park
73. Mount Kenya National Park
74. Nairobi National Park
75. Nakuru National Park
76. Mount Elgon National Park
77. Amboseli Game Reserve
78. Masai Mara Game Reserve
79. Samburu Uaso Nyiro Game Reserve
80. Marsabit National Reserve
81. Shimba Hills Forest Reserve
82. South West Mau Nature Reserve
83. Murchison Falls National Park
84. Queen Elizabeth National Park
85. Kidepo National Park
86. Toro Game Reserve
87. Kigezi Game Reserve
88. Aswa Lolim Game Reserve
89. Lomunga Game Reserve
90. Kigezi Gorilla Sanctuary
91. Mount Kei White Rhino Sanctuary
92. Mount Otze White Rhino Sanctuary
93. Kagera National Park
94. Albert National Park, Rwanda Sector
95. Upemba National Park
96. Albert National Park, Congo Sector
97. Garamba National Park

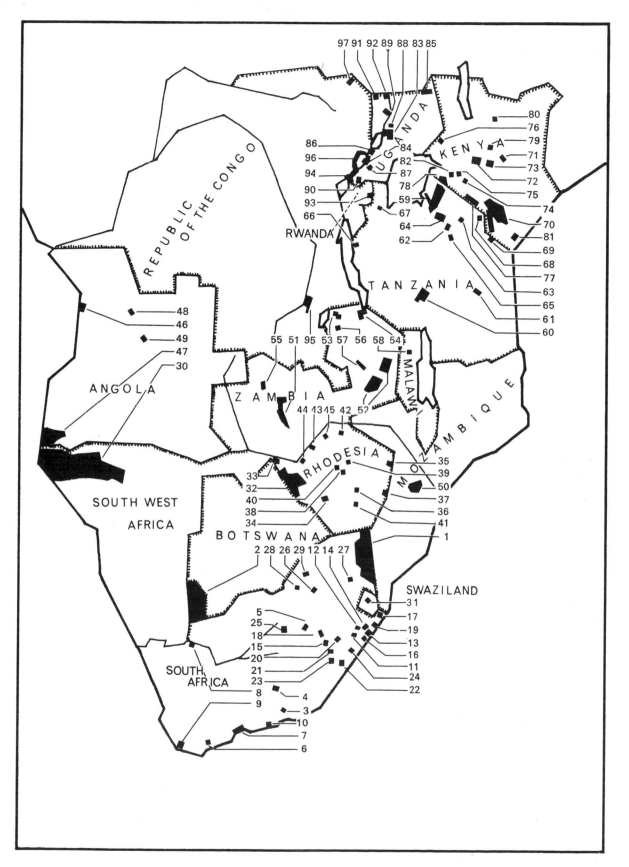

173

African National Parks and Wildlife Reserves

South Africa

Kruger National Park, 7,016 sq. m. Eastern Transvaal. Bushveld and savannah. Very good place to see greater kudu, nyala, sable antelope, roan, tsesseby. Many other antelopes, also giraffe, buffalo, zebra, hippo, lion, leopard, cheetah, hunting dog, elephant. White rhino have been · re-introduced. Bird life very rich.

Kalahari Gemsbok National Park, 3,456 sq. m. North Western Cape Province. Semi-desert, with red sand dunes and dry river beds. Springbok, gemsbok (South African oryx), red hartebeest, eland, lion. Colonies of sociable weavers. An adjoining area of Botswana, 3,705 sq. m., was declared a game reserve in 1940.

Addo Elephant National Park, 24·7 sq. m. Approximately 40 elephants, fenced in. Buffalo, various antelopes. Black rhino and hippo (introduced).

Mountain Zebra National Park, 19·3 sq. m. Mountain area near Craddock. Created for the protection of the Cape mountain zebra. Also black wildebeest, blesbok.

Golden Gate Highlands National Park, 15·4 sq. m. Blesbok, black wildebeest, eland, red hartebeest, springbok.

Bontebok National Park, 5·3 sq. m. On the Breede River near Swellendam. Bontebok, red hartebeest, springbok, buffalo.

Tsitsikama Forest Coastal National Park, 37 sq. m. Protects part of the famous Tsitsikama Forest as well as the fauna and flora of the coast. First marine national park in South Africa.

Aughrabies Falls National Park, 17·75 sq. m. Of mainly scenic interest.

Provincial Reserves

Cape Province

Cape of Good Hope Nature Reserve, 25·8 sq. m. Cape Peninsula. Of great botanical interest. Zebra, red hartebeest, eland, bontebok.

Goukama Nature Reserve, 6·3 sq. m. Coastal area.

Natal

Umfolozi Game Reserve, 185 sq. m. Acacia country, between the White and Black Umfolozi Rivers. Thriving population of white rhino. Also black rhino, greater kudu, waterbuck, reedbuck, warthog, lion.

Hluhluwe Game Reserve, 88 sq. m. Close to Umfolozi Reserve. Black rhino, some white rhino. Nyala, impala, waterbuck, greater kudu, blue wildebeest, buffalo, giraffe, Burchell's zebra, cheetah (introduced).

St. Lucia Game Reserve, 141 sq. m. Coastal forest, lagoons. Hippo, crocodile. Of great ornithological interest.

Mkuzi Game Reserve, 95 sq. m. Black rhino, white rhino (introduced), zebra, greater kudu, impala, leopard.

Giant's Castle Game Reserve, 92 sq. m. Drakensberg. Grassland with eland, oribi, reedbuck, leopard.

St. Lucia Park, 47·8 sq. m. Adjoining St. Lucia Game Reserve. Hippo, crocodile. Of great ornithological interest.

Ndumu Game Reserve, 38·6 sq. m. On Mozambique border. Bush, savannah. Elephant, hippo, crocodile. Bird life very rich and varied.

Royal Natal National Park and Rugged Glen Nature Reserve, 30·8 sq. m. and 2·9 sq. m. respectively. Mountain area. Some antelopes.

False Bay Park, 8·6 sq. m. Peninsula north of St. Lucia. Hippo, bush pig, nyala, bushbuck, impala, reedbuck, crocodile. Bird life very rich.

Kamberg Nature Reserve, 8·5 sq. m. Drakensberg.

Gemsbok in Kalahari Gemsbok National Park

Impala at water-hole, Mkuzi Game Reserve

Loteni Nature Reserve, 8·2 sq. m. Drakensberg.
Oribi Gorge Nature Reserve, 6·8 sq. m. Forested gorge. Oribi, two species of duiker, leopard.
Coleford Nature Reserve, 4·8 sq. m. Grassland.
Umlalazi Nature Reserve, 3·4 sq. m. Lagoon and coastal forest. Crocodile.

Orange Free State

Willem Pretorius Game Reserve, 34·7 sq. m. Artificial lake. High veld vegetation. Black wildebeest, blesbok, eland, springbok, white rhino (introduced).

Transvaal

Loskop Dam Nature Reserve, 47·8 sq. m. Alluvial plains, hills and mountains. White rhino (introduced), sable antelope, greater kudu, blue wildebeest, impala, eland, zebra, giraffe.
Hans Merensky Nature Reserve, 15·8 sq. m. Hilly area with acacia and combretum trees. Sable antelope, tsesseby. waterbuck, eland, giraffe, leopard.
Barberspan Nature Reserve, 13·8 sq. m. Of great ornithological interest. Greater and lesser flamingo, spoonbill, goliath heron.
Percy Fyfe Nature Reserve, 9·5 sq. m. Blesbok, greater kudu, impala, black wildebeest.

There are several smaller Provincial Reserves, a number of Municipal Reserves, and 67 Forest Nature Reserves. Seals and penguins are protected on 33 State Guano islands.

South West Africa

Etosha Game Park, 25,090 sq. m. Extending from coastal Namib Desert to bush, grassland, and mopane forest of interior. Elephant, black rhino, Hartmann's mountain zebra giraffe, eland, impala, greater kudu, red hartebeest, blue wildebeest, gemsbok, lion.

Swaziland

Milwane Game Sanctuary, 1·8 sq. m. To be enlarged in near future. Situated on Mount Nyongane. White rhino (introduced), giraffe, impala, waterbuck, greater kudu, black wildebeest, zebra.

Rhodesia

Wankie National Park, 5,540 sq. m. Mopane forest, Kalahari sand vegetation. Elephant, black rhino (reintroduced), white rhino (reintroduced), Burchell's zebra, hippo, giraffe, buffalo, eland, greater kudu, sable antelope, roan, tsesseby, impala, waterbuck, a few gemsbok near Botswana border. Lion, leopard, cheetah, hunting dog.
Victoria Falls National Park, 229 sq m. On Zambesi River. Kalahari sand vegetation. Elephant, hippo, buffalo, sable antelope, roan, greater kudu, waterbuck, lion, leopard, crocodile. Of great ornithological interest.
Rhodes Matopos National Park, 167 sq. m. Interest mainly scenic and archaeological (Bushman paintings). Game park with white and black rhino, various antelopes.

Elephants and giraffe in Wankie National Park

Rhodes Inyanga National Park, 133·6 sq. m. Plateau near Mozambique border. Greater kudu, waterbuck, bushbuck, klipspringer, reedbuck, leopard.

Mushandike National Park, 49·7 sq. m. Artificial lake. Sable antelope, greater kudu and other ungulates. Of great ornithological interest.

Chimanimani National Park, 31·5 sq. m. Chimanimani Mountains on Mozambique border. Eland, sable antelope, greater kudu, klipspringer, leopard.

Ngesi National Park, 22·4 sq. m. Ngesi Dam. Antelopes. Of ornithological interest. Breeding site of dwarf goose.

Robert McIlwaine National Park, 22·1 sq. m. Lake near Salisbury. Fenced-in game park. Of ornithological interest.

Sebakwe National Park, 10·2 sq. m. Hills covered with brachystegia forest. Greater kudu, impala, zebra, leopard.

Zimbabwe National Park, 2·8 sq. m. Of mainly archaeological interest. Some game.

In addition to the National Parks there are six Game Reserves. **Chewore, Matusadona, Chizarira** and **Mana Pools** give shelter to black rhino. The **Kyle Game Reserve,** 15·6 sq. m., on Kyle Lake, has white rhino, introduced from South Africa, also many antelopes, partly indigenous, partly introduced.

Angola

Quiçama National Park, 3,844 sq. m. Near coast, south of São Paulo de Luanda. Elephant, hippo, roan, eland, leopard.

Iôna National Park, 1,045 sq. m. In the south western corner of the country, near mouth of Cunene River. Elephant, black rhino, gemsbok, Hartmann's mountain zebra, Burchell's zebra, leopard.

Cangandala and Luando Nature Reserves, 231 and 3,196 sq. m. respectively, serve as refuges for the giant sable antelope.

Mozambique

Gorongoza National Park, 2,134 sq. m. Savannah, gallery forests, swamps. Elephant, black rhino, hippo, buffalo, blue wildebeest, waterbuck, impala, sable antelope, lion. An abandoned camp has been 'taken over' by lions and forms a great attraction of this park.

There are several partial and special reserves, for instance a buffalo reserve of 579 sq. m. and an elephant reserve of 289 sq. m.

Zambia

Kafue National Park, 8,492 sq. m. On the Kafue River. Elephant, black rhino, Burchell's zebra, hippo, buffalo, sable antelope, roan, greater kudu, red lechwe, situtunga, eland, impala, lion, leopard. Of great ornithological interest.

Luangwa Valley Game Reserve. This reserve is split into two areas of 1,776 and 3,204 sq. m. respectively. It is the main Zambian stronghold of the black rhino; also elephant, Burchell's zebra, hippo, giraffe, greater kudu, eland, buffalo, lion, leopard, crocodile.

Mweru Marsh Game Reserve, 1,196 sq. m. Near Lake Mweru. Elephant, some black rhino, Burchell's zebra, hippo, sable antelope, eland, roan, puku, situtunga, buffalo, lion.

Sumbu Game Reserve, 772 sq. m. At southern end of Lake Tanganyika. Elephant, hippo, sable antelope, eland, puku.

Lunga Game Reserve, 637 sq. m. Elephant, hippo, Burchell's zebra, sable antelope, roan, puku, buffalo, lion, cheetah.

Red lechwe on the Kafue Flats

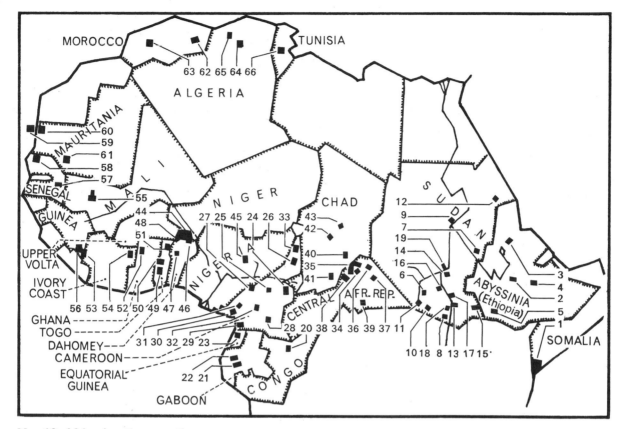

Map 12: Africa (northern part)

 1. Bubasci Reserve
 2. Menagasha National Park
 3. Simien Reserve
 4. Awash National Park
 5. Maji or Omo Reserve
 6. Southern National Park
 7. Dinder National Park
 8. Nimule National Park
 9. Sabaloka Game Reserve
10. Mbari-Zunga Game Reserve
11. Bire Kpatuos Game Reserve
12. Tokar Game Reserve
13. Mongalla Game Reserve
14. Zeraf Game Reserve
15. Boma Game Reserve
16. Shambe Game Reserve
17. Badigeru Game Reserve
18. Juba Game Reserve
19. Fanyikang Game Reserve
20. Odzala National Park
21. Ofoué Reserve
22. Okanda National Park
23. Mount Raices Park
24. Boubandijidah National Park
25. Benoué National Park
26. Waza National Park
27. Faro Forest Reserve
28. Dja Faunal Reserve
29. Campo Faunal Reserve
30. Douala Faunal Reserve
31. Edea Faunal Reserve
32. Bafia Faunal Reserve
33. Kala-Maloué Faunal Reserve

34. Vassako-Bolo Nature Reserve
35. Bamingui-Bangoran National Park
36. Saint Floris National Park
37. André Félix National Park
38. Gribingui-Bamingui Faunal Reserve
39. Nana Barya Faunal Reserve
40. Zakouma National Park
41. Manda National Park
42. Siniaka-Minia Game Reserve
43. Abou Telfane Partial Reserve
44. W-du-Niger National Park (Niger)
45. Yankari Game Reserve
46. W-du-Niger National Park (Dahomey)
47. Pendjari Bend National Park
48. W-du-Niger National Park (Upper Volta)
49. Koué Total Faunal Reserve
50. Kamassi Game Reserve
51. Keran Game Reserve
52. Mole Game Reserve
53. Mount Nimba Total Reserve
54. Bouna Total Reserve
55. Baoulé National Park
56. Mt. Nimba Total Nature Reserve
57. Niokolo Koba National Park
58. Djovol Total Reserve
59. Mauretanian Islands Total Reserve
60. Lévrier Bay Total Faunal Reserve
61. El Agher Partial Faunal Reserve
62. Tazekka National Park
63. Toubkal National Park
64. Chréa National Park
65. Ouarsenis National Park
66. Bou-Hedma Park

Lusenga Game Reserve, 308 sq. m. Elephant, Burchell's zebra, sable antelope, roan, eland, buffalo.

Kasanka Game Reserve, 146 sq. m. Grassland, marsh, forest. Elephant, hippo, sable antelope, roan, puku, buffalo, lion. Some whaleheaded storks.

The Zambian Government has recently bought Farm Lochinvar on the Kafue Flats, the main stronghold of the red lechwe, and it is hoped that it will be turned into a Lechwe National Park. The area is also of great ornithological interest.

Malawi

Malawi National Park, 325 sq. m. Nyika Plateau. Burchell's zebra, eland, sable antelope, roan, Lichtenstein's hartebeest, buffalo, lion.

There are several game reserves:

Kasungu, 772 sq. m.
Nkhota-Kota, 656 sq. m.
Majete, 69·5 sq. m.
Mwabvi, 57·9 sq. m.
Lengwe Game Reserve, 48·2 sq. m., of special interest as a haunt of the beautiful nyala antelope.

Tanzania

All National Parks and Game Reserves are in Tanganyika, the mainland part of the Republic.

Serengeti National Park, approx. 5,600 sq. m. Grassland, savannah. Elephant, black rhino, Burchell's zebra, giraffe, white-bearded wildebeest, topi, Coke's hartebeest, a few roan, impala, Thomson's and Grant's gazelle, waterbuck, buffalo, lion, cheetah. The vicinity of Seronera Lodge is

perhaps the best place in all Africa to see leopard. Hunting dogs, spotted hyaena. Patas monkey can be met with in the savannah near Banagi.

Ruaha National Park, 5,000 sq. m. On the Great Ruaha River. Savannah woodland, rocky ridges, depressions flooded during the rains. Elephant, black rhino, Burchell's zebra, hippo, giraffe, Lichtenstein's hartebeest, waterbuck, sable antelope, roan, greater kudu, lesser kudu, eland, buffalo, lion, leopard, cheetah.

Mikumi National Park, 450 sq. m. Brachystegia savannah, wooded hills. Elephant, black rhino, giraffe, wildebeest, waterbuck, sable antelope, greater kudu, lion, leopard, cheetah.

Lake Manyara National Park, 123 sq. m. of which approximately 80 sq. m. are lake. At the foot of the western escarpment of Great Rift Valley. Elephant, black rhino, Burchell's zebra, hippo, giraffe, Coke's hartebeest, white-bearded wildebeest, waterbuck, impala, buffalo, lion (often in trees!), leopard. Of great ornithological interest: flamingoes, white and pink-backed pelicans, saddle-billed stork, goliath heron.

Ngurdoto Crater and Momela Lakes National Park, 20 sq. m. At foot of Mount Meru. Elephant, black rhino, Burchell's zebra, hippo, giant forest hog, giraffe, impala, bushbuck, waterbuck, buffalo, leopard. Ngurdoto Crater is an excellent place to watch the guereza colobus monkey. The Momela Lakes are of great ornithological interest.

Ngorongoro Crater Conservation Area, 3,000 sq. m., about three quarters of which are effectively protected. Elephant, black rhino, Burchell's zebra, hippo, giant forest hog, giraffe, Coke's hartebeest, white-bearded wildebeest, waterbuck (common and defassa), Thomson's and Grant's gazelle, bushbuck, eland, buffalo, lion, leopard,

Wildebeest herd in Serengeti National Park

C. A. W. Guggisberg/Bruce Coleman Ltd

C. A. W. Guggisberg/Bruce Coleman Ltd

Gerenuk in Tsavo National Park

Courting lions in Nairobi National Park

serval, cheetah, spotted hyaena, golden jackal. Ngorongoro Crater is of great ornithological interest.

Tarangire Game Reserve, 525 sq. m. Acacia bush. Elephant, black rhino, fringe-eared oryx, lesser kudu, eland, impala, white-bearded wildebeest, waterbuck.

Gombe Stream Game Reserve, 61 sq. m. North-eastern shore of Lake Tanganyika. Chimpanzee, red colobus.

Further Game Reserves:

Biharamulo, sable antelope, Lichtenstein's hartebeest;
Kilimanjaro, 720 sq. m. interesting high altitude vegetation. Elephant, black rhino, eland, Abbot's duiker, buffalo, leopard, guereza colobus; . . . . . .
Mkomazi, black rhino, lesser kudu, gerenuk, fringe-eared oryx.

Kenya

Tsavo National Park, 8·034 sq. m. Thornbush, bushy savannah, acacia woodlands. Elephant, black rhino, hippo, Burchell's zebra, Grevy zebra (introduced), Masai giraffe, Coke's hartebeest, Hunter's hartebeest (introduced), white-bearded wildebeest, eland, gerenuk, Grant's gazelle, fringe-eared oryx, lesser kudu, waterbuck, klipspringer, lion, leopard.

Meru National Park, 700 sq. m. North-east of Mount Kenya. Bush, savannah. Elephant, black rhino, white rhino (introduced), Burchell's zebra, Grevy zebra, hippo, reticulated giraffe, Coke's hartebeest, waterbuck, impala, Grant's and Thomson's gazelle, gerenuk, beisa oryx, lesser kudu, eland, buffalo, lion, leopard, cheetah.

Aberdare National Park, 228 sq. m. Aberdare Range. Forest, high altitude moorlands. Elephant, black rhino, giant forest hog, bush pig, waterbuck, bongo, bushbuck, eland, lion, leopard, serval, guereza colobus. Of great ornithological interest. Contains the famous 'Treetops Hotel'.

Mount Kenya National Park, 227 sq. m. Part of forest zone, bamboo forest, high altitude moorlands, snow peaks. Elephant, black rhino, giant forest hog, bongo, bushbuck, buffalo, leopard, serval, guereza colobus. Ornithologically very interesting: green ibis, lammergeyer, Mackinder's eagle owl.

Nairobi National Park, 44 sq. m. adjoining a reserve which offers possibilities of extension. Grassland, whistling thorn, highland forest. A park probably unique in the whole world, swarming with game and situated only four miles from the centre of Kenya's capital. Black rhino, Burchell's zebra, hippo, warthog, Masai giraffe, Coke's hartebeest, white-bearded wildebeest, steinbok, waterbuck (common and defassa), Bohor reedbuck. Chanler's reedbuck, impala, Thomson's and Grant's gazelle, bushbuck, eland, buffalo (reintroduced), lion, leopard, cheetah, crocodile. The various artificial lakes attract many water birds. The park is fenced on the Nairobi side, but open towards the south.

Nakuru National Park, 24 sq. m. Mainly a bird sanctuary. Around 370 species have been recorded. Greater and lesser flamingo, white- and pink-backed pelican, stilt, avocet. Visited by numerous migrants.

Mount Elgon National Park. Most recent Kenya National Park, gazetted 1968. Elephant, buffalo, several species of duiker, colobus, lammergeyer.

179

Amboseli Game Reserve, 1,259 sq. m. At foot of Kilimanjaro. Thorn bush, acacia woodlands, grassland, swamps. Elephant, black rhino, Burchell's zebra, hippo, Masai giraffe, Coke's hartebeest, white-bearded wildebeest, waterbuck, impala, Thomson's and Grant's gazelle, gerenuk, fringe-eared oryx, lesser kudu, buffalo, lion, leopard, cheetah. This wonderful game reserve is still used as pastureland by the Masai herdsmen. At the time of writing, there are hopes of giving total protection to 200 sq. m.

Masai Mara Game Reserve, 700 sq. m., of which 200 sq. m. are closed to the Masai pastoralists. Elephant, black rhino, Burchell's zebra, hippo, Masai giraffe, topi, Coke's hartebeest, white-bearded wildebeest, waterbuck, Thomson's and Grant's gazelle, roan, eland, buffalo, lion, leopard, cheetah.

Samburu Uaso Nyiro Game Reserve, 40 sq. m. and **Isiolo**

Buffalo Springs Reserve, 75 sq. m. On both sides of Uaso Nyiro River. Dry bush and savannah. Elephant, black rhino, Grevy's zebra, Burchell's zebra, hippo, reticulated giraffe, waterbuck, impala, Grant's gazelle, gerenuk, beisa oryx, lesser kudu, buffalo, lion, leopard, cheetah. Of great ornithological interest. Big flocks of vulturine guinea fowl, pygmy falcon, blue-necked ostrich.

Marsabit National Reserve, 800 sq. m. Mount Marsabit, covered with cloud forest, surrounded by semi-desert. Several craters. 'Lake Paradise'. Elephant, black rhino, Grevy's zebra, reticulated giraffe, Grant's gazelle, gerenuk, beisa oryx, greater kudu, buffalo, lion, leopard.

Shimba Hills Forest Reserve. Hilly country near Mombasa. Sable antelope, elephant.

South West Mau Nature Reserve, 164 sq. m. Forest area. Elephant, giant forest hog, bongo, yellow-backed duiker, buffalo, leopard, golden cat.

Assortment of game in Nairobi National Park

New-born zebra struggling to its feet—Amboseli Reserve

An old buffalo bull—Amboseli Reserve

Uganda

Murchison Falls National Park, 1,557 sq. m. Part of Victoria Nile. Riveraine forest, undulating grasslands, forest patches, swamps. Elephant, black rhino, white rhino (introduced from west bank of Albert Nile), hippo, Rothschild's giraffe, lelwel hartebeest, oribi, kob, waterbuck, Bohor reedbuck, lion, leopard, colobus, chimpanzee, crocodile, monitor lizard. Of great ornithological interest. Whale-headed stork, goliath heron, open-billed stork, skimmer.
Queen Elizabeth National Park, 767 sq. m. Between Lakes Edward and George. Grassland, savannah, dense forest, swamp. Elephant, hippo, giant forest hog, topi, kob, waterbuck, buffalo, lion, leopard, chimpanzee, red and black-and-white colobus. Of great ornithological interest.
Kidepo National Park, 486 sq. m. On Uganda-Sudan border. Dry savannah, acacia country. Elephant, black rhino, Burchell's zebra, Rothschild's giraffe, lelwel hartebeest, oribi, waterbuck, Bohor and Chanler's reedbuck, Bright's gazelle, roan, lesser kudu, eland, buffalo, lion, leopard, cheetah, patas monkey.
Toro Game Reserve, 202 sq. m. Semliki Valley. Elephant, hippo, giant forest hog, kob, lelwel hartebeest, waterbuck, buffalo, lion, leopard.
Kigezi Game Reserve, 200 sq. m. Adjoining southern part of Queen Elizabeth Park. Elephant, hippo, kob, topi, giant forest hog.
Aswa Lolim Game Reserve, 40 sq. m. North of Murchison Falls Park. Savannah. Elephant, kob, buffalo.
Lomunga Game Reserve, 35 sq. m. West of Albert Nile. White rhino. Also elephant, lelwel hartebeest, kob, lion, leopard.

Crocodile—Murchison Falls National Park

There are several other small reserves, and 12 game sanctuaries, of which the most important are:

Kigezi Gorilla Sanctuary, 17 sq. m. Mounts Muhavura and Mgahinga. Forest, bamboo forest. Mountain gorillas occasionally come over from the Albert Park. Elephant, buffalo, giant forest hog, colobus, Kandt's golden monkey.
Mount Kei White Rhino Sanctuary, 170 sq. m. and **Mount Otze White Rhino Sanctuary,** 80 sq. m. —Both situated to the west of the Albert Nile, close to the Sudan border. They have in the past suffered very badly from the inroads of poachers.

Somalia

Bubasci Reserve, 2,412 sq. m. An area of acacia bush in the southernmost part of the country. Elephant, black rhino, Hunter's hartebeest, lesser kudu, beisa oryx, buffalo, lion, leopard.
There are several partial reserves, of which one, situated on the Abyssinian border, is said to harbour some black rhino.

Abyssinia (Ethiopia)

Menagasha National Park, 11·5 sq. m. On the slopes of Mount Nochoda. Extinct volcano. Colobus, various antelopes (Arusi bushbuck), leopard. Bird life very rich and varied.
Awash National Park, over 385 sq. m. In the Abyssinian part of the Great Rift Valley. Beisa oryx, Soemmering's gazelle, greater and lesser kudu.

There are in addition, several reserves:

Simien Reserve, over 385 sq. m. of mountain country in Simien. Walia ibex.

Maji or **Omo Reserve,** 617 sq. m. Near north end of Lake Rudolf. Lesser kudu, beisa oryx, eland, lelwel hartebeest, lion.

Sudan

Southern National Park, 6,176 sq. m. Bush, gallery forests. Elephant, white rhino, eland, lelwel hartebeest, roan. This park is unfortunately situated in a politically disturbed area and is sure to have suffered badly.

Dinder National Park, 2,509 sq. m. On the Dinder River. Bush and savannah. Giraffe, tora hartebeest, tiang, roan, oribi, waterbuck, greater kudu, several species of gazelle, buffalo, lion, leopard.

Nimule National Park, 96·5 sq. m. Plateau west of Albert Nile, close to Uganda border. Elephant, white rhino, hippo, lelwel hartebeest, waterbuck, buffalo.

Sabaloka Game Reserve. 444 sq. m. Hilly country on left bank of the Nile, north of Khartoum. Barbary sheep, Nubian ibex.

Mbari-Zunga Game Reserve, 58 sq. m. On Congo-Nile watershed. Gallery forests. Giant forest hog, bongo, chimpanzee.

Bire Kpatuos Game Reserve, approximately 48 sq. m. On Congo-Nile watershed. Dense forest. Bongo. In a politically disturbed area.

Tokar Game Reserve, 48 sq. m. Red Sea Hills. Nubian ibex; also Soemmering's gazelle, roan, leopard.

Rahad Game Reserve, 48 sq. m. Close to Dinder National Park. Same fauna.

Mongalla Game Reserve, 29 sq. m. Along Nile. Riveraine plain, sparsely set with trees. Said to harbour some black rhino. Elephant, giraffe, roan, buffalo.

Zeraf Game Reserve, 2,600 sq. m. Between Bahr-el-Jebel and Bahr-el-Zeraf. Created for the protection of Nile lechwe.

Boma Game Reserve, 521 sq. m. Mountain area and high plateau near Abyssinian border. Said to be very good game country.

Shambe Game Reserve, 386 sq. m. Marshes. White rhino, Nile lechwe, giraffe. Also elephant and buffalo.

Badigeru Game Reserve, 193 sq. m. Marshes and dry savannah. Black rhino.

Juba Game Reserve, 115 sq. m. On Nile. White rhino.

Fanyikang Game Reserve, 50 sq. m. Island in Nile, east of Lake No. Nile lechwe, situtunga.

Rwanda

Kagera National Park, 968 sq. m. Hilly savannah. Hippo, various antelopes, Burchell's zebra, lion, leopard. Black rhino (reintroduced).

Albert National Park, Rwanda Sector, 88 sq. m. Virunga Volcanoes. Mountain gorilla, chimpanzee, Kandt's golden monkey.

Congo

Upemba National Park, 3,667 sq. m. Katanga. Savannah, light forest, marshes. Elephant, hippo, Burchell s zebra, sable antelope, roan waterbuck, Lichtenstein's hartebeest, buffalo. Of great ornithological interest. Has suffered badly owing to political troubles.

Albert National Park, 3,088 sq. m. Virunga Volcanoes, Rwindi Plain, Semliki Valley, Ruwenzori. Elephant, hippo, giant forest hog, topi, kob, waterbuck, okapi, lion, leopard, mountain gorilla. Of great ornithological interest.

A young greater kudu bull—Marsabit National Reserve

Hippopotamus in Queen Elizabeth National Park

C. A. W. Guggisberg/Bruce Coleman Ltd.

183

Garamba National Park, 1,899 sq. m. On Congo-Sudan border. Elephant, white rhino, hippo, giraffe, lelwel hartebeest, lion, leopard. Has suffered badly owing to political troubles.

Congo (former Middle Congo, capital Brazzaville)

Odzala National Park, 425 sq. m. Equatorial rain forest, uninhabited, except for some pygmy groups. Elephant, bongo, dwarf buffalo, gorilla.

Gaboon

Ofoué Reserve, 579 sq. m. Rain forest on Ofoué River. Forest fauna.
Okanda National Park, 733 sq. m. Forest area north of Ofoué.

Equatorial Guinea

Mount Raices Park, 100 sq. m. Equatorial forest. Gorilla, chimpanzee, buffalo.
Pico de Santa Isabel Total Reserve, 20–40 sq. m.
Rio Ekuku Game Reserve, 29 sq. m. Situtunga.
Mount Alen Partial Reserve, 366 sq. m. Gorilla.

Cameroon

Boubandijidah National Park, 850 sq. m. Savannah. Elephant, black rhino, hippo, giant eland, korrigum, lelwel hartebeest, roan, waterbuck, buffalo, lion, leopard, cheetah, crocodile.
Benoué National Park, 694 sq. m. In the valley of the Benue River. Savannah, gallery forests. Elephant, black rhino, hippo, giraffe, giant eland, waterbuck, kob, korrigum, lelwel hartebeest, lion, leopard, cheetah.
Waza National Park, 656 sq. m. In the Lake Chad depression. Forest, grassland, flooded during the rains. Elephant, giraffe, roan, kob, korrigum, gazelles, lion, leopard, cheetah. Of great ornithological interest.
Faro Forest Reserve, 1,274 sq. m. Not yet adequately guarded. Elephant, black rhino, hippo, various antelopes, buffalo, lion.
There are six faunal reserves (Dja, Campo, Douala, Edea, Bafia, Nango-Eboko, Kala-Maloué), hippo reserves on the Sanaga and Faro Rivers, and a bird sanctuary on Lakes Ossa and Mevia.
In Western Cameroon there is the Kimbe River Game Reserve, 19 sq. m. and the Mbi Crater Game Reserve, 1·4 sq. m.

Central African Republic

Vassako-Bolo Nature Reserve, 580 sq. m. Savannah, gallery forests. Elephant, hippo, some black rhino, giant eland, roan, lelwel hartebeest, lion, leopard.
Bamingui-Bangoran National Park, 3,860 sq. m. Savannah, plains, flooded during the rains. Same fauna as Vassako-Bolo. Some black rhino, also kob, waterbuck, giant eland.

Giraffe and calf

Roan antelope

Saint Floris National Park, 388 sq. m. Upper basin of the River Shari. Savannah, plains flooded during the rains. Elephant, giraffe, various antelopes, buffalo, lion, leopard, cheetah. Of great ornithological interest.

André Félix National Park, 656 sq. m. Upper basin of the River Shari. Same fauna as Saint Floris.
There are a number of not very well protected faunal reserves, of which **Gribingui-Bamingui,** 1,930 sq. m. is the largest and **Nana Barya,** 850 sq. m. the best guarded. The latter harbours black rhino and giant eland.

Chad

Zakouma National Park, 1,146 sq. m. Savannah plains flooded during the rains. Elephant, some black rhino, roan, korrigum, lelwel hartebeest, kob, a few greater kudu, lion, leopard, cheetah.
Manda National Park, 424 sq. m. On upper Shari. Bushy savannah. Elephant, hippo, giant eland, roan, korrigum, lelwel hartebeest, kob, buffalo, lion, leopard.
Siniaka-Minia Game Reserve, 1,644 sq. m. Black rhino, greater kudu.
Abou Telfane Partial Reserve, 424 sq. m. Greater kudu.

Niger

W-du-Niger National Park, 1,158 sq. m. Savannah gallery forest. The name of the park is derived from a double bend of the River Niger.

Nigeria

Yankari Game Reserve, 720 sq. m. Savannah. Elephant, hippo, giraffe, roan, waterbuck, lion, leopard, crocodile.

There are several other reserves, of these:

Borgu, 1,400 sq. m. is inadequately guarded.
Natural Forest Inviolate Plot seems still to be in the planning stage.

Dahomey

W-du-Niger National Park, 1,938 sq. m., adjoining Niger park of same name. Elephant, hippo, roan, western hartebeest, kob, lion, cheetah, crocodile.
Pendjari Bend National Park, 1,061 sq. m. Savannah. Elephant, hippo, various antelopes, lion, leopard. Of ornithological interest.

Upper Volta

W-du-Niger National Park, 1,273 sq. m. Adjoining the Niger and Dahomey parks of the same name. Elephant, hippo, roan, kob, korrigum, western hartebeest, lion, cheetah.
Three faunal reserves:
Singou, 741 sq. m.
Arly, 293 sq. m.
Bontioli, 49 sq. m.

Togo

Koué Total Faunal Reserve, 154 sq. m. Forest, savannah. Hippo, bongo, roan, situtunga, lion, leopard, gorilla.
Kamassi Game Reserve, 65·6 sq. m. Adjoining the above. Gorilla.
Keran Game Reserve, 25·8 sq. m. Savannah, gallery forests. Roan, kob, waterbuck, buffalo.
Two more reserves are being developed.

Ghana

Mole Game Reserve, 868 sq. m. Hills, savannah country, near Ghana-Ivory Coast border. Elephant, roan, waterbuck, bushbuck, kob, lion, leopard, cheetah, crocodile.
Several game sanctuaries which are not yet sufficiently guarded.

Ivory Coast

Mount Nimba Total Reserve, 19·3 sq. m. Forested mountain area. Chimpanzee.
Bouna Total Reserve, 3,475 sq. m. Savannah. Elephant, hippo, roan, western hartebeest, kob, buffalo, lion, leopard.

Mali

Baoulé National Park, 1,351 sq. m. Sudanese savannah, gallery forests. Elephant, giant eland, korrigum, western hartebeest, roan, gazelles, buffalo, giraffe, lion.
Several faunal reserves.

Liberia

Three National Parks are projected and mapped.

Guinea

Mount Nimba Total Nature Reserve, 50 sq. m. Adjoining Mount Nimba Reserve of Ivory Coast. Chimpanzee, dwarf buffalo.

Senegal

Niokolo Koba National Park, 1,582 sq. m. On the upper Gambia. Savannah. Elephant, hippo, giant eland, roan, kob, waterbuck, western hartebeest, oribi, lion, leopard, crocodile.
Djovol Total Reserve, 7·4 acres. Marshy area of great ornithological interest.

Mauretania

Mauretanian Islands Total Reserve, 38·6 sq. m. A number of small islands of great ornithological interest. Flamingoes, big breeding colonies of cormorants, terns, gulls, spoonbills, egrets, herons.
Lévrier Bay Total Faunal Reserve, 1,196 sq. m., Coast opposite Mauretanian Islands.
El Agher Partial Faunal Reserve. Fairly good game country; approximately 40 elephants.

Morocco

Tazekka National Park, 2·2 sq. m. Cedar forest. Poor fauna. Wild boar, leopard said to occur occasionally.
Toubkal National Park, 139 sq. m. Uninhabited, but used for pasturing livestock. Barbary sheep and mountain gazelle now rare. Leopard has disappeared.

A number of faunal reserves, especially bird sanctuaries.

Algeria

Chréa National Park, 5·2 sq. m. Pic Sidi Abd el Kader. Wild boar, jackal.
Ouarsenis National Park, 4 sq. m. Ouarsenis Mountains. Hyaena, jackal, lynx.
There are 11 further reserves. It is gratifying to learn that the Algerian Government has recently put a ban on the hunting of Barbary stags, Barbary sheep, gazelles, scimitar-horned oryx, and addax. If the ban can be implemented, these species, now exceedingly rare in Algeria, may have a chance of recovery.

Tunisia

Bou-Hedma Park, 40 sq. m. Acacia country. Dorcas gazelle, Barbary sheep, interesting birds.

Projected:

Ghardimaou Park, for the protection of the Barbary stag.

Banded duiker, *Cephalophus zebra*—endangered

Barbary sheep

Indian Ocean Islands

Madagascar

Madagascar, is usually regarded as some kind of an appendage of the African Continent, but the huge island is really a world of its own, its fauna differing greatly from that of Mozambique, only 250 miles across the sea. Like so many other islands, it has suffered badly at the hands of man. The first invaders killed off the gigantic ostriches they encountered. Civilization brought the usual measure of ruthless devastation in its wake, depriving Madagascar's unique wildlife of most of its original habitat. Losses have not been very heavy, but a considerable number of mammals and birds are seriously threatened, and great efforts will be needed if many of them are not to vanish from the face of the earth in the near future.

Map 13: Madagascar

1. Isalo National Park
2. Mount Ambre National Park
3. Tsingy du Bemaraha Total Nature Reserve
4. Ankarafantsika Total Nature Reserve
5. Andohahelo Total Nature Reserve
6. Zahamena Total Nature Reserve
7. Tsaratanana Total Nature Reserve
8. Andringitra Total Nature Reserve
9. Tsingy de Namoroka Total Nature Reserve
10. Lake Tsimanampetsotsa Total Nature Reserve
11. Betampona Total Nature Reserve
12. Lokobè Total Nature Reserve

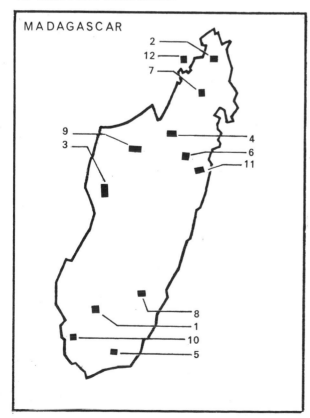

Delalande's Coucal, *Coua delalandei*—extinct

Madagascar species extinct:

Elephant bird, *Aepyornis maximus;*
Delalande's coucal, *Coua delalandei.*

Madagascar mammals and birds in danger:

Grey gentle lemur, *Hapalemur griseus;*
Broad nosed gentle lemur, *Hapalemur simus;*
Acoumba lemur, *Lemur macaco;*
Mongoose lemur, *Lemur m. mongoz;*
Weasel lemur, *Lepilemur mustelinus;*
Hairy eared dwarf lemur, *Cheirogaleus trichotis;*
Fat-tailed lemur, *Cheirogaleus medius;*
Coquerel's mouse lemur, *Microcebus coquereli;*
Fork-marked mouse lemur, *Phaner furcifer;*
Sifaka, *Propithecus verreauxi* (5 subspecies);
Indris, *Indri indri;*
Aye-aye, *Daubentonia madagascariensis;*
Malagassy civet, *fossa fossa;*
Falanouc, *Eupleves guodoti;*
Aloatra grebe, *Tachybaptus rufolavatus;*
Madagascar teal, *Anas bernieri;*
Long-tailed ground roller, *Uratelornis chimaera;*
Small-billed false sunbird, *Neodrepanis hypoxantha.*

National Parks and Wildlife Reserves of Madagascar

Isalo National Park, 314 sq. m. Of mainly historical interest.
Mount Ambre National Park, 70·2 sq. m. Ancient volcano covered with rain forest rich in epiphytes and lichens. Many crater lakes. Mouse lemur, grey gentle lemur, Acoumba lemur, mongoose lemur.

Total Nature Reserves

Tsingy du Bemaraha, 577 sq. m. Dry deciduous forest. Mouse lemur, Coquerel's mouse lemur, fat-tailed dwarf lemur, fork-marked mouse lemur, sportive lemur, Acoumba lemur, grey gentle lemur, sifaka.

Ankarafantsika, 236 sq. m. Sandy plateau with dry deciduous forest. Fauna very rich. Mouse lemur, fat-tailed dwarf lemur, sportive lemur, Acoumba lemur, mongoose lemur, woolly lemur, sifaka.
Andohahelo, 236 sq. m. Forest area. Mouse lemur, weasel lemur, ring-tailed lemur, sifaka, small-toothed mongoose.
Zahamena, 223 sq. m. Tropical cloud forest, bamboo forest. Fauna very rich. Mouse lemur, greater dwarf lemur, weasel lemur, grey gentle lemur, ruffed lemur, Acoumba lemur, woolly lemur, sifaka, indris.
Tsaratanana, 175 sq. m. Forest-covered mountain. Acoumba lemur, fossa, ring-tailed mongoose.
Andringitra, 115 sq. m. Forested mountain area, which contains the sources of many rivers. Ring-tailed lemur, sifaka.
Tsingy de Namoroka, 89·6 sq. m. Dry deciduous forest. Mouse lemur, fat-tailed dwarf lemur. Acoumba lemur, mongoose lemur, Decken's sifaka, crowned sifaka.
Lake Tsimanampetsotsa, 58·9 sq. m. Limestone plateau with dry bush. One of the most interesting reserves of Madagascar. Mouse lemur, fat-tailed dwarf lemur, fork-marked mouse lemur, sportive lemur, ring-tailed lemur, sifaka. Of great ornithological importance. Greater and lesser flamingo, many other water birds.
Betampona, 8·5 sq. m. Tropical rain forest north of Tamatave. Mouse lemur, greater dwarf lemur, woolly lemur, ruffed lemur, Acoumba lemur, grey gentle lemur, sifaka, aye-aye.
Lokobé, 2·9 sq. m. Only remaining vestige of forest on Nosy-Bé Island.
In addition to the national parks and total nature reserves mentioned above, there are 18 special reserves.

Mauritius blue pigeon, *Alectroenas nitidissima*—extinct

Mascarenes

Madagascar, being the world's fourth largest island, can almost qualify as a small continent, and its losses in terms of outright extermination have as yet been moderate. The small islands of the Indian Ocean have, on the other hand, had their wildlife savagely depleted, and none more so than the Mascarenes.

Réunion, Mauritius and Rodriguez lost the following species of birds:

Large coot, *Fulica newtoni*, known only from bones;
Van den Broeck's red rail, *Aphanapteryx bonasia*, last seen about 1675;
Flightless blue rail, *Aphanapteryx leguati*, last seen about 1730;
Flightless night heron, *Nycticorax megacephalus*, last seen about 1730;
Bourbon pink pigeon, *Columbo duboisii*, last seen about 1669;
Mauritius blue pigeon, *Alectroenas nitidissima*, last seen about 1830;
Dodo, *Raphus cucullatus*, last seen about 1681;
Réunion solitaire, *Raphus solitarius*, last seen about 1791;
Rodriguez solitaire, *Pezophaps solitaria*, extinct about 1746;
Mascarene parakeet, *Mascarinus mascarinus*, last seen about 1834;

Broad-billed parrot, *Lophopsittacus mauritianus*, last seen about 1638;
Exiled ring-necked parakeet, *Psittacula exsul*, last seen about 1872;
Bourbon parakeet, *Necropsittacus borbonicus*, last seen about 1669;
Rodriguez parakeet, *Necropsittacus rodericanus*, last seen about 1837;
Commerson's scops owl, *Otus commersoni*, last seen 1837;
Rodriguez little owl, *Athene murivora*, last seen about 1730;
Leguat's eagle owl, *Bubo leguati*, known only from bones;
Leguat's starling, *Fregilupus rodericanus*, last seen about 1832;
Bouron crested starling, *Fregilupus varius*, last seen about 1862;
Réunion fody, *Foudia bruante*, last seen about 1776.
A bird which may have been a chough and a big rail from Réunion have been named on inconclusive evidence.

Mascarene species in danger:

Réunion petrel, *Pterodroma aterrima*;
Réunion harrier, *Circus m. maillardi*;
Mauritius kestrel, *Falco punctatus*;
Mauritius pigeon, *Nesoenas mayeri*;
Mauritius ring-necked parakeet, *Psittacula krameri echo*;
Mauritius cuckoo shrike, *Coquus newtoni*;
Réunion olivaceous bulbul, *Hypsipetes bulbul borbonicus*;
Mauritius olivaceous bulbul, *Hypsipetes b. bulbul*;
Rodriguez warbler, *Bebrornis rodericanus*.

Comoro

The Comoro islands have fared considerably better than the Mascarenes. There have been no losses, and only two subspecies are considered as threatened:

Anjouan red sparrow hawk, *Accipiter francesii pusillus;*
Moheli green pigeon, *Treron australis griveaudi.*

Seychelles

The Seychelles have lost one subspecies:

Seychelles whiteye, *Zosterops mayottensis semiflava.*

Several species and subspecies must be considered as endangered:

Seychelles kestrel, *Falco araea;*
Seychelles turtle dove, *Streptopelia picturata rostrata;*
Seychelles Vasa parrot, *Coracopsis nigra barklyi;*
Seychelles owl, *Otus insularis;*
Seychelles warbler, *Bebrornis sechellensis;*
Seychelles black flycatcher, *Terpsiphone corvina;*
Seychelles fody, *Foudia sechellarum;*
Magpie robin, *Copsychus seychellarum.*

Assumption Island

Exploitation of guano deposits has turned this island into a desert and wiped out all the resident sea birds. The following land birds have become extinct:

Assumption whiteye, *Zosterops maderaspatana* subspecies;
Assumption turtle dove, *Streptopelia picturata assumptionensis;*
Coucal, *Centropus toulou assumptionis;*
Abbott's rail, *Dryolimnas cuvieri abbotti* (this flightless bird survives, however, on Aldabra, and possibly on Cosmoledo and Astove).

Sacred ibis on Aldabra

Aldabra

Aldabra, with its large population of giant tortoises and its interesting birds, has so far miraculously escaped large-scale settlement and exploitation. A serious threat developed recently, when it was proposed to establish an air-base on the island. This would have meant the speedy extermination of the tortoises and most of the birds. Owing to defence cuts the danger has receded, at least for the moment. There seems to be no reason why Aldabra should not be declared a national park.

Christmas Island

Christmas Island has lost three mammals:

Christmas Island shrew, *Crocidura fuliginosa trichura;*
Maclear's rat, *Rattus macleari;*
Bulldog rat, *Rattus nativitatis.*
Two of the island's birds have declined to danger point:
Abbott's booby, *Sula abbotti* (exterminated on Assumption);
Christmas Island goshawk, *Accipiter fasciatus natalis.*

Wildlife Reserves in the Indian Ocean
Mascarenes
There are two reserves on Mauritius:

Bel-Ombre, 3·5 sq. m. and **Macabe-Mare Longue**, 1·9 sq. m., both protecting patches of natural climax forest.

Seychelles

The 67-acre island **Cousin** has recently been turned into a sanctuary. This will give protection to about 500 Seychelles fodys, 50 Seychelles warblers and to a still fairly pure population of Seychelles turtle doves.

Asia

We now have to turn to Asia, an enormous land mass which extends from the edge of the Arctic Ocean to sunny coral seas, fringed all round by archipelagos of innumerable islands, large and small. In the northern parts of the continent, the march of civilization has taken a course similar to that in Canada and Alaska, with intensive exploitation and industrialization setting in rather later than in the northernmost regions of America. The impact has, in the last few decades, been somewhat tempered by legislation aimed at the conservation of wildlife and of samples of natural habitat.

The deserts and high plateaus of central Asia have for a long time remained very sparsely inhabited. During the first two or three decades of the present century, explorers such as Sven Hedin, Captain C. G. Rawling, Sir Henry Hayden, R.C. Andrews and E. Schäfer still encountered large herds of antelopes, gazelles, wild asses and yaks. According to their descriptions there must have been almost as much game in certain areas of Tibet and Mongolia as on the plains of Africa. These countries—hardly known to Europeans only sixty or seventy years ago—have since been devastated by revolutions and civil wars, during which modern means of transport were introduced and firearms of western manufacture spread to the remotest regions. Whenever politics turn into orgies of senseless revolutionary destruction, wildlife is made to suffer, and this has been the case in many of the innermost recesses of the Asian Continent. Animals which were extremely numerous when Sven Hedin carried out his daring exploration of Tibet are now verging on extinction.

In southern and south-eastern Asia and on many of the large islands, centres of civilization have long existed next to jungles and forests inhabited by primitive agriculturists, or even by roaming hunters and food gatherers. In many areas, wildlife was therefore able to co-exist with man until quite recently. It was unfortunate that the population explosion and the large-scale introduction of western technology into eastern lands should have coincided with a decline, in many countries even with a breakdown, of order and discipline. There has been a tremendous destruction of wildlife, and the fauna of southern Asia, once so rich and varied, is today being wiped out with horrifying speed. Nowhere in the world are there so many endangered species, and a considerable number of them have already been reduced to such a low level that their future can only be viewed with the utmost concern. The conservationists of south-eastern Asia—such as the late E. P. Gee in India and Boonsong Lekagul in Siam (Thailand)—have been fighting an especially hard and difficult battle, fortunately not without at least some successes. Indian rhinos, for instance, have shown a slight, but very gratifying increase, and if this can be maintained, the species

may yet be saved. Most of the sanctuaries created by the colonial governments are still in existence, and additional ones have been established. There is, in fact, no lack of reserves, and some are well run and adequately guarded, but from what one hears, this by no means applies to all of them.

Asia and the islands adjacent have lost the following mammals and birds:

Japanese wolf, *Canis hodophilax;*
Pygmy hog, *Sus salvanius;*
Syrian wild ass, *Equus hemionus hemionus;*
Schomburgk's deer, *Cervus duvauceli schomburgki;*
Crested shelduck, *Tadorna cristata;*
Pink headed duck, *Rhodonessa caryophyllacea;*
Himalayan mountain quail, *Ophrysia superciliosa;*
Jerdon's courser, *Cursorius bitorquatus;*
Riukiu kingfisher, *Halcyon miyakoensis;*
Spectacled cormorant, *Phalacrocorax perspicillatus.*

If the number of lost species and subspecies is not unduly large, the list of mammals and birds which must be considered as seriously endangered, and in many cases as approaching extinction, cannot but fill every lover of the animal world with utmost horror:

Mindanao gymnure, *Podogymnura truei;*
Snub-nosed monkey, *Rhinopithecus roxellanae;*
Orang-utan, *Pongo pygmaeus;*
Riukiu rabbit, *Pentalagus furnessi;*
Assam rabbit, *Caprolagus hispidus;*
Short-eared hare, *Nesolagus netscheri;*
Four-striped ground squirrel, *Lariscus hosei;*
Giant panda, *Ailuropoda melanoleuca;*
Owston's banded civet, *Chrotogale owstoni;*
Hose's palm civet, *Diplogale hosei;*
Otter civet, *Cynogale bennetti;*
Indian lion, *Panthera leo persica;*
Caspian tiger, *Panthera tigris virgata;*
Java tiger, *Panthera tigris sondaica;*
Amur tiger, *Panthera tigris altaica;*
Chinese tiger, *Panthera tigris amoyensis;*
Sumatra tiger, *Panthera tigris sumatrae;*
Bali tiger, *Panthera tigris baliae;*
Amur leopard, *Panthera pardus orientalis;*
Snow leopard, *Felis uncia;*
Clouded leopard, *Felis nebulosa;*
Flat-headed cat, *Felis planiceps;*
Asian cheetah, *Acynonix jubata venatica;*
Banded linsang, *Priodon linsang;*
Ceylon elephant, *Elephas m. maximus;*
Przewalski's horse, *Equus caballus przewalskii;*
Mongolian wild ass, *Equus hemionus onager;*
Indian wild ass, *Equus hemionus khur;*
Tibetan wild ass, *Equus hemionus kiang;*
Indian rhinoceros, *Rhinoceros unicornis;*
Java rhinoceros, *Rhinoceros sondaicus;*
Sumatran rhinoceros, *Didermoceros sumatrensis;*
Babirusa, *Babirussa babirussa;*
Wild camel, *Camelus bactrianus ferus;*
Musk deer, *Moschus moschiferous;* (Chinese, Sakhalin and Manchurian subspecies);

Black muntjac, *Muntiacus crinifrons;*
Fea's muntjac, *Muntiacus feae;*
Persian fallow deer, *Dama mesopotamica;*
Thai hog deer, *Axis porcinus annamiticus;*
Swamp deer, *Cervus duvauceli duvauceli;*
Manipur thamin or Eld's deer, *Cervus eldi eldi;*
Burmese thamin, *Cervus eldi thamin;*
Siamese thamin, *Cervus eldi siamensis;*
Formosan sika, *Cervus nippon taionanus;*
North China sika, *Cervus nippon mandarinus;*
South China sika, *Cervus nippon kopschi;*
Shansi sika, *Cervus nippon grassianus;*
Riukiu sika, *Cervus nippon keramae;*
White-lipped deer, *Cervus albirostris;*
Kashmir stag, *Cervus elaphus hanglu;*
Bactrian wapiti, *Cervus elaphus bactrianus;*
McNeill's deer, *Cervus elaphus macneilli;*
Yarkand deer, *Cervus elaphus yarkandensis;*
David's deer, *Elaphurus davidianus,* (only surviving in captivity);
Wild water buffalo, *Bubalus bubalus;*
Tamarau, *Anoa mindorensis;*
Lowland anoa, *Anoa d. depressicornis;*
Mountain anoa, *Anoa d. fergusoni;*
Quarles' anoa, *Anoa d. quarlesi;*
Seladang or Malayan gaur, *Bos gaurus hubbacki;*
Kouprey, *Bos sauveli;*
Wild yak, *Bos grunniens mutus;*
Arabian oryx, *Oryx leucoryx;*
Arabian dorcas gazelle, *Gazella dorcas saudiya;*
Arabian gazelle, *Gazella gazella arabica;*
Arabian sand gazelle, *Gazella leptoceras marica;*
Red goral, *Nemorhaedus cranbrooki;*
Sumatra serow, *Capricornis s. sumatraensis;*
Japanese serow, *Capricornis c. crispus;*
Formosa serow, *Capricornis c. swinhoei;*
Golden takin, *Budorcas taxicolor bedfordi;*
Szetchwan takin, *Budorcas taxicolor tibetana;*
Arabian tahr, *Hemitragus jayakari;*
Nilgiri tahr, *Hemitragus hylocrius;*
Markhor, *Capra falconeri,* (several sub-species);
Cyprian mouflon, *Ovis orientalis ophion;*
Punjab mouflon or urial, *Ovis orientalis punjabiensis.*
Chinese egret, *Egretta eulophotes;*
Japanese white stork, *Ciconia ciconia boyciana;*
Giant ibis, *Thaumatibis gigantea;*
Japanese crested ibis, *Nipponia nippon;*
Monkey-eating eagle, *Pithecophaga jefferyi;*
Maleo, *Macrocephalus maleo;*
White-eared pheasant, *Crossoptilon mantschuricus;*
Chinese monal, *Lophophorus ihuysii;*
Sclater's monal, *Lophophorus sclateri;*
Swinhoe's pheasant, *Lophura swinhoeii;*
Edward's pheasant, *Lophura edwardsi;*
Imperial pheasant, *Lophura imperialis;*
Palawan peacock pheasant, *Polyplectron emphanum;*
Malayan brown peacock pheasant, *Polyplectron m. malacense;*
Borneo peacock pheasant, *Polyplectron m. schliermacheri;*
Burmese grey peacock pheasant, *Polyplectron bicalcaratum;*
Elliot's pheasant, *Syrmaticus ellioti;*
Mikado pheasant, *Syrmaticus mikado;*
Lady Hume's pheasant, *Syrmaticus humiae;*
Blyth's tragopan, *Tragopan blythii;*
Cabot's tragopan, *Tragopan caboti;*
Western tragopan, *Tragopan melanocephalus;*
Platen's Celebes rail, *Aramidopsis plateni;*
Japanese crane, *Grus japonensis;*

Przewalski's horse, *Equus caballus przewalskii* — endangered

Kandahar markhor, *Capra falconeri megaceros* — endangered

Punjab urial, *Ovis orientalis punjabiensis* — endangered

Indian rhinoceroses, *Rhinoceros unicornis*—endangered

Siberian white crane, *Grus leucogeranus;*
Hooded crane, *Grus monacha;*
Black-necked crane, *Grus nigricollis;*
Sharp's sarus crane, *Grus antigone sharpi;*
Great Indian bustard, *Choriotis nigriceps;*
Japanese ancient murrelet, *Synhliboramphus wumizusume;*
Mindoro imperial pigeon, *Ducula mindorensis;*
Tristram's woodpecker, *Dryocopus javensis richardsi;*
Red-faced malkoha, *Phaenicophaeus pyrrhocephalus;*
Giant scops owl, *Otus gurneyi;*
Narcondam hornbill, *Aceros narcondami;*
Rothschild's blue starling, *Leucopsar rothschildi;*
Cebu black shama, *Copsychus niger cebuensis;*
Ashy ground thrush, *Zoothera cinerea;*
Rueck's blue flycatcher. *Niltava ruecki;*
Rufous-headed robin, *Erithacus ruficeps.*

It is particularly sad to have to record the catastrophic decline of so many of those strikingly beautiful birds, the pheasants and their close allies, the monals and tragopans. They mostly breed well in captivity, and one must hope that the birds already in zoos or in private aviaries will be registered and kept under careful control. It may become necessary to use some of them for the propagation of species which have become extinct in their native habitat. It should also be possible to ensure the survival of many of the threatened ungulates, such as deer, wild yak, wild water buffalo, seladang, kouprey, anoa and straight-horned

markhor in suitable zoos and game parks. Snow leopards and clouded leopards, too, can quite easily be bred.

Urgent and strict protection is required for the **Komodo dragon**, *Varanus komodoensis*, of the Komodo and Rintja Islands, which has been very seriously reduced in numbers. The **big-headed tortoise**, *Platysternum megalocephalum* of the Siamese and Laotian rivers is getting rare, owing to the pet trade, while the **giant frog**, *Rana macrodon*, of southern Siam, is being rapidly exterminated by the natives who consider it as a great delicacy.

Asian National Parks and Game Reserves

Turkey (See map on page 150).

Uludag National Park, 104 sq. m. On Mount Uludag. Bear, wolf, wild boar.
Kusadasi National Park, 61·7 sq. m. Wild boar, striped hyaena. Leopard said to occur.
Karatepe National Park, 29·7 sq. m. Of mainly historical interest. Roedeer, wild boar, wolf, jackal.
Yedigöller National Park, 7·8 sq. m. Forest-covered mountain range along Black Sea. Deer, roedeer, wild boar, wolf, jackal.
Kizilçahaman National Park, 3·9 sq. m. Partly forested plateau. Wild boar, wolf, bear.
Yosgat National Park, 1·1 sq. m.
Lake Manyas National Park, 128·4 acres. Bird sanctuary. Herons, egrets, pelicans, spoonbill, glossy ibis.

Cyprus

There are several game reserves, and the Government has accepted responsibility for ensuring the survival of the Cyprian mouflon.

Israel

Mount Carmel National Park and Nature Reserve, 27 sq. m. Mediterranean bush (maquis) and patches of coniferous forest. Of ornithological interest.
Mount Meron Reserve, 40·5 sq. m. Karst area. Of great botanical interest. Leopards were seen in the reserve in 1966.
Wadi Shorek Reserve, 3·8 sq. m. Of mainly botanical interest.
Ein Gedi (Dead Sea) Nature Reserve, 3·2 sq. m. Refuge for Nubian ibex. Some interesting birds: See-see partridge, Tristram's grackle.
Wadi Tabor Nature Reserve, 3 sq. m. Of botanical interest. Cliffs offering nesting sites to various birds of prey.
Wadi Amud Nature Reserve, 2·7 sq. m. Griffon vulture, Bonelli's eagle.
Wadi Dishon Nature Reserve, 2·3 sq. m. Griffon vulture.
Huleh Swamp Nature Reserve, 1·2 sq. m. Marshland. Swamp lynx, wild boar. Of ornithological interest.
Solelim Forest Nature Reserve, 1·15 sq. m. Of botanical interest.
Eilat Gulf Nature Reserve, 247 acre. Coral reefs.

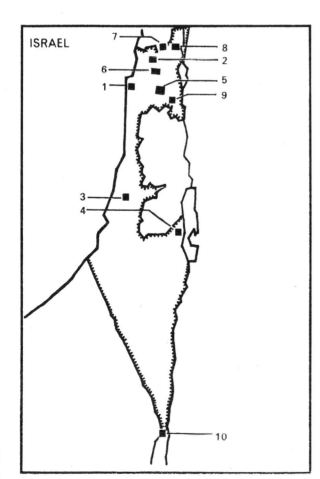

Persia

There is a 'Wildlife Park' of 386 sq. m., situated in a mountain area in north-eastern Iran, between Bojnours and Goubad Kabus. Agricultural exploitation or pasturing of livestock are not allowed, but there is some controlled hunting. Urial, ibex, maral stag, bear, leopard, some Caspian tigers.

Pakistan

Chittagong Hill Tracts National Park, East Pakistan, 100 sq. m. Deer, tiger.
Madhupur National Park, East Pakistan, 40 sq. m. Various game animals have been introduced; Cheetal, muntjac, swamp deer. Others are to follow.
The Changa-Manga and Shogran National Parks, of West Pakistan, 19·3 and 11 sq. m. respectively, are not yet sufficiently protected.
Kalabagh Wildlife Reserve, West Pakistan. Situated in the Salt Range Mountains, this reserve has been established by the Nawab of Kalabagh at the instigation of the World Wildlife Fund in order to give protection to the last 500 Punjab mouflon or urial.

India

Manas Wildlife Sanctuary, Assam, 233 sq. m. Indian rhino, buffalo, gaur, hog deer, muntjac or barking deer.
Kaziranga National Park, Assam, 166 sq. m. Indian rhino, elephant, buffalo, hog deer, muntjac, swamp deer, tiger, leopard, bear.
Shivpuri National Park, 61 sq. m., Madhya Pradesh. Sambhar, cheetal, nilgai, chinkara, tiger.
Hazaribagh National Park, Bihar, 71 sq. m. Sambhar, muntjac, tiger, leopard, bear.
Gir Wildlife Sanctuary, Gujarat, 1,229 sq. m. Last refuge of Indian lion; also sambhar, cheetal, nilgai, chinkara, bear.
Periyar Wildlife Sanctuary, Kerala, 300 sq. m. Elephant, gaur, sambhar, muntjac, wild pig, tiger, bear.
Taroba National Park, Maharashtra, 45 sq. m. Gaur, sambhar, cheetal, tiger, leopard.
Kanha National Park, Madhya Pradesh, 122 sq. m. Swamp deer, sambhar, cheetal, blackbuck, nilgai, gaur, tiger, leopard, peafowl, red jungle fowl. According to a recent report this reserve is suffering from illicit grazing of livestock, and from poaching. The gaur is the only ungulate which, at the moment, is showing some increase.
Mudumalai Wildlife Sanctuary, Madras, 124 sq. m. Elephant, gaur, sambhar, cheetal, muntjac, tiger, leopard, bear, langur.
Bandipur Wildlife Sanctuary, Mysore, 22 sq. m. Elephant, gaur, sambhar, cheetal, muntjac, tiger, leopard.

Map 14: Israel

 1. Mount Carmel National Park and Reserve
 2. Mount Meron Reserve
 3. Wadi Shorek Reserve
 4. Ein Gedi (Dead Sea) Nature Reserve
 5. Wadi Tabor Nature Reserve
 6. Wadi Amud Nature Reserve
 7. Wadi Dishon Nature Reserve
 8. Huleh Swamp Nature Reserve
 9. Solelim Forest Nature Reserve
10. Eilat Gulf Nature Reserve

Sariska Wildlife Sanctuary, Rajasthan, 80 sq. m. Sambhar, chinkara, nilgai, tiger, leopard.
Jaisamand Wildlife Sanctuary, Rajastan, 20 sq. m. Sambhar, cheetal, gazelle, tiger, leopard, bear.
Corbett National Park, Uttar Pradesh, 183 sq. m. Elephant, sambhar, cheetal, hog deer, tiger, leopard, crocodile, ghavial.
Jaldapara Wildlife Sanctuary, West Bengal. 93 sq. m. Indian rhino, a few elephants, sambhar, swamp deer, tiger, bear.
Bharatpur or Keoladeo Ghana Bird Sanctuary, Rajasthan, 10·8 sq. m. Spoonbill, painted stork, openbill stork, darter, sarus crane, little egret; also cheetal, blackbuck.
In Kashmir a national park is to be established in order to protect the last few surviving Kashmir stags.

Nepal

Chitawan Rhinoceros Sanctuary, 293 sq. m. Indian rhinoceros, elephant, sambhar, cheetal, muntjac, tiger, bear.
Sukla Phanta Sanctuary, 48·2 sq. m. Elephant, sambhar, swamp deer, muntjac, cheetal, blackbuck, tiger, leopard.

Ceylon

Wilpattu National Park, 250 sq. m. Forest. Elephant, buffalo, cheetal, sambhar, leopard, bear.
Ruhunu National Park, 88·7 sq. m. Elephant, sambhar, cheetal, leopard, crocodile.
Wasgomuwa Strict Natural Reserve, 108 sq. m. Elephant, sambhar, cheetal, leopard, bear.
Ritigala Strict Natural Reserve, 5·6 sq. m. Of mainly botanical interest. Mountain vegetation.
Gal Goya National Park, 96·5 sq. m. Protected area around a big artificial lake. Elephant, buffalo, deer, leopard.

Burma

Pidaung Game Sanctuary, 278 sq. m. Kachin State. Elephant, gaur, a few tsine (banteng), sambhar, hog deer, muntjac, a few tiger, leopard, bear.

There are 11 other game reserves, among them:

Mulayit Game Reserve in southern Burma, with hog deer, wild pig, tiger, leopard.
Kayatthin Game Reserve in northern Burma, established mainly to protect thamin.
Yegauk Game Reserve, Arakan Forest. Serow, tiger, possibly Sumatran rhino.
Shwezettaw Game Reserve in western Burma. Gaur, sambhar, thamin, muntjac.
Taunggyi Bird Sanctuary also serves to protect muntjac.

Malaya

King George V (Taman Negara) National Park, 1,698 sq. m. Elephant, a few Sumatran rhino, seladang (Malayan gaur), sambhar, tapir, tiger, leopard, Malayan bear.
Templer Park, 4·6 sq. m. Tapir, tiger and other game.

There are several other reserves, one of the most important being:

Krau Reserve of 193 sq. m.

Singapore
Four small reserves. Interesting birds. Various monkeys, mouse deer, otter, flying lemur, pangolin.

Eric Hosking

Hog deer

Malayan leathery turtle

M. W. F. Tweedie/Bruce Coleman Ltd.

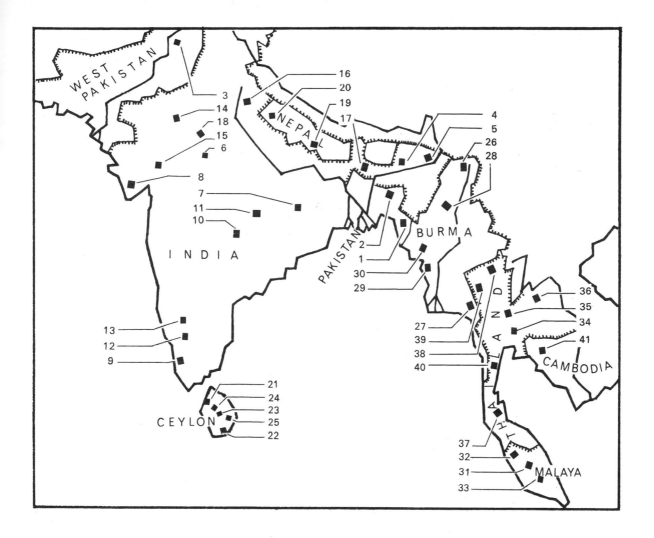

Map 15: Pakistan, India, Nepal, Ceylon, Burma, Malaya, Siam (Thailand) and Cambodia

1. Chittagong Hill Tracts National Park
2. Madhupur National Park
3. Kalabagh Wildlife Sanctuary
4. Manas Wildlife Reserve
5. Kaziranga National Park
6. Shivpuri National Park
7. Hazaribagh National Park
8. Gir Wildlife Sanctuary
9. Periyar Wildlife Sanctuary
10. Taroba National Park
11. Kanha National Park
12. Mudumalai Wildlife Sanctuary
13. Bandipur Wildlife Sanctuary
14. Sariska Wildlife Sanctuary
15. Jaisamand Wildlife Sanctuary
16. Corbett National Park
17. Jaldapara Wildlife Sanctuary
18. Bharatpur or Keoladeo Ghana Bird Sanctuary
19. Chitawan Rhinoceros Sanctuary
20. Sukla Phanta Sanctuary
21. Wilpattu National Park

22. Ruhuna National Park
23. Wasgomuva Strict Natural Reserve
24. Ritigala Strict Natural Reserve
25. Gal Goya National Park
26. Pidaung Game Sanctuary
27. Mulayit Game Reserve
28. Kayatthin Game Reserve
29. Yegauk Game Reserve
30. Shwezettaw Game Reserve
31. King George V (Taman Negara) National Park
32. Templer Park
33. Krau Reserve
34. Khao Yei National Park
35. Tung Slang Luang National Park
36. Pukradeung National Park
37. Khao Luang National Park
38. Doi Pui National Park
39. Larn Sang National Park
40. Khao Samroi National Park
41. Angkor National Park

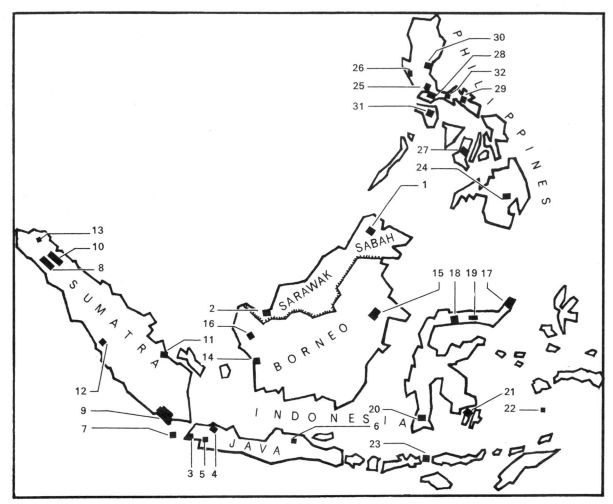

North Borneo (Sabah)

Kinabalu National Park, 266 sq. m. On Mount Kinabalu. Orang-utan, gibbon, sambhar, perhaps a few Sumatran rhino. Bird life very rich and varied.

Sarawak

Bako National Park, 9·8 sq. m. Situated on a pensinsula. Proboscis monkey. Of great ornithological interest.
Ten further national parks are planned, the biggest of them to have an area of 239 sq. m.

Siam (Thailand)

Khao Yei National Park, 837 sq. m. Elephant, gaur, deer, tiger, bear, gibbon.
Tung Slang Luang National Park, 494 sq. m. Elephant, gaur, sambhar, thamin, gibbon.
Pukradeung National Park, 134 sq. m. Sambhar, thamin, wild pig, gibbon, langur.
Khao Luang National Park, 793 sq. m. Elephant, gaur, banteng, sambhar, thamin, bear.
Doi Pui National Park, 61·7 sq. m. Sambhar, thamin, wild pig, gibbon, langur.
Larn Sang National Park, 55 sq. m. Elephant, gaur, sambhar, thamin, serow.
Khao Samroi National Park, 38·4 sq. m. Sambhar, thamin, wild pig, bear, langur.

Indonesia

There are 113 reserves in Indonesia; 68 of them in Java, 25 in Sumatra, seven in Celebes, and six in various other islands. Only a few can be mentioned here:

Udjung Kulon Nature Reserve, Java, 158 sq. m. Last refuge of Javan rhinoceros! Also banteng, Timor sambhar, mouse deer, leopard.
Tjikepuh, Western Java, 38·6 sq. m. Banteng, sambhar, leopard. Possibly a few tiger. Of great ornithological interest.
Tjibodias, Java, 4 sq. m. Forested mountain area of great botanical interest. A few leopard. Bird life very rich and varied.
Ardjuna Lalidjiva, Java, 2·2 sq. m. Situated among the volcanoes of Eastern Java. Timor sambhar, muntjac.
Pulau Panaitan, Java, 67·5 sq. m. Forested island near Udjung Kulon Peninsula. Banteng, muntjac, mouse deer, wild pig.
Pulau Dua, Pulau Bokar and **Pulau Rambut,** Java. Three coral islands totalling 113·6 acres. Bird sanctuaries. Breeding colonies of spoonbills, egrets, ibis.
Saobi, Java, 1·6 sq. m. Of great ornithological interest. Several species of brush turkey.
Sigogor, Java, 469 acres. Forest area. Leopard, wild pig.
Gunung Löser Game Reserve, northern Sumatra. 1,607 sq. m. Elephant, Sumatran rhino, tapir, sambhar, tiger, orang-utan.

Map 16: Malay Archipelago and Philippines

1. Kinabalu National Park
2. Bako National Park
3. Udjung Kulon Nature Reserve
4. Tjikepuh
5. Tjibodias
6. Ardjuna Lalidjiva
7. Pulau Panaitan
8. Gunung Löser Game Reserve
9. Sumatera Selatan
10. Langkat
11. Berbak
12. Indrapura
13. Rafflesia Serbodjadi
14. Kotawaringin—Sampit
15. Padang Luwai
16. Mandor
17. Tangkoko Batuangus
18. Panua
19. Tanggala
20. Bantimurung
21. Napabalano
22. Gunung Api
23. Komodo Island Reserve
24. Mount Apo National Park
25. Mount Makiling National Park
26. Bataan National Park
27. Mount Canlaon National Park
28. Mounts Banahao—San Cristobal National Park
29. Mount Isarog National Park
30. Aurora Memorial National Park
31. Naujan Lake National Park
32. Quezon National Park

British Museum (Natural History)

Orang-utan

Proboscis monkey

Russ Kinne/Bruce Coleman Ltd.

Sumatera Selatan, south-western Sumatra, 1,377 sq. m. Elephant, Sumatran rhino, sambhar, tapir, macaque, gibbon.

Langkat, eastern Sumatra, 823 sq. m. Elephant, tapir, sambhar, serow, tiger, orang-utan.

Berbak, Central Sumatra, 733 sq. m. Swampy forest. Sumatran rhino, tapir, banteng.

Indrapura, Sumatra, 48·3 sq. m. Among the island's highest mountains. Elephant, serow. Possibly some Sumatran rhinos.

Rafflesia Serbödjadi, Sumatra, 741 acres. One of several reserves established for the protection of the giant-flowered plant *Rafflesia arnoldi*. The area harbours some orang-utan.

Kotawaringin-Sampit, south-eastern Borneo, 1,351 sq. m. Banteng, orang-utan, proboscis monkey. Of great ornithological interest.

Padang Luwai, Borneo. 4·1 sq. m. Of botanical and ornithological interest. Malay lorikeet, blue-naped parrot.

Mandor, Borneo, 482 acres. Proboscis monkey.

Tangkoko Batuangus, northern Celebes, 17·1 sq. m. Anoa, babirusa, maleo brush turkey.

Panua, northern Celebes, 5·8 sq. m. Coastal plain. Reserve created for the protection of maleo brush turkey.

Tanggala, Celebes, 308·9 acres. Anoa.

Bantimurung, Celebes, 24·7 acres. Black ape, anoa.

Napabalano, Celebes, 22·2 acres. Timor sambhar, buffalo.

Gunung Api, volcanic island of the Moluccas. Bird sanctuary. Three species of boobies, three species of terns, frigate bird, tropic bird.

In 1965 a reserve was established on Komodo Island to protect the famous Komodo dragons.

Philippines

The Philippine Islands have 42 national parks, of which 23 are considered as coming up to international specifications. This seems a somewhat optimistic view, if regarded in the light of what Lee Talbot, the well-known American conservationist, recently had to report: 'Since the war there has apparently been no effective return to game hunting laws and any effective wildlife consciousness,' Talbot wrote, 'In the same period the number of firearms in the hands of private citizens has increased greatly, and the Philippines probably has one of the highest percentages of actively armed non-military citizenry of any country in the world . . . These factors, combined with the impermanence of park refuge and forest land, and the very rapidly increasing human population, have resulted in unlimited exploitation of the wildlife and modification of habitat.'

This state of affairs is all the more regrettable, as quite a number of Philippines species, such as tamarau, monkey eating eagle, Palawan peacock pheasant and giant scops owl, are approaching extinction and are in urgent need of effective protection. It must be hoped that Talbot's remarks have already been taken to heart by the Philippines Government, and that the archipelago's nature reserves will, in future, be properly safeguarded.

Only a few of them shall be mentioned here:

Mount Apo National Park, Mindanao, 297 sq. m. Extinct volcano covered with dense forest. Hot springs, waterfalls. Mindanao gymnure, monkey-eating eagle.
Mount Makiling National Park, Lucon, 14·5 sq. m. Dense forest. Sambhar, wild pig, brush turkey.
Bataan National Park, Luçon, 121·2 sq. m. On Bataan Peninsula. Sambhar, wild pig, macaque, civet cat. Bird life rich and varied.
Mount Canlaon National Park, Negros, 94·8 sq. m. Extinct volcano, covered with dense forest. Sambhar, wild pig, civet cat, macaque.
Mounts Banahao—San Cristobal National Park, Luçon, 42·9 sq. m. Forest covered volcano. Sambhar, wild pig, red jungle fowl. Bird life very rich.
Mount Isarog National Park, Luçon, 39 sq. m. Mountain area with dense forest, inhabited by primitive Negrito. Sambhar, wild pig, macaque, red jungle fowl and other interesting birds.
Aurora Memorial National Park, Luçon, 9·1 sq. m. Forested mountain area. Sambhar, tamaran, civet cat, macaque, monitor lizard, python. Bird life very rich and varied.
Naujan Lake National Park, 8·4 sq. m. Surrounding Lake Naujan. Sambhar, wild pig crocodile. Of great ornithological interest.
Quezon National Park, Luçon, 3·8 sq. m. Forest area. Sambhar, wild pig, macaque. Of ornithological interest.

Komodo dragon

Besides the national parks, there are seven wildlife refuges, totalling some 770 sq. m. Of some interest is the **Liguasan Game Refuge and Bird Sanctuary.**

Cambodia

Angkor National Park, 41·3 sq. m. Of mainly archaeological interest. It is, however, planned to re-introduce some mammals and birds, such as monkeys, deer and peafowl, into the forest surrounding the famous ruins.

There are five faunal reserves which might one day be turned into national parks. It is to be hoped that the Cambodian Government will safeguard the survival of the kouprey, a wild ox which became known to scientists in 1937, and of which probably only about 200 are now in existence.

Japan

Of the numerous national parks, 23 are regarded as coming up to international specifications. Most of the Japanese parks are, however, inhabited, and in some, there is a certain amount of controlled exploitation.

Daisetsuzan National Park, Hokkaido, 895 sq. m. Including 7,694 ft. Asahi Volcano. Coniferous forests. Brown bear, raccoon-dog, blue hare, Japanese macaque.
Bandai-Asahi National Park, Honshu. 732 sq. m. Gassan Volcano. Deciduous and coniferous forest. Alpine flora. Japanese black bear, serow, macaque.
Joshin-Etsu Kogen National Park, Honshu, 729 sq. m. Hot springs. Sika deer, serow, Japanese black bear, raccoon-dog.
Chubu Sangaku National Park, Honshu, 655 sq. m. In the Japanese Alps. Lakes, hot springs. Serow, wild pig, Japanese black bear, Japanese macaque, golden eagle, mountain hawk eagle.
Nikko National Park, Honshu, 543 sq. m. Volcanic area. Sika deer, serow, Japanese black bear, raccoon-dog, Japanese macaque.
Fuji-Hakone-Izu National Park, Honshu, 472 sq. m. Mount Fuji and surrounding area. Sika deer, wild pig, raccoon-dog, Japanese macaque.
Chichibu-Tama National Park, Honshu, 469 sq. m. Densely forested mountain area. Sika deer, serow, wild pig, Japanese black bear, raccoon-dog, Japanese macaque.
Shikotsu-Toya National Park, Hokkaido, 380 sq. m. Volcanic mountain area with crater lakes, hot springs. Sika deer, brown bear, blue hare.
Akan National Park, Hokkaido, 337 sq. m. Volcanic area with active craters, mud volcanoes, hot springs, lakes. Coniferous forest. Ainu settlements. Sika deer, brown bear, raccoon-dog, sable, ermine, otter, blue hare.

Raccoon-dogs

Towada-Hachimantai National Park, Honshu, 321 sq. m. Mountain area with crater lake. Serow, Japanese black bear, raccoon-dog, Japanese macaque.
Aso National Park, Kyushu, 282 sq. m. Of great scenic beauty. Sika deer, Japanese black bear, Japanese macaque.
Yoshino-Kumano National Park, Honshu, 215 sq. m. Southern coast. Hot springs. Sika deer, serow, Japanese black bear.
Kirishima-Yako National Park, Kyushu, 213 sq. m. Mountain area with hot springs. Sika deer, wild pig, Soemmering's pheasant.

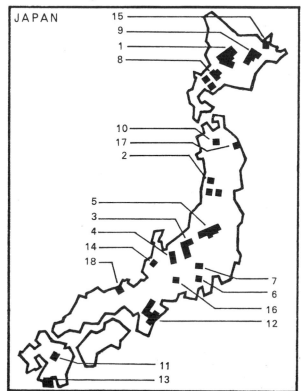

Map 17: Japan

1. Daisetsuzan National Park
2. Bandai-Asahi National Park
3. Joshin-Etsu Kogen National Park
4. Chubu Sangaku National Park
5. Nikko National Park
6. Fuji-Hakone-Izu National Park
7. Chichibu-Tama National Park
8. Shikotsu-Toya National Park
9. Akan National Park
10. Towada-Hachimantai National Park
11. Aso National Park
12. Yoshino-Kumano National Park
13. Kirishima-Yako National Park
14. Hakusan National Park
15. Shiretoko National Park
16. Minami-Alps National Park
17. Rikuchu Kaigan National Park
18. San-in Kaigan National Park

Hakusan National Park, 183 sq. m. This park has a 'wilderness area'. Sika deer, serow, Japanese black bear, Japanese macaque, golden eagle, mountain hawk eagle.
Shiretoko National Park, Hokkaido, 159 sq. m. Japan's wildest and most untouched national park. Mountainous area. Sika deer, brown bear, sea eagle, Steller's sea eagle.
Minami-Alps National Park, Honshu. 138 sq. m. Mountainous area. Japanese macaque, golden eagle, mountain hawk eagle.
Rikuchu Kaigan National Park, Honshu, 44·7 sq. m. Coastal cliffs. Sika deer, serow, sea birds.
San-in Kaigan National Park, Honshu, 34·7 sq. m. Coastal area. Japanese macaque, sea birds, Japanese white stork. Besides the national parks, Japan has over a hundred faunal reserves and many bird sanctuaries. Great efforts are made to preserve threatened species, such as the Japanese crested ibis (12 individuals left alive in 1965), the Japanese crane (180 in Japan and 200 to 300 on the Asian mainland in 1964), and the hooded crane (921 surviving in Japan in 1964).

China
A reserve is said to have been established in Hsifan, Szechwan, to protect the giant panda.

Mongolia
The once plentiful wildlife of this interesting country suffered very badly during the thirties and forties. Przewalski's horse, the wild ass and the wild camel are now very rare. There are no reserves yet, but game laws have been introduced, and the above mentioned animals have been declared protected. Uncontrolled hunting of argali and ibex has been stopped, and both species have recently increased in numbers.

Soviet Union (Asian part)
Sikhote Alin, Tatjuche, 1,196 sq. m. Mountain area along Sea of Japan. Taiga, Manchurian forest. Manchurian wapiti, sika deer, elk, musk deer, goral, wild boar, Amur tiger, leopard brown bear, Asian black bear, sable, yellow-throated marten.
Barguzin, Russian Mongolia, 957 sq. m. Mountainous area adjoining Lake Baikal. Coniferous forests. Elk, musk deer, brown bear, sable, Lake Baikal seal, capercaillie.
Zeya, Russian Manchuria, 317 sq. m. River Zeya. Tukuringa Mountains. Elk, roedeer, musk deer, bear, sable.
Hingan, Amur, 225 sq. m. Right bank of River Amur. Hingan Mountains. Bear.
Stolby, Yenissei, 182 sq. m. Kuissunsk Mountains. Baikal wapiti, roedeer, musk deer, brown bear, wolverine, sable.
Komsomolski, Amur, 123 sq. m. Taiga, Manchurian forest. Elk, brown bear, wolverine.
Kiedrovaja Padj, Coast near Vladivostok, 69 sq. m. Forested mountain area. Sika deer, roedeer, musk deer, wild boar, leopard, brown bear, yellow-throated marten, mandarin duck.
Suputinsk, near Vladivostok, 65·6 sq. m. Taiga. Manchurian wapiti, roedeer, wild boar, Amur tiger, sable, capercaillie.
Kronotzk, Kamtchatka, 3,721 sq. m. Kronotzk Peninsula. Birch forests, active volcanoes, hot springs. Reindeer, Asian bighorn, brown bear, sable, Steller's sea lion. Colonies of sea birds.

Giant panda

Argali

Asiatic musk deer—hunted for its scent glands—faces extinction in many areas

Altai, 3,531 sq. m. Altai Mountains. Deciduous forest, coniferous forest, alpine vegetation. Siberian wapiti, elk, musk deer, reindeer, snow leopard, sable, capercaillie, blackcock, hazelhen, ptarmigan.

Naurzum, Kazakhstan, 694 sq. m. Steppe with patches of forest and lakes. Roedeer, wild boar, bustard.

Barsakeljemess, Kazakhstan, 76·4 sq. m. Island in Lake Aral. Saiga antelope, goitred gazelle, onager (introduced). About 200 species of birds.

Alma-Ata, Kazakhstan, 497 sq. m. Tien-shan Mountains; Siberian wapiti, argali, goitred gazelle, brown bear.

Aksu-Dzhabagly, Kazakhstan, 289 sq. m. Valley of Aksu River and adjoining mountains. Siberian ibex, argali, roedeer, snow leopard, wolf.

Badchyz, Turkmenistan, 513 sq. m. Hilly steppe. Goitred gazelle, onager, leopard, cheetah.

Gassankuli, Turkmenistan, 269 sq.m. On Caspian Sea. Of ornithological interest.

Repetek, Turkmenistan, 133 sq. m. Eastern part of Kara-Kum Desert. Goitred gazelle. Desert monitor.

Amu-Darja, Uzbekistan, 231 sq. m. Delta of Amu Darja. Steppe, marshy forests. Saiga, goitred gazelle, pelican, and many other species of water birds.

Chatkal, Uzbekistan, 135 sq. m. Forested mountain area in Tashkent Province. Siberian ibex, snow leopard, brown bear, porcupine, marmot, lammergeyer.

Zaamin-Guralash, Uzbekistan, 41 sq. m. Mountain area in Samarkand Province. Siberian ibex, argali, wild boar, snow leopard, lynx, brown bear, wolf.

There are many reserves and game parks, serving to preserve and propagate such animals as European bison, elk, saiga, sable and beaver.

Map 18: Soviet Union (Asian part)

1. Sikhote Alin
2. Barguzin
3. Zeya
4. Hingan
5. Stolby
6. Komsomolski
7. Kedrovaja Padj
8. Suputinsk
9. Kronotzk
10. Altai
11. Naurzum
12. Barsakeljemess
13. Alma-Ata
14. Aksu-Dzhabagly
15. Badchyz
16. Gassankuli
17. Repetek
18. Amu-Darja
19. Chatkal
20. Zaamin-Guralash

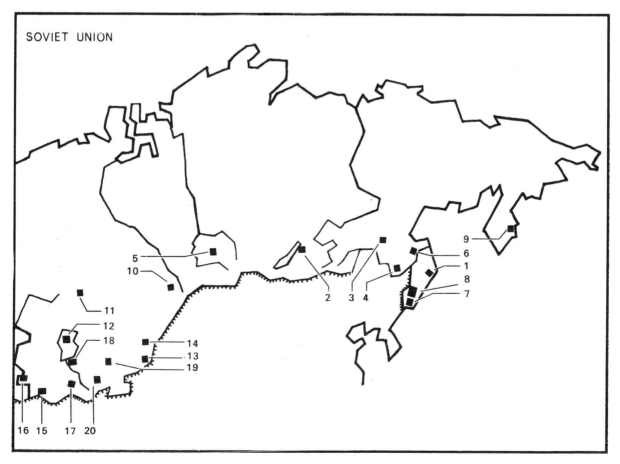

Australia and Tasmania

Zoologically, Australia has often been called a 'Continent of Living Fossils'. Its mammalian fauna is even stranger than that of Madagascar, consisting almost entirely of marsupials with a few monotremes (egg-laying mammals). Most of these primitive animals were only able to survive because Australia became isolated from all other land-masses before it could be invaded by the more highly developed placental mammals. The monotremes never got very far, being today represented only by the platypus and the spiny anteater, but the marsupials went through a process of adaptive radiation and successfully occupied all the ecological niches the Australian continent had to offer.

It seems likely that the advent of man, in the form of the aborigines, and of the dingo, which probably made its appearance at the same time, had an adverse effect on certain species. The Tasmanian tiger may well have disappeared from the mainland owing to competition from the more vigorous and more efficient dingo. A state of balance soon became established between the aborigines, who never passed beyond the stage of primitive hunters and food-gatherers, and their surroundings. They became a part of the ecological pattern and had no more than a controlling effect upon animal populations.

Civilization fortunately arrived late, but when it did come, it had a truly devastating effect through hunting pressure, habitat destruction and through the introduction of predators, creating absolute havoc among the highly vulnerable Australian animals. As in North America and South Africa, a more sophisticated appreciation of wildlife came only just in time, but the energetic conservation measures of the last few decades have slowed down the decline and repaired some of the damage done by ruthless exploitation.

Eastern native cat, *Dasyurus viverrinus*—endangered

The following mammals and birds have become extinct:
Gilbert's rat kangaroo, *Potorous gilberti;*
Broad faced bandicoot, *Potorous platyops;*
Eastern barred bandicoot, *Perameles fasciata;*
Western barred bandicoot, *Perameles bougainvillei myosura;*
Southern barred bandicoot, *Perameles bougainvillei notina;*
Gaimard's rat kangaroo, *Bettongia gaimardi;*
Nalpa bilby, *Macrotis lagotis grandis;*
Toolach wallaby, *Wallabia greyi;*
White-tailed rat, *Zyzomys argurus argurus;*
(this is not a marsupial, but a rodent; subspecies *indutus* is still common in northern Australia.
Tasmanian emu, *Dromaeius novaehollandiae diemenensis;*
Kangaroo Island emu, *Dromaeius n. diemenianus* (exterminated by aborigines).

The following species and subspecies must be regarded as endangered; some of them have not been seen for a considerable time and may be extinct:
Dusky planigale, *Planigale tenuirostris;*
Kimberley planigale, *Planigale subtilissima* (extinct?);
Wambenger, *Phascogale calura;*
Long-tailed sminthopsis, *Sminthopsis longicaudata* (extinct?);
Eastern jerboa marsupial, *Antechinomys laniger;*
Speckled marsupial mouse, *Antechinus apicalis;*
Eastern native cat, *Dasyurus viverrinus;*
Western native cat, *Dasyurus geoffroyi;*
Tasmanian tiger, *Thylacinus cynocephalus;*
Rusty numbat, *Myrmecobius fasciatus rufus;*
Rabbit bandicoot, *Marcrotis lagotis;*
Pig-footed bandicoot, *Chaeropus ecaudatus* (extinct?);
Leadbeater's opossum, *Gymnobelideus leadbeateri;*
Scaly-tailed opossum, *Wyulda squamicaudata;*
Ring-tail, *Pseudocheirus occidentalis;*
Hare wallaby, *Lagorchestes hirsutus;*
Banded hare wallaby, *Lagostrophus fasciatus;*
Bridled nail-tail wallaby, *Onychogalea fraenata;*
Crescent nail-tail wallaby, *Onychogalea lunata;*
Parma wallaby, *Wallabia dosalis parma;* (extinct in Australia, but has recently been found to be surviving in New Zealand, where it was introduced);
Brush tailed rat kangaroo, *Bettongia penicillata;*

Lesueur's rat kangaroo, *Bettongia lesueuri;*
Desert rat kangaroo, *Caloprymnus campestris;*
True rat kangaroo, *Potorous tridactylus;*
Cape Barren goose, *Cereopsis novae-hollandiae;*
Australian night parrot, *Geopsittacus occidentalis;*
Orange bellied parakeet, *Neophema pulchella;*
Superb parakeet, *Neophema splendida;*
Ground parrot, *Pezoporus wallicus;*
Golden shouldered paradise parakeet, *Psephotus ch. chrysptergyius;*
Hooded paradise parakeet, *Psephotus ch. dissimilis;*
Beautiful parakeet, *Psephotus pulcherrimus;*
Noisy scrub bird, *Atrichornis clamosus;*
Rufous scrub bird, *Atrichorus rufuscens;*
Western whipbird, *Psophodea nigrogularis;*
Eyrian grass wren, *Amytornis goyderi;*
Bristle tail, *Dasyornis brachypterus longirostris;*
Helmeted honeyeater, *Meliphaga cassidix.*

Cape Barren Goose, *Cereopsis novae-hollandiae—* endangered

The two marsupial giants, the **great grey kangaroo**, *Macropus giganteus*, and the **red kangaroo**, *Macropus rufus*, are not on the list of threatened species, but they might have to be included at some future date, if the present hunting pressure continues.

Man has never been at a loss for a cheap excuse whenever he was out to commit murder for the sake of personal gain, and would-be kangaroo hunters have long ago thought up a tale to justify the slaughter of those wonderful animals. Without really knowing the first thing about their prospective victims' feeding habits, they let it be known that one of the great kangaroos eats four times as much grass a day as a sheep. How harrowing for a sheep baron to have 'mobs' of these voracious creatures on his immense lands, and what a charitable act to free him of these pests, the meat and skins of which bring in such a tidy bit of money! The preposterous story was widely believed and has been uncritically repeated in innumerable books and articles. A scientific study of the grey kangaroo's food requirements has now been made, and what was the result? The daily food-intake is actually slightly less than half as much as that of an average sheep.

Moreover, the kangaroo has no food preferences, subsisting on what is readily available, and a considerable percentage of its food consists of plants which sheep and cattle will not touch under normal conditions. They do not migrate to areas where there has been a fall of rain, as has so often been stated, for they are well adapted to the almost permanent state of drought so prevalent in many parts of Australia. It has, in fact, been noted that they lose condition when forced to feed for any length of time on really high grade pasture, for instance, on lucerne or oats.

There is, thus, no valid reason for a continued massacre of grey and red kangaroos—except, of course, to fill the pockets of certain citizens who prefer thoughtless shooting to doing a more constructive day's work. If there has to be a certain amount of control in some areas, this can be done by Government hunters and in accordance with a strict game management scheme.

Remains of red kangaroo after the shooters have left

Australian National Parks and Wildlife Reserves

New South Wales

Mount Kosciusko State Park, 2,316 sq. m. Australian Alps. Magnificent eucalyptus forests. Various species of kangaroos, wombat, platypus, spiny anteater, lyrebird, emu.

Blue Mountains National Park, 262 sq. m. Sandstone mountains with deep gorges. Bush, dense rain forests. Grey kangaroo, platypus, spiny anteater, lyrebird, bowerbird.

New England National Park, 86·7 sq. m. Forested mountain area. Platypus, satin bowerbird, lyrebird, brush turkey.

Morton National Park, 69·5 sq. m. Mountain area, Platypus, spiny anteater, lyrebird.

Ku Ring Gai Chase National Park, 58·6 sq. m. Near Sidney. Grey kangaroo, platypus, spiny anteater, satin bowerbird, lyrebird.

Royal National Park, 56·4 sq. m. On Pacific Coast. Grey kangaroo, platypus, spiny anteater, lyrebird, satin bowerbird, sea birds.

Gibraltar Range National Park, 53·2 sq. m. Grey kangaroo, wombat, spiny anteater, lyrebird.

Mount Kaputar National Park, 23·9 sq. m. Mountain area, Nandewa Range. Koala, brush turkey.

Brisbane Water National Park, 23·4 sq. m. Mountain ridges parallel to coast. Forest patches. Grey kangaroo, platypus, spiny anteater, bowerbird, lyrebird, sea birds.

Australian News/Bruce Coleman Ltd.

Wombat

Map 19: Australia and Tasmania

1. Mount Kosciusko State Park
2. Blue Mountain National Park
3. New England National Park
4. Morton National Park
5. Ku Ring Gai Chase National Park
6. Royal National Park
7. Gibraltar Range National Park
8. Mount Kaputar National Park
9. Brisbane Water National Park
10. Warrumbungle National Park
11. Dorrigo National Park
12. Macquarie Marshes Reserve
13. Wyperfeld National Park
14. Wilson's Promontory National Park
15. Kulkuyne National Park
16. Hattah Lakes National Park
17. Mount Buffalo National Park
18. Mallacoota Inlet National Park
19. Fraser National Park
20. King Lake National Park
21. Alfred National Park
22. Lakes National Park
23. Wingan Inlet National Park
24. Lind National Park
25. Port Campbell National Park
26. Mount Richmond National Park
27. Fern Tree Gully National Park
28. Sir Colin Mackenzie Sanctuary
29. Sherbrook Forest Reserve
30. Belair National Park
31. Hincks, Murlong and Nicholls Wildlife Reserve
32. Flinders Chase Reserve
33. Hambidge Wildlife Reserve
34. Billiatt Wildlife Reserve
35. Archibald Makin Wildlife Reserve
36. Lincoln Wildlife Reserve
37. Wilpena Pound Wildlife Reserve
38. Peebinga Wildlife Reserve
39. Chauncey's Line
40. Stirling Ranges National Park
41. Nornalup National Park
42. Yanchep National Park
43. Porongorups National Park
44. John Forrest National Park
45. Ayer's Rock-Mount Olga National Park
46. Katherine Gorge National Park
47. Howard Springs Recreation Reserve
48. Coburg Peninsula Sanctuary
49. Daintree Gorge National Park
50. Eungella National Park
51. Hinchinbrook Island National Park
52. Bellenden-Ker National Park
53. Carnarvon National Park
54. Salvator Rosa National Park
55. Mount Elliot National Park
56. Lamington National Park
57. Conway Range National Park
58. Whitsunday Island National Park
59. Bunya Mountains National Park
60. Robinson Gorge National Park
61. Crystal Creek National Park
62. Mount Barney National Park
63. Isla Gorge National Park
64. Mount Walsh National Park
65. Flinders Island National Park
66. Barron Falls National Park
67. Castle Rock National Park
68. Palmerston National Park
69. Magnetic Island National Park
70. Bald Rock National Park
71. Gloucester Island National Park
72. Thornton National Park
73. Cradle Mountain—Lake St. Clair National Park
74. Mount Field National Park
75. Freycinet Peninsula National Park

Warrumbungle National Park, 12·8 sq. m. Mountain area. Kangaroo, wallaroo, rock wallaby, koala, opossum, spiny anteater, wedge-tailed eagle.

Dorrigo National Park, 5·9 sq. m. Mountain area close to coast. Lyrebird, satin bowerbird, brush turkey.

Macquarie Marshes Reserve, 77·2 sq. m. Swamps and lagoons along the Macquarie River. Ibis, spoonbill, various herons, black swan and other water birds.

Victoria

Wyperfeld National Park, 216 sq. m. Semi-desert eucalyptus bush ('mallee'). Black-faced kangaroo, spiny anteater, emu, brush turkey, ('mallee hen'), Mitchell's pink cockatoo.

Wilson's Promontory National Park, 158 sq. m. Mountain area close to south coast. Gorges overgrown with tree ferns. Kangaroo, wallaby, koala, opossum, marsupial mouse, spiny anteater, ground parrot.

Kulkuyne National Park, 84·9 sq. m. On Murray River. Mallee, spinifex-scrub. Grey kangaroo, platypus. Of great ornithological importance. Brush turkey, emu, bustard. Along river, pelicans and other water birds.

Hattah Lakes National Park, 77·2 sq. m. Mallee bush. Five lakes. Black faced kangaroo, mallee hen, pelican, egret, avocet.

Mount Buffalo National Park, 42·1 sq. m. North-east Victoria. Granite plateau with forest. Grassland in the valleys. Various species of kangaroo and wallaby, wombat, spiny anteater, lyrebird.

Mallacoota Inlet National Park, 17·3 sq. m. Bird sanctuary. Various species of herons, pelican, cormorant.

Fraser National Park, 11·9 sq. m. Area adjoining Eildon Reservoir. Kangaroo, wombat.

King Lake National Park, 21·7 sq. m. Forest area. Black-tailed wallaby, wombat, koala, opossum, platypus, lyrebird.

Alfred National Park, 8·3 sq. m. Mountain area with sub-tropical rain forest. Wallaby, barred bandicoot.

Lakes National Park, 8·1 sq. m. Gippsland Lakes. Kangaroo, koala, opossum.

Wingan Inlet National Park, 7·3 sq. m. On Wingan River. Of ornithological interest.

Lind National Park, 4·4 sq. m. Forest area of great botanical interest.

Port Campbell National Park, 2·7 to 3·1 sq. m. Coastal area. Fairy penguin, mutton bird.

Mount Richmond National Park, 2·3 sq. m. Of great botanical interest, approximately 50 species of orchids. Bird life rich and varied. May contain some rat kangaroo.

Fern Tree Gully National Park, 1·4 sq. m. Forest area near Melbourne. Wallaby, wombat, opossum, spiny anteater. Bird life very rich.

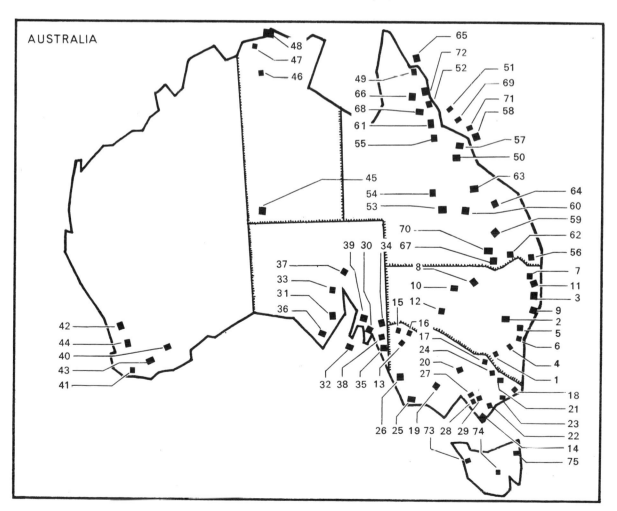

AUSTRALIA

Sir Colin Mackenzie Sanctuary. Kangaroos and many other marsupials.
Sherbrook Forest Reserve, 3·8 sq. m. Close to Melbourne. Dense eucalyptus forests, tree ferns. Best place to see lyrebirds and watch their fascinating display.

South Australia

Belair National Park, 3·4 sq. m. In the Mount Lofty Ranges.
Hincks, Murlong and Nicholls Wildlife Reserve, 252 sq. m. Mallee bush. Wallaby, grey kangaroo.
Flinders Chase Reserve, 209 sq. m. Eastern part of Kangaroo Island. Grey kangaroo, wallaby, koala (introduced), opossum, spiny anteater, platypus (introduced), brush turkey, emu (reintroduced), black swan, pelican.
Hambidge Wildlife Reserve, 145 sq. m. Mallee bush.
Billiatt Wildlife Reserve, 85·8 sq. m. Mallee bush. Kangaroo, mallee hen.
Archibald Makin Wildlife Reserve, 67·2 sq. m. Mallee bush, eucalyptus woods.
Lincoln Wildlife Reserve, 54·8 sq. m. On Eyre Peninsula.
Wilpena Pound Wildlife Reserve, 30·6 sq. m. Flinders Range.
Peebinga Wildlife Reserve, 6·2 sq. m. Mallee bush. Kangaroo, mallee hen.
Chauncey's Line, 3 sq. m. Eastern slope of Lofty Range. Kangaroo, mallee hen.

Western Australia

Stirling Ranges National Park, 416 sq. m.
Nornalup National Park, 50·9 sq. m.
Yanchep National Park, 10·2 sq. m. Grey kangaroo, koala, opossum, emu. Caverns with interesting cave fauna.
Porongorups National Park, 8·3 sq. m. Eucalyptus forest.
John Forrest National Park, 5·6 sq. m. Darling Range, near Perth. Dry eucalyptus forest with grass trees and cycads. Black-gloved wallaby, striped numbat, spiny anteater.

Northern Territory

Ayer's Rock—Mount Olga National Park, 481 sq. m. Semi-desert country with isolated granite mountains. Kangaroo, roan wallaroo, barred bandicoot, dingo, emu.
Katherine Gorge National Park, 86·5 sq. m. Wallaby, Johnston's crocodile.
Howard Springs Recreation Reserve, 1·1 sq. m. Patch of sub-tropical jungle near Darwin. Wallaby, parrots.
Coburg Peninsula Sanctuary, 743 sq. m. Peninsula on coast of Arnhem Land. Savannah. Various species of kangaroos. Of ornithological interest.

Queensland

Daintree Gorge National Park, 207 sq. m. Tropical forest.
Eungella National Park, 191 sq. m. Forested mountain area. Tree fern jungle. Interesting fauna. Bird life very rich and varied.
Hinchinbrook Island National Park, 151 sq. m. Forested island in Hinchinbrook Channel.
Bellenden-Ker National Park, 125 sq. m. Forested mountain area. Tree kangaroo, many other marsupials. 200 species of birds, among them Freycinet's brush turkey, Australian carroway.
Carnarvon National Park, 103 sq. m. East slope of Great Dividing Range. Grey kangaroo, wallaby, koala, opossum, platypus.
Salvator Rosa National Park, 100 sq. m. Eastern part of Great Dividing Range.

Emu

Red kangaroo

Mount Eliott National Park, 93 sq. m. Tropical rain forest, eucalyptus forest.
Lamington National Park, 75·7 sq. m. MacPherson Range. Subtropical rain forest with eucalyptus and casuarinas. Several species of kangaroo, koala, dormouse, opossum, platypus. Bird life very rich. Albert's lyrebird, black cockatoo, rufous scrub bird.
Conway Range National Park, 75 sq. m. Mountain area.
Whitsunday Island National Park, 42·1 sq. m. Forested island.
Bunya Mountains National Park, 37·8 sq. m. Rain forest.
Robinson Gorge National Park, 34·3 sq. m.
Crystal Creek National Park, 27·6 sq. m.
Mount Barney National Park, 20·2 sq. m. Eucalyptus forest.
Isla Gorge National Park, 17·9 sq. m. Eucalyptus forest.
Mount Walsh National Park, 11·5 sq. m. Eucalyptus forest.
Flinders Island National Park, 11·4 sq. m.
Barron Falls National Park, 10·9 sq. m.
Castle Rock National Park, 10·6 sq. m. Mountain area. Wombat, opossum, lyrebird.
Palmerston National Park, 9·8 sq. m. North Queensland jungle. Buff-breasted pitta, Australian cassowary.
Magnetic Island National Park, 9·7 sq. m. Island covered with dense vegetation.
Bald Rock National Park, 9·6 sq. m. Mountain area. Wombat, opossum, lyrebird.
Gloucester Island National Park, 9·4 sq. m.
Thornton National Park, 9 sq. m.

Tasmania

Cradle Mountain—Lake St. Clair National Park, 514 sq. m. Dense eucalyptus forest with nothofagus and tree ferns, subalpine forest, savannah. Eastern native cat, tiger cat, or spotted native cat, Tasmanian devil, wombat, wallaby, kangaroo, bandicoot. Possibly Tasmanian tiger.
Mount Field National Park, 64·8 sq. m. Mountain area with dense eucalyptus forest. Nothofagus and tree ferns. Marshes, lakes. Platypus, spiny anteater, Bennett's kangaroo, Tasmanian devil, wombat, native cat. Possibly Tasmanian tiger.
Freycinet Peninsula National Park, 24·7 sq. m. East coast. Kangaroo, wallaby, wombat, platypus. Possibly Tasmanian tiger.
Ben Lomond National Park, 61 sq. m. and Hartz Mountains National Park, 34·4 sq. m. are not yet adequately guarded.

New Zealand and adjacent Islands
Human invasion has very badly depleted the fauna of New Zealand and its neighbouring islands. The Polynesians—Moa hunters and Maoris— exterminated the ostrich-like moas. European settlement brought extensive habitat destruction and the introduction of a great number of predators. The complete absence of indigenous mammals— apart from a few bats—encouraged the colonists to stock the two main islands with deer, chamois and other game animals, which have been very destructive to the vegetation. In much of New Zealand the flora and fauna has, in rather less than a century, been changed beyond recognition, and many interesting species have become either extinct or reduced to danger level. Great efforts are now being made to preserve what is not yet lost.

Wallaby feeding

The following list will show that, as far as actual extermination within the last 200 years or so goes, the smaller islands have suffered more than the two main ones:

Lesser moa, *Megalapteryx didinus* (South Island);
Auckland Island merganser, *Mergus australis;*
New Zealand quail, *Coturnix n. novaezelandiaa* (both main islands);
Chatham Island banded rail, *Rallus dieffenbachii;*
Chatham Island rail, *Rallus modestus;*
New Zealand fruit pigeon, *Hemiphaga novaeseelandiae spadicea,* (Norfolk Island);
Norfolk Island kea, *Nestor meridionalis productus;*
Macquarie parakeet, *Cyanoramphus novaezelandiae erythrotis* (Macquarie Island);
North Island laughing owl, *Sceloglau albifacies rufifacies;*
Stephen Island wren, *Xenicus lyalli;*
New Zealand bellbird, *Anthornis melanura melanocephala* (Chatham Island);
Huia, *Heteralocha acustirostris* (North Island);
Poa swan, *Cygnus sumnerensis,* (Chatham Island), extinct between 1590 and 1690.

The list of endangered species is, unfortunately, very long:
King Shag, *Phalacrocorax carunculatus* (Marlborough Island);

Auckland Island flightless teal, *Anas a. aucklandica;*
New Zealand brown teal, *Anas a. chlorotis;*
Campbell Island flightless teal, *Anas a. nesiotis* (extinct?);
Auckland Island rail, *Rallus pectoralis muelleri;*
Eastern weka rail, *Gallirallus australis hectori* South Island
(extinct?), introduced Chatham Island;.
Takahé, *Notornis mantelli,* (South Island);
New Zealand shore plover, *Thinornis novae zealandicae*
(Chatham Island);
New Zealand snipe, *Coenocorypha aucklandica* (a few
small islands south and south east of South Island);
Chatham Island pigeon, *Hemiphaga novaeseelandiae
chathamensis;*
Orange-fronted parakeet, *Cyanoramphus malherbi,*
(Southern Alps);
Mangare Island parakeet, *Cyanoramphus auriceps forbesi;*
Antipodes Island parakeet, *Cyanoramphus unicolor;*
Norfolk Island parakeet, *Cyanoramphus novaezelandiae
cookii;*
Kakapo, *Strigops habroptilus* (Fjordland, South Island);
New Zealand laughing owl, *Sceloglaux a. albifacies*
(Southern Alps, extinct?);
New Zealand bush wren, *Xenicus longipes;*
South Island kokako, *Callaeas c. cinera;*
North Island kokako, *Callaeas c. wilsoni;*
South Island saddleback, *Creadion c. carunculatus;*
North Island saddleback, *Creadion c. rufusater* (Taranga
Island only);
Popio, *Turnagra capensis;*
Chatham Island robin, *Petroica traversi;*
Stitchbird, *Notiomystis cincta* (Barrier Island);
Chatham Island tiu, *Prosthemadera novaeseelandiae
chathamensis.*

New Zealand National Parks and Wildlife Reserves

Fjordland National Park, South Island, 4,667 sq. m.
Mountain area of great scenic beauty with fjords, lakes,
rivers and waterfalls. Last refuge of takahé and kakapo.
Many other interesting birds. Seals in the fjords.
Urewera National Park, North Island, 763 sq. m.
Forest-covered mountains with many streams and
waterfalls. Kiwi.
Mount Aspiring National Park, 760 sq. m. South Island
Southern Alps. Dense forest.
Arthur's Pass National Park, South Island, 375 sq. m.
Southern Alps. Nothofagus forests, glaciers. Bird life rich
and varied. Grey kiwi, kea parrot.
Westland National Park, South Island, 324 sq. m. Southern
Alps.
Mount Cook National Park, South Island, 267 sq. m.
Southern Alps. Magnificent mountain scenery. Seventeen
summits over 9,000 ft. Many glaciers. Kea parrot.
Tongariro National Park, North Island, 252 sq. m. Mount
Ruapehu and other volcanoes. Forest, grassland. Thermal
area. Bird life of great interest.
Nelson Lakes National Park, South Island, 215 sq. m.
Two lakes in mountainous setting.
Egmont National Park, North Island, 127 sq. m. Mount
Egmont. Subtropical forests, sphagnum moors. Bird life of
great interest. Kiwi.
Abel Tasman National Park, South Island. 67·4 sq. m.
Tasman Bay. Forests. Many small islands. Of great
ornithological interest.

There are 29 additional reserves. Some of them are bird
sanctuaries, others protect certain rare species of animals
and plants.

North Island kiwi and chick

Map 20: New Zealand

1. Fjordland National Park
2. Urewera National Park
3. Mount Aspiring National Park
4. Arthur's Pass National Park
5. Westland National Park
6. Mount Cook National Park
7. Tongariro National Park
8. Nelson Lakes National Park
9. Egmont National Park
10. Abel Tasman National Park

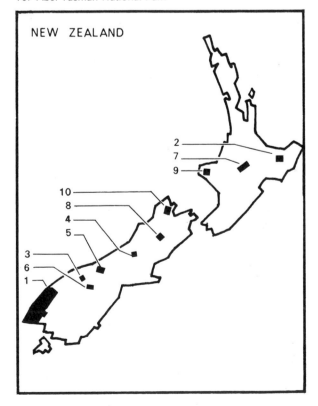

NEW ZEALAND

Pacific Islands

The widely scattered archipelagos of the Pacific have suffered as much as the islands of the Caribbean. Habitat destruction, the introduction of predators and, in some cases, hunting pressure, have wiped out a great number of species and subspecies of birds. Of all the Pacific Islands, the Hawaiian group has been by far the worst affected.

Hawaiian Islands
Extinct:

Laysan Island rail, *Porzanula palmeri;*
Hawaiian rail, *Pennula sandwichensis;*
Lanai thrush, *Phaeornis obscurus lanaiensis;*
Molokai thrush, *Phaeornis o. rutha;*
Oahu thrush, *Phaeornis o. oahensis;*
Laysan reed warbler or millerbird, *Acrocephalus f. familiaris;*
Molokai oo, *Moho bishopi;*
Hawaii oo, *Moho nobilis;*
Oahu oo, *Moho apicalis;*
Kioea, *Chaetoptila augustipluma;*
Great amakilu, *Loxops sagittirostris;*
Lanai creeper, *Loxops maculata montana;*
Molokai creeper, *Loxops m. flammea;*
Akialoa, *Hemignathus obscurus;*
Oahu honeycreeper, *Hemignathus lucidus lucidus;*
Maui honeycreeper, *Hemignathus l. affinis;*
Hopue, *Psittacirostris palmeri;*
Lesser koa finch, *Psittacirostris flaviceps;*
Kona finch, *Psittacirostris kona;*
Ula-ai-hawane, *Oiridops auna;*
Mamo, *Drepanis pacifica;*
Black mamo, *Drepanis funerea;*
Blood red starling, *Himatione sanguinea freethii.*

Endangered:

Hawaii shearwater, *Puffinus p. newelli;*
Laysan teal, *Anas laysanensis;*
Hawaii mallard, *Anas platyrhynchos wyvilliana;*
Ne-Ne, *Branta sandvicensis* (increasing in numbers, can probably be regarded as safe!);
Hawaii hawk, *Buteo solitarius;*
Hawaiian gallinule, *Gallinula chloropus sandvicensis;*
Hawaiian stilt, *Himantopus himantopus knudseni;*
Hawaiian crow, *Corvus tropicus;*
Kanai thrush, *Phaeornis obscurus myadestina;*
Hawaii thrush, *Phaeornis o. obscurus;*
Phaioki, *Phaeornis palmeri;*
Nihoa millerbird, *Acrocephalus kingi;*
Kanai oo, *Moho braccata;*
Nukupuu, *Hemignathus lucidus hanapepe;*
Kanaiakialoa, *Hemignathus procerus;*
Hawaiian nukupuu, *Hemignathus wilsoni;*
Kanai alauwahio, *Loxops maculata bairdi;*
Molokai creeper, *Loxops maculata flammea;*
Oahu creeper, *Loxops m. maculata;*
Maui creeper, *Loxops m. newtoni;*
Maui parrot-bill, *Pseudonestor xanthophrys;*
Palila, *Psittirostra bailleui;*
Ou, *Psittirostris psittacea.*

Wake Island
Extinct:

Wake Island rail, *Rallus wakensis.*

Ne-Ne, *Branta sandvicensis*—endangered

Bonin Islands
Extinct:

Bonin wood pigeon, *Columba versicolor;*
Kittlitz thrush, *Zoothera terrestris;*
Bonin grosbeak, *Chaunoproctus ferreirostris.*

Endangered:

Short-tailed albatros, *Diomedea albatrus.*

Iwo Jima (Volcano Island)
Extinct:

Iwo Jima rail, *Poliolimnas cinereus breviceps.*

Marianas
Endangered:

Marianas megapode, *Megapodius l. lapérouse;*
Truk monarch, *Matabolus rugensis;*
Tinian monarch, *Monarcha takasukase;*
Truk great whiteye, *Rukia ruki.*

Carolinas
Extinct:

Kusaie Island crake, *Aphanolimnas monasa;*
Kusaie starling, *Aplonis corvina.*

Endangered:

Palau megapode, *Megapodius lapérouse senex;*
Palau ground dove, *Gallicolumba canifrons;*

Palau owl, *Otus podargina;*
Ponape mountain starling, *Aplonis pelzelni;*
Palau fantail, *Rhipidura lepida;*
Ponape whiteye, *Rukia sanfordi.*

New Hebrides
Extinct:
Tanna ground dove, *Gallicolumba ferruginea.*

Choiseul (Solomon Islands)
Extinct:
Crested Choiseul pigeon, *Microgoura meeki.*

Nauru
Endangered:
Nauru nightingale warbler, *Acrocephalus luscinia rehsei.*

New Caledonia and Uvea
Extinct:
New Caledonia wood rail, *Tricholimnas lafresnayauus;*
New Caledonia parakeet, *Charmosyna diadem.*

Endangered:
Kagu, *Rhynochetos jubatus;*
Cloven-feathered dove, *Drepanoptila holosericea;*
Giant imperial pigeon, *Ducula goliath;*
Horned parakeet, *Eunymphicus c. cornutus;*
Uvea horned parakeet, *Eunymphicus c. uveaensis.*

Lord Howe Island
Extinct:
White gallinule, *Porphyrio p. albus;*
Lord Howe pigeon, *Columba vitiensis godmanae;*
Lord Howe parakeet, *Cyanoramphus novaezelandiae subflavescens;*
Lord Howe thrush, *Turdus poliocephalus vinitinctus;*
Lord Howe flycatcher, *Gergyone igata insularis;*
Lord Howe whiteye, *Zosterops strenua;*
Lord Howe fantail, *Rhipidura fuliginosa cervina;*
Mountain starling, *Aplonis fuscus hullianus.*

Endangered:
Wood rail, *Tricholimnas sylvestris.*

Galapagos land iguana, *Conolophus subcristatus—*
endangered

Fiji
Extinct:
Fiji bar winged rail, *Nesoclopeus poecilopterus;*

Endangered:
Macgillivray's petrel, *Pterodroma macgillivrayi;*
Masked parrot, *Prosopeia personata.*

Society Islands
Extinct:
Tahiti red-billed rail, *Rallus ecaudatus;*
Tahitian sandpiper, *Prosobonia leucoptera;*
Tahiti parakeet, *Cyanoramphus zealandicus;*
Raiatea thrush, *Turdus ulietensis;*
Tongatabu flycatcher, *Pomarea nigra tabuensis.*

Endangered:
Tahiti flycatcher, *Pomarea n. nigra.*

Line Islands
Extinct:
Washington Island gadwall, *Anas strepera couesi;*
Sharp-billed sandpiper, *Aechmorhynchus cancellatus.*

Samoan Islands
Extinct:
Samoan wood rail, *Pareudiastes pacificus.*

Endangered:
Tooth-billed pigeon, *Didunculus strigirostris.*

Galapagos Islands
Extinct:
James Island rice rat, *Nesoryzomys swarthi;*
Darwin's large billed finch, *Geospiza m. magnirostris.*

Endangered:

Flightless cormorant, *Nannopterum harrisii;*
Galapagos penguin, *Spheniscus mendiculus;*
Galapagos hawk, *Buteo galapagoensis;*
Charles Island mockingbird, *Nesomimus t. trifasciatus;*
Galapagos land iguana, *Conolophus subcristatus;*
Galapagos giant tortoise, *Testudo elephantopus.*

Galapagos giant tortoise, *Testudo elephantopus—*
endangered

Philippa Scott/Bruce Coleman Ltd.

Russ Kinne/Bruce Coleman Ltd.

Guadalupe Island

Extinct:

Guadalupe storm petrel, *Oceanodroma macrodactyla;*
Guadalupe caracara, *Polyborus lutosus;*
Guadalupe flicker, *Colaptes cafer rufipileus;*
Guadalupe wren, *Thryomanes bewicki brevicauda;*
Guadalupe bunting, *Pipilo erythrophthalmus consobrinus.*

Locality unknown, probably extinct:

Mysterious starling, *Aplonis mavornata.*

National Parks and Wildlife Reserves on Pacific Islands

Hawaiian Islands

Hawaii National Park, on the islands of Hawaii and Maui, totalling 340 sq. m. Within the park are the volcanoes Mauna Loa, Kilauea (both Hawaii) and Haleakala (Maui). With its craters, lava lakes, lava formations, fern jungles and yucca-like silverswords, the park is of great scenic, geological and botanical interest. It is also a refuge for a number of survivors of the once-rich Hawaiian bird fauna, such as aakiapolaau, amo thrush, elepaio flycatcher, amakili, apapano, iiwi, and ne-ne.

Hawaiian Islands National Wildlife Refuge. A number of islands and coral reefs at the western end of the Hawaiian Archipelago. Laysan, the largest of these islands, has been famous for its bird life ever since Rothschild published his *Avaifauna of Laysan.* In 1909, tragedy struck, when, to quote Devereux Butcher, 'one Max Schlemmer, catering for the millinery trade, rounded up a group of Japanese workers and came to the island and slaughtered the birds by countless thousands for their wings . . . Fortunately, Schlemmer was interrupted by officers of a U.S. revenue cutter in time to prevent total extermination of the bird colonies. Schlemmer, his Japs and the wings of more than 300,000 birds were taken to Honolulu for legal action.' Laysan was declared a bird sanctuary shortly after this outrage. The unfortunate introduction of rabbits caused further havoc and brought about the extinction of three land birds. The sea birds, however, have recovered, and Laysan still has spectacular colonies of Laysan and black-footed albatrosses, frigate birds, tropic birds, shearwaters, Bonin Island petrels, grey-backed, white and sooty terns.

At the time of writing an underwater reserve near the Hawaii Oceanographic Institute is in the planning stage.

Carolinas

An underwater reserve has recently been established at Palau Island.

Solomon Islands

Queen Elizabeth Park, 23·4 sq. m. Mountain area, covered with tropical vegetation. Of considerable ornithological interest. There are seven bird sanctuaries on small islands.

Fiji

Ravilevu Nature Reserve, 15·3 sq. m. On Taveuni Island. three separate areas, totalling 6·4 sq. m. on Mount Victoria. Virgin forest. Rare orchids. Golden pigeon.

There are several small nature reserves and twenty forest reserves.

Galapagos Islands

Galapagos National Park, extending over the islands of Albemarle, Indefatigable, James, Chatham and Charles, came into being in 1934. But it was only in 1963 and 1964, after negotiations between the Government of Equador and the Charles Darwin Foundation, that 38·6 sq. m. of Albemarle received effective protection, exerted through the personnel of the Charles Darwin Research Station. It is hoped that other islands will, in due course, also come under the direct control of the Station.

The Galapagos National Park is one of the most important reserves in the Pacific, safeguarding the survival of many interesting birds, such as the flightless cormorant and Darwin's finches, of the land and sea iguanas so characteristic of these islands, and of the giant tortoises. Early in the last century, whaling ships, visiting the archipelago for provisioning, often took on board from six to nine hundred tortoises. The log books of 79 New England whalers, who paid 151 visits to the islands, show that they took off no less than 10,373 tortoises. No wonder that the reptiles were nearly exterminated! It may be mentioned that the San Diego Zoo has recently succeeded in breeding Galapagos tortoises in captivity.

Flightless cormorant, *Nannopterum harrisii*—endangered

Arctic

Despite many forbidding aspects, the more accessible parts of the arctic regions have long ago come under intensive exploitation. Even though whales and seals were the main objects of northern enterprises, wildlife in general was brought under considerable hunting pressure. The effects of this were all the more disastrous, as arctic animals have to cope with a difficult and hostile environment, living very near to what must be considered as a marginal basis of stability.

The **musk ox**, *Ovibos moschatus*, was at one time thought to be nearing extinction. Protective measures in northernmost Canada, on the Canadian Arctic Islands and in Greenland have brought about a fair recovery, and the animals are now also bred in captivity. The Russians have recently bought some musk oxen from Canada, in order to establish a herd on Wrangel Island.

An arctic animal which has to be considered as endangered, is the **polar bear**, *Thalarctos maritimus*. Since the nineteen-thirties its range has been considerably reduced through over-hunting, and sealers still bring back great numbers of skins, for which there is a ready sale in Europe and America. Estimates of the total polar bear population vary from 5,000 to well over 10,000. It is difficult to give the animals effective protection, as they have a tendency to wander over the pack ice, far away from land, thus putting themselves at the mercy of any gunman that comes along. There are pilots who fly sportsmen—if they can be called that—out over the arctic seas. When a bear is spotted, the plane is set down on a nearby ice floe, and all the sportsman has to do is to shoot straight. If he does not, the pilot will probably do it for him. King Charles' Land, east of Spitsbergen, and Wrangel Island, have been declared bear sanctuaries, and there are several reserves in Canada, where the much persecuted 'King of the Arctic' can find refuge.

Young polar bears in the Wrangel Island Reserve

Novosti Press Agency

The Oceans

The exploitation of marine life dates back a very long time, and technological improvements have unfortunately made it more and more ruthless and destructive.

Extinct:

Juan Ferandez fur seal, *Arctocephalus p. philippii.*
Steller's sea cow, *Hydrodamalis gigas;*

The list of endangered species is of considerable length:

Fin whale, *Balaenoptera physalus;*
Blue whale, *Balaenoptera m. musculus;*
Pygmy blue whale, *Balaenoptera m. brevicauda;*
Humpback whale, *Megaptera novaeangliae;*
Greenland right whale, *Balaena mysticetus;*
North Atlantic right whale, *Eubalaena glacialis;*
North Pacific right whale, *Eubalaena sieboldii;*
Southern right whale, *Eubalaena australis;*
Galapagos fur seal, *Arctocephalus australis galapagoensis;*
Guadalupe fur seal, *Arctocephalus philippii townsendi;* ·
Japanese sea lion, *Zalophus californianus japonicus;*
Atlantic walrus, *Odobenus rosmarus rosmarus;*
Pacific walrus, *Odobenus r. divergens* (still fairly numerous, but in danger of over-hunting);
Ribbon seal, *Phoca fasciata;*
Kurile, harbour seal, *Phoca kurilensis;*
Mediterranean monk seal, *Monachus monachus;*
Caribbean monk seal, *Monachus tropicalis;*
Hawaiian monk seal, *Monachus schauinslandi;*
Dugong, *Dugong dugong* (still fairly common on Queensland coast);
West Indian manatee, *Trichechus manatus manatus;*
Florida manatee, *Trichechus manatus latirostris.*

The threat of extinction also hangs over the large sea tortoises:

Green turtle, *Chelonia mydas* (the 'most valuable reptile in the world');
Loggerhead turtle, *Thalassochelys caretta;*
Hawksbill turtle, *Chelone imbricata;*
Leathery turtle or luth, *Dermochelys coriacea.*

Conservation measures outside territorial waters are only possible by way of international negotiations.

Young green turtle, *Chelonia mydas*—endangered

Graham Pizzey/Bruce Coleman Ltd.

Every newspaper reader knows that exercises of this kind, for whatever purpose they may have been instigated, are usually very protracted and rarely lead to any really satisfactory results. To give a certain amount of protection to the whales and to those seals which spend all their lives at sea, breeding on the ice floes of the arctic and antarctic waters, is one of the most difficult and · arduous tasks conservationists are faced with. Seals breeding on land, congregating in big rookeries, are more vulnerable than the pelagic species, but they can also be much better protected, once the necessity of intelligent conservation has been fully realised. The Galapagos and Guadalupe fur seal, both thought to be extinct not so long ago, have made a come-back and are, at present, showing satisfactory increases.

Antarctic

After having been badly devastated by whalers and sealers, most of the subantarctic and antarctic islands have now become virtual reserves, and their wildlife has gone through a very gratifying period of recovery. With scientific stations having been established on practically all of them, there is little chance of anybody being able to sneak in for a quick bout of illicit slaughter. Whatever exploitation of animal resources there is, such as killing elephant seals for oil, operates under strict control.

In 1925, the French established two national parks in the Kerguelen Archipelago, one on three small islets, the other on the main island. These reserves were re-sited in 1938, and it is difficult to understand the reasoning behind this measure, for the new areas chosen were, in fact, already extremely well protected through their inaccessibility. No real harm was, however, done, as there has been no hunting on Kerguelen since 1931.

Until a very short time ago the Antarctic continent was only visited by the occasional exploring expedition. Small groups of men spent a year or two in this inhospitable world of ice and storms, and whatever seals and birds they killed for scientific purposes or to provide themselves with fresh meat, hardly counted at all. After they had departed, years probably went by until another ship forced its way through the pack. Things have changed enormously during the last twenty years or so, and there are now a considerable number of permanent bases on the sixth continent, the existence of which, though vaguely guessed by Captain Cook, was only fully established during the 1840s.

Ten to a dozen nations are participating in an all-out effort to unveil the last mysteries of Antarctica, and it gives one pleasure to record that they have all recognized the urgent need to 'preserve and conserve' the living resources of the last continent to be conquered by man. International agreement has, for once, been reached over measures to be taken, and lists of particularly protected species and areas have been drawn up. Let us hope that now that Antarctica is getting 'inhabited', the impact will be less fatal than it has been almost everywhere else, that man will, for once, overcome his destructive tendencies and live in amicable co-existence with the Weddell seals, the penguins, skuas, petrels and prions.

One Antarctic seal already figures on the official Red List of endangered animals; this is the **Ross seal**, *Ommatophoca rossi*, with an estimated total population of 50,000. There is no reason to assume that it was ever more numerous, for all Antarctic explorers considered it as the rarest of the seals they encountered. The **crab eater**, *Lobodon carcinophaga*, can be regarded as the most common Antarctic seal, but it is, perhaps, the one that should be put on the Red List. Its breeding grounds have been found to be on the pack ice, far from land and outside the area covered by the Antarctic treaty, and it is now in danger of exploitation for skins.

Weddell seal on King George Island—Antarctica

Index

Figures in bold type indicate illustrations

215

216

217

220

Bibliography

It would be easy to fill fifty pages or more with titles touching upon conservation, hunting, game management, commercial exploitation of animal resources, extinction, habitat destruction, pollution and kindred subjects. Not having fifty pages at my disposal, I have restricted this bibliography to books, papers and articles which provided me with specific items of information as well as publications dealing in more detail with some of the points that have been especially stressed in the text of this book.

Akeley, Carl E. In Brightest Africa. London 1924
Akeley, Mary L. Jobe. Restless Jungle. London 1937
Akeley, Mary L. Jobe. The Wilderness Lives Again. New York 1940
Anon. Wildlife in Thailand. Oryx VII, 6, 1964
Anon. Encouraging Report on the Congo. Oryx VIII, 5, 1966
Anon. Vicuna Reserve in Peru. Oryx VIII, 5, 1966
Anon. Fun Furs. The New Yorker Magazine Inc. Reprinted Oryx IX, 3, 1967
Ardrey, Robert. African Genesis: A Personal Investigation into the Animal Origins and Nature of Man. London 1961
Atkinson-Willes, G. L. (Editor). Wildfowl in Great Britain. London 1963
Attenborough, David. Zoo Quest to Madagascar. London 1961
Audubon, John James. Audubon's Wildlife. Edited by Edward Way Teale. London 1965
Audubon, John James. Audubon and his Journals. Edited by Maria R. Audubon and Elliott Coees. Reprint New York 1960
Augusta, Josef, and Zdanek, Burian. Prehistoric Man. London 1960
Augusta, Josef, and Zdanek, Burian. A Book of Mammoths. London 1962
Baechler, Emil. Das Drachenloch ob Vaettis im Taminatal. St. Gallen 1921
Baechler, Heinz. Die ersten Bewohner der Schweiz. Bern 1947
Bailey, Alfred M. and J. H. Sorensen. Subantarctic Campbell Island. Proceedings No. 10, Denver Museum of Natural History. 1962
Baillie-Grohman, W. A. Sport in the Alps, Past and Present. London 1896
Bannikov, A. G. Die Saiga Antilope. Wittenberg Lutherstadt 1963
Barnett, Lincoln. (Editor). The Wonders of Life on Earth. New York 1956
Beebe, William. Galapagos—World's End. New York/London 1924
Beebe, William. High Jungle. London 1950
Berger, Arthur. Die Jagd aller Voelker im Wandel der Zeit. Berlin 1928
Bertram, Colin and Kate. Dugongs in Australian Waters. Oryx VIII, 4, 1966
Bertram, Colin and Kate. The Sirenia: A vanishing Order of Mammals. Animal Kingdom LXIX, 6, 1966
Boolootian, Richard A. California's Sea Otter. Animals, 3, 12, 1962
Bourne, Arthur. Sealing in Canada: Cruel or Humane? Animals, 9, 6, 1966
Braun, Bernhard, P. Der neuentdeckte Australische Schlaf-mausbeutler. Kosmos 63, 5, 67
Breeden, Stanley and Kay. The Life of the Kangaroo. Sydney 1967
Brentjes, Burchard. Die Haustierwerdung im Orient. Wittenberg Lutherstadt 1965
Bridges, T. C. Les Réserves de Bêtes Sauvages. Paris 1938
Broderick, Alan Houghton. Man and his Ancestry. London 1964
Brown, Leslie. Ethiopian Episode. London 1965
Brown, Leslie. Africa. London 1965
Brown, Philip and George Waterton. The Return of the Osprey. London 1962

Bruggen, A. C. van. Illustrated Notes on some extinct South African Ungulates. S. A. Journal of Science. Vol. 55, No. 8, 1959
Bruemer, Fritz. Helft der Sattelrobbe. Kosmos 63, 6, 67
Brunies, S. Der Schweizerische Nationalpark. Basel 1918
Butcher, Devereux. Exploring our National Parks and Monuments. New York 1947
Butcher, Devereux. Seeing America's Wildlife in our National Refuges. New York 1955
Carr, Archie. The Turtle: A Natural History of Sea Turtles. London 1968
Carrington, Richard. Elephants. London 1958
Carrington, Richard. Great National Parks. London 1967
Catlin, George. Letters and Notes on the Manners, Customs and Conditions of the North American Indians. New York 1841
Cattrick, Alan. Spoor of Blood. Cape Town 1959
Clark, Eugenie. The Need for Conservation in the Sea. Oryx IX, 2, 1967
Conway, William G. The Opportunities for Zoos to save vanishing Species. Oryx IX, 2, 1967
Conway, William G. A close look at Argentine Wildlife. Animal Kingdom. LXVIII, 5, 1965
Couturier, Marcel A. L'Ours brun. Grenoble 1954
Cowles, Raymond B. Zulu Journal. Berkeley and Los Angeles 1959
Crowe, Philip K. What's happening to the Wildlife of South America? Oryx VIII, 1, 1965
Dall, William Healy. The Discovery and Exploration of Alaska. In: Harriman Alaska Expedition. Vol. II. New York 1901
Darling, F. Fraser. Wild Life in an African Territory. London 1960
Darwin, Charles. Journal of Researches into the Natural History and Geology of the Countries visited during the Voyage of H.M.S. Beagle around the World. London 1889
Decary, Raymond. La Faune Malgache. Paris 1950
Dembeck, Hermann. Mit Tieren leben. Duesseldorf/Wien 1961
De Voto, Bernard. Westward the Course of Empire; The Story of the Exploration of North America from its Discovery to 1805. London 1953
Dorst, Jean. Natur in Gefahr. Zuerich 1966. (English transl.: Before Nature Dies. London 1969)
Dorst, Jean. South American and Central America: A Natural History. London 1967
Dufresne, Frank. No Room for Bears. London 1966
Dugmore, A. Radclyffe. The Romance of the Beaver: Being a History of the Beaver in the Western Hemisphere. London 1914
Eibl-Eibesfeldt, Irenaeus. Galapagos: Die Arche Noah im Pazifik. Muenchen 1960
Eibl-Eibesfeldt, Irenaeus. Die Charles Darwin Station auf den Galapagos Inseln. Kosmos. 63, 1, 1967
Engelhardt, Wolfgang. Die letzten Oasen der Tierwelt. Frankfurt 1961
Findeisen, Hans. Das Tier als Gott, Daemon und Ahne. Stuttgart 1956
Fisher, James, and Roger Tory Peterson. The World of Birds. London 1964
Frauca, Harry. Encounters with Australian Animals. London/Melbourne/Toronto
Garretson, Martin S. The American Bison. New York 1938
Garut, W. E. Das Mammut. Wittenberg Lutherstadt 1964
Gaymer, Roger. Aldabra—The Case for Conserving this Coral Atoll. Oryx VIII, 6, 1966
Gee, E. P. Report on a Survey of the Rhinoceros Area of Nepal, March and April 1959. Oryx V, 2, 1959

Gee, E. P. The Wild Life of India. London 1964

Gerlach, Richard. Bedrohte Tierwelt. Darmstadt 1959

Gill, F. B. Birds of Rodriguez Island (Indian Ocean). Ibis, 109, 1967

Gilmore, D. P. Wallabies in New Zealand. Animals 11, 2, 1968

Greenway, James C. Extinct and Vanishing Birds of the World. New York 1958

Grey, Zane. The Thundering Herd. 1925. (This novel gives an excellent account of how the bison were slaughtered)

Grimwood, Ian. Operation Oryx: The Three Stages of Captive Breeding. Oryx IX, 2, 67

Grimwood, Ian. Endangered Mammals of Peru. Oryx IX, 6, 68

Grosvenor, Gilbert (Editor). The Book of Birds. Washington 1927

Grosvenor, Gilbert, and Alexander Wetmore (Editors). The Book of Birds. Washington 1937

Grzimek, B. Serengeti Shall Not Die. London 1960

Guggisberg, C. A. W. Das Tierleben der Alpen. Bern 1954/1955

Guggisberg, C. A. W. Simba, the Life of the Lion. Cape Town 1961

Guggisberg, C. A. W. The Wilderness is Free. Cape Town 1963

Guggisberg, C. A. W. S.O.S. Rhino. London 1966

Guggisberg, C. A. W. Tierwelt Afrikas: Affen, Raubtiere, Huftiere. Neuenburg 1967

Guiler, Eric R. In Pursuit of the Thylacine. Oryx VIII, 5, 66

Gulland, J. A. The Plight of the Whales. Oryx VIII, 1, 65

Happold, D. C. D. The Future for Wildlife in the Sudan. Oryx VIII, 6, 66

Hardy, Sir Alister. The Open Sea II: Fish and Fisheries. London 1959

Hardy, Sir Alister. Great Waters: A Voyage of Nature History to study Whales, Plankton and the Waters of the Southern Ocean in the old Royal Research Ship Discovery. London 1967

Harper, Francis. Extinct and Vanishing Mammals of the Old World. New York 1945

Harrington, C. R. The Life and Status of the Polar Bear. Oryx VIII, 3, 1965

Harris, C. J. Otters. London 1968

Harrison, Jeffery. A Wealth of Wildfowl. London 1967

Harrisson, Barbara. Orang Utan. London 1962

Harrisson, Tom. A Future for Borneo's Wildlife? Oryx VIII, 2, 65

Haroy, Jean-Paul. Liste des Nations Unies des Parcs Nationaux et Réserves Analogues. Morges 1967

Hayes, G. D. How Independence Saved an African Reserve. Oryx IX, 1, 67.

Heck, Lutz. Grosswild im Etoschaland. Berlin 1955

Heck, Lutz. Fahrt zum Weissen Nashorn. Stuttgart 1957

Heim, Roger. Derniers Réfuges: Atlas Commenté des Réserves Naturelles dans le Monde. Amsterdam 1956

Hewitt, Gordon. The Conservation of the Wildlife of Canada. New York 1921

Hibbert, R. A. Wildlife Protection in Mongolia. Oryx IX, 3, 67

Hislop, J. A. Rhinoceros and Seladang—Malaya's Vanishing Species. Oryx VIII, 6, 66

Hornaday, William T. A Wild Animal Round-up. New York/London 1925

Hubback, Theodore. Malayan Gaur or Seladang. Journ. Bombay Nat. Hist. Soc. Vol. XL

Hubback, Theodore. The two-horned Asiatic Rhinoceros. Journ. Bombay Nat. Hist. Soc. Vol. XL

Hubback, Theodore. Principles of Wild Life Conservation. Journ. Bombay Nat. Hist. Soc. Vol. XL

Huxley, Julian. La Protection de la Grande Faune et des Habitats Naturels en Afrique Centrale et Orientale. UNESCO Paris 1961

Jarvis, Caroline. The Value of Zoos for Science and Conservation. Oryx IX, 2, 67

Johnston, Sir Harry. Pioneers in Canada. London 1912

Kaszab, Z. New Sighting of Przewalski Horses. Oryx VIII, 6, 66

Keast, Allen. Australia and the Pacific Islands: A Natural History. London 1966

Kenney, Nathaniel T. Big Bend, Jewel of the Texas Desert. Nat. Geogr. Mag. 133, No. 1, 1968

Keller, C. Reisebilder aus Ostafrika und Madagaskar. Leipzig 1887

Keller, C. Madagascar, Mauritius and the other East African Islands. London 1901

Kersten, Otto. Baron Carl Claus von der Decken's Reisen in Ost-Afrika in der Jahren 1859 bis 1961. Leipzig/Heidelberg 1869

King, F. Wayne. Ora—Giants of Komodo. Animal Kingdom XXI, 4, 1968

Kinloch, Bruce. Kagera—Cinderella of Africa's Parks. Animals. 10, 5, 1964

Koch, Wilhelm. Die Jagd in Vergangenheit und Gegenwart. Stuttgart 1961

Koford, Carl B. The California Condor. New York 1966

Konitzky, Gustav A. Bisonjaeger. Stuttgart 1959

Konitzky, Gustav A. Arktische Jaeger. Stuttgart 1961

Krasheninnikow, S. P. The History of Kamtschatka and the Kurilski Islands with the Countries adjacent. Glocester 1764. Reprint Chicago 1962

Kroesche, Otto. Die Moa Strausse. Wittenberg Lutherstadt 1961

Kuehn, Herbert. On the Track of Prehistoric Man. London 1955

Kuehn, Herbert. The Rock Pictures of Europe. London 1956

Kuehn, Herbert. Eiszeitkunst. Goettingen 1965

Kunhenn, Paul. Pygmäen und andere Primitivvoelker. Stuttgart 1952

Labuschagne, R. J. Our National Parks. Pretoria 1958

Labuschagne, R. J. Sixty Years Kruger Park. Pretoria 1958

La Farge, Oliver. A Pictorial History of the American Indian. London 1963

Lehmann, F. Carlos. The Pet Trade and Extinction. Oryx IX, 2, 1967

Lekagul Boonsong. The Wildlife of South-east Asia: How Zoos can help to serve it. Oryx IX, 2, 67

Lengerken, Hanns von. Der Ur und seine Beziehung zum Menschen. Leipzig 1953

Le Vaillant, François. Travels from the Cape of Good Hope into the Interior Parts of Africa. London 1790

Lichtenstein, Henry. Travels in Southern Africa in the Years 1803, 1804, 1805, 1806. London 1815. Reprint Cape Town 1928/1930

Lindner, Kurt. La Chasse Préhistorique. Paris 1950

London, Jack. The Sea Wolf. 1904. (A novel dealing with the slaughter of fur seals)

Luettschwager, J. Die Drontevoegel. Wittenberg Lutherstadt 1961

Macpherson, A. H. Grizzly Bears in Danger. Oryx VIII, 5, 1966

Mallinson, J. J. C. Bolivia and the Vicuna. Oryx VIII, 5, 1966

Martin, P. S., and Wright, H. E. (Editors). Pleistocene Extinction: The Search for a Cause. New Haven and London 1967

Matthiessen, Peter. Wild Life in America. New York 1964

Mazak, Vratislav. Der Tiger. Wittenberg Lutherstadt 1965

Maxwell, Gavin. Seals of the World. London 1967

McCracken, Harold. The Beast That Walks Like Man: The Story of the Grizzly Bear. London 1957

McCracken, Harold. George Catlin and the Old Frontier. New York 1959

McKie, Ronald. The Company of Animals. (A Game Warden's experiences in Malaya). Sydney 1965

McNulty, Faith. A fight against Extinction: The Whooping Crane. London 1967

Meissner, H. O. Bezaubernde Wildnis: Wandern, Jagen, Fliegen in Alaska. Stuttgart 1966

Meissner, H. O. Im Alleingang zum Mississippi: Die Abenteuer des Pierre Radisson. Stuttgart 1966

Mohr, Erna. Der Wisent. Leipzig 1952

Mohr, Erna. Sirenen oder Seekuehe. Wittenberg Lutherstadt 1957

Mohr, Erna. Das Urwildpferd. Wittenberg Lutherstadt 1959

Montague, Ivor. The Wild Horse. Animals 4, 16, 1964

Moore, Audrey. Serengeti. London 1938

Moorhead, Alan. The Fatal Impact: An Account of the Invasion of the South Pacific 1767—1840. New York 1966

223

Mountfort, Guy. Portrait of a Wilderness: The Story of the Ornithological Expedition to the Coto Doñana. London 1958

Mowat, Farley. People of the Deer. London 1954

Mowat, Farley. Never Cry Wolf. London 1963

Murie, Adolph. A Naturalist in Alaska. New York 1963

Newton, Alfred. A Dictionary of Birds. London 1893–1896

Nogueira-Neto, Paulo. Saving Forests for Wildlife in Brazil. Oryx VIII, 5, 66

Nottebohm, Fernando. Argentine Fauna: Time of Decision. Animal Kingdom, LXX, 4, 1967

Oliver, J. The Extinct Blue-buck. African Wild Life, 8, 3, 1954

Paulian, Patrice. La Vie Animale aux Iles Kerguelen. Paris 1953

Pedersen, Alwin. Der Eisbaer. Wittenberg Lutherstadt 1957

Pedersen, Alwin. Der Moschusochse. Wittenberg Lutherstadt 1958

Pedersen, Alwin. Das Walross. Wittenberg Lutherstadt 1962

Perry, Richard. The World of the Polar Bear. London 1966

Peterson, Roger Tory, and James Fisher. Wild America. London 1956

Pfeiffer, Pierre. Auf den Inseln des Drachen. Stuttgart 1954

Pfeiffer, Pierre. Asia. London 1968

Player, Ian. Translocation of White Rhinoceros in South Africa. Oryx IX, 2, 67

Poertner, Rudolf. Bevor die Roemer kamen; Staedte und Staetten deutscher Urgeschichte. Muenchen/Zuerich 1965

Prater, S. H. The Book of Indian Animals. Bombay 1965

Preble, Edward A., and W. L. McAtee. A Biological Survey of the Pribiloff Islands, Alaska. North American Fauna No. 46. Washington 1923

Rankin, Niall. Antarctic Isle. London 1951

Roberts, Brian. Wildlife Conservation in the Antarctic. Oryx VIII, 4, 66

Robin, Louis. Le Livre des Sanctuaires de la Nature. Paris 1954

Roure, G. La Haute Gambie et le Parc National du Niokolo Koba. Dakar 1956

Rutgers, Abram. John Gould's Birds of Australia. Grosset 1967

Sanderson, Ivan T. Follow the Whale. London 1956

Savidge, J. M. Catching and Carting White Rhino in Uganda. Oryx VIII, 2, 65

Schaller, George B. The Mountain Gorilla. Chicago and London 1963

Schaller, George B. The Deer and the Tiger. Chicago and London 1967

Schenk, Paul. (Editor). Jagd und Naturschutz in der Schweiz. Basel 1966

Scheppe, Walter (Editor). First Man West: Alexander Mackenzie's Journal of his Voyage to the Pacific Coast of Canada in 1793. Berkeley and Los Angeles 1962

Schumacher, Eugen. Die letzten Paradiese: Auf den Spuren seltener Tiere. Guetersloh 1966 (English Edition: The Last of the Wild. London 1967)

Schultze-Westrun, Thomas. Wildziegen in den Weissen Bergen Kretas. Kosmos 63, 9, 67

Scott, Peter. The Launching of the New Ark: First Report of the World Wildlife Fund. London 1965

Seebeck, John. Rediscovery of two 'extinct' Mammals. Animals, 10, 6, 67

Serventy, Vincent. A Continent in Danger. London 1966

Severy, Merle. (Editor). America's Wonderlands: the Scenic National Parks and Monuments of the United States. Washington 1959

Severy, Merle. (Editor). Wild Animals of North America. Washington 1960

Sharell, Richard. The Tuatara, Lizards and Frogs of New Zealand. London 1966

Sharland, Michael. Tasmanian Wild Life. Melbourne 1963

Shaw, Charles E. Breeding the Galapagos Tortoise—Success Story. Oryx IX, 2, 67

Shepherd, Anthony. The Flight of the Unicorns. London 1965

Sidney, John. New Zealand's Flightless Birds. Animals, 10, 8, 1967

Simon, Noel. Between the Sunlight and the Thunder: The Wild Life of Kenya. London 1962

Simon, Noel. Red Data Book I: Mammalia. Published by I.U.C.N. Morges, 1966

Snow, D. W. The Giant Tortoises of the Galapagos Islands: Their Present Status and Future Chances. Oryx VII, 6, 64

Snow, H. J. In Forbidden Seas: Recollections of Sea Otter Hunting in the Kuriles. London 1910

Soergel, W. Die Jagd der Vorzeit. Jena 1922

Sollas, W. J. Ancient Hunters and their Modern Representatives. London 1924

Spilett, Juan. Pesticide Poisoning of Tigers. Oryx IX, 3, 67

Steller, George Wilhelm. Von Kamtschatka nach Amerika. Leipzig 1926

Stevenson-Hamilton, J. South African Eden: From Sabi Game Reserve to Kruger National Park. London 1952

Stivens, Dal. A New Zealand Oddity: The Flightless Takahe. Animal Kingdom LXX, 1, 1967

Stockley, C. H. Stalking in the Himalayas and Northern India. London 1936

Street, Philip. Vanishing Animals: Preserving Nature's Rarities. London 1961

Swinton, W. E. Fossil Birds. London 1958

Talbot, Lee Meriam. A Look at Threatened Species: A report on some animals of the Middle East and southern Asia which are threatened with extermination. Fauna Preservation Society, London 1959

Tanner, James. The Ivory-billed Woodpecker. New York 1966

Tenger, E. Zehn Jahre Aletschbann. Schweizer Naturschutz IX, 45, 1943

Thomson, A. Landsborough. (Editor). A New Dictionary of Birds. London 1964

Troughton, Ellis. Furred Animals of Australia. Sydney 1965

Ucko, Peter J. and Andree Rosenfeld. Palaeolithic Cave Art. London 1967

U.S. Fish and Wildlife Service. Wildlife Research Problems—Programs—Progress 1965. Washington 1966

U.S. Fish and Wildlife Service. Wildlife Research Problems—Programs—Progress 1966. Washington 1967

Vaucaire, Michel. Histoire de la Pêche à la Balaine. Paris 1941

Verschuren, J. Report from the Congo. Animals 4, 9, 1964

Vincent, Jack. Red Data Book II Aves. Published by I.U.C.N. Morges 1966

Walker, Ernest P. Mammals of the World. Baltimore 1964

Wayre, Philip. Saving the World's Rarest Pheasants. Animals 9, 8, 1967

Wayre, Philip. In Search of Swinhoe's Pheasant. Animals 11, 2, 1968

Weinzierl, Hubert. Europas groesste Wildnis: Streifzuege durch einige der schoensten Nationalparks im Norden Schwedens. Kosmos 64, 12, 1968

Wendt, Herbert. Entdeckungsfahrt durchs Robbenmeer: Georg Wilhelm Stellers Reise ans 'Ende der Welt'. Stuttgart 1952

Wendt, Herbert. Das bedrohte Paradies: Kampf um die Erhaltung der Tierwelt. Wien/Heidelberg 1965

Wetmore, Alexander. Re-creating Madagascar's Giant Extinct Bird. Nat. Geogr. Mag. 132, 4, 1967

Willan, R. S. M. Rhinos increase in Nepal. Oryx VIII, 3, 65

Williams, John G. A Field Guide to the National Parks of East Africa. London 1967

Ziswiler, Vinzenz. Bedrohte und ausgerottete Tiere. Berlin/Heidelberg 1965